# HISTORY OF A SMALL SCOTTISH TOWN
## close-up on
## COUPAR ANGUS

a social history of the town from
the Reformation to the year 2000

*Margaret Laing*

Margaret Laing

© Margaret Laing 2002

All rights reserved. No part of this book may be reproduced in any form or by any means without the express permission of the publisher, except by a reviewer wishing to quote passages in a review either written or broadcast.

I, Margaret Laing, hereby assert and give notice of my right under Section 77 of the Copyright, Design and patents Act 1988 to be identified as the author of this work.

ISBN 0 905452 37 2

*Published by*
Perth & Kinross Libraries
AK Bell Library
York Place
Perth
PH2 8EP

*Tolbooth, built in 1762*

# CONTENTS

| | page |
|---|---|
| Foreward | 7 |
| The Parish and Town of Coupar Angus | 8 |
| From the Reformation to the Present | 9 |
| The Hanging Judge | 13 |
|     Bailie Ogilvie's chair | 13 |
| The Steeple | 14 |
|     The Auld Steeple Bell *(Poem)* | 16 |
| The Provost's Robes, Chain of Office | 17 |
|     The Burgh Seal | 19 |
| The Town, or Victoria Hall | 20 |
| Church Development in Scotland | 22 |
|     The Early Church | 23 |
|     Chart of the Kirks | 23 |
|     The Parish/Established/Abbey Kirk | 24 |
|     The Communion Silver | 26 |
|     The Manses | 26 |
|     The Abbey Kirkyard | 28 |
|     The Secession or Antiburgher Church | 28 |
|     The Relief/Ecumenical/Congregational Church | 29 |
|     The Burgher Church | 30 |
|     United Presbyterian or South Free Church | 30 |
|     The North Church/St Andrews | 31 |
|     A Deed of Settlement | 31 |
|     The Scottish Episcopal Church | 32 |
|     St Anne's Scottish Episcopal Church | 32 |
|     The Roman Catholic Religion | 34 |
|     St Mary's Roman Catholic Church | 34 |
| Agriculture | 36 |
|     The Farmers' or Horse Show | 40 |
| The Country Estate as a Source of Employment | 41 |
|     Hallyburton Estate | 41 |
|     Keithick Estate | 43 |
| The Railway | 46 |
|     Coal Supplies and the Railways | 47 |
| Industry - Linen and Jute | 48 |
|     The Bucky | 49 |
|     The Manufactury | 50 |
|     The First Power Loom Factory | 51 |
|     The Second Power Loom factory | 51 |
|     The Third Power Loom Factory | 52 |
| Commerce | 53 |
|     Professions in 1794 | 53 |
|     Business Directory 1906 | 54 |
|     Shops and Businesses 1914 into the 1960s | 55 |
|     Business Directory 2000 | 56 |
|     Culross the Printers | 57 |
|     Davidson, Chemists | 59 |
| Scottish Education - in the Beginning | 61 |
|     The School Board | 62 |
|     Evening Classes | 65 |
|     The Burgh School (Mr Loutet) | 67 |
|     1900 to 1932 (Mr Strain) | 67 |
|     The School during two world wars | 69 |
|     The Home Guard | 70 |
|     1932 to 1939 (Mr Robertson) | 71 |
|     The Post War Era | 72 |
|     1954 to 1964 (Mr Tuckwell) | 73 |
|     1964 to 1978 (Mr Black) | 74 |
|     1978 to 1982 (Mr Johnston) | 74 |
|     1982 to 1996 (Mrs Pratt) | 75 |
|     The School Savings Bank | 76 |
|     Edwin Sturrock | 77 |
|     The School I Remember | 78 |
| Banks in the Town | 78 |
|     The Union Bank of Scotland | 80 |

|  | page |
|---|---|
| The National Bank of Scotland and | |
|     The Royal Bank of Scotland | 80 |
|     The Bank of Scotland | 81 |
|     The Savings Bank | 81 |
| **Community Services** | 82 |
|     The Fire Service & police | 82 |
| **Communications** | 84 |
|     The Post Office & telephones | 84 |
| **In Sickness and Health** | 85 |
|     The Health Centre and Red Cross | 85 |
| **Roads in Town and District** | 91 |
|     Street names old and new | 97 |
| **Holidays & Festivals** | 98 |
|     The Coupar Fair | 100 |
| **Entertainment over the Years** | 102 |
|     Music music music | 102 |
|     The War Years | 103 |
|     The DYBBC | 104 |
|     The post War Years | 105 |
|     Adam Rennie | 107 |
|     The Pipe Band | 108 |
|     The Instrumental Band | 110 |
| **Sporting Activities** | 111 |
|     Curling | 111 |
|     Cricket | 113 |
|     Quoiting | 114 |
|     Bowling | 116 |
|     Tennis | 117 |
|     Football | 118 |
|     Hockey | 121 |
| **Larghan Victory Park** | 122 |
| **Coupar Angus Highland Games** | 123 |
| **In Memorium** | 124 |
|     School Memorial | 125 |
|     Abbey Church Memorial | 126 |
|     South & St Andrews Church Memorials | 127 |
| **The Anglo Boer War** | 128 |
|     Boer War Casualties | 129 |
|     General Wimberley | 130 |
| **Group Activities** | 131 |
|     The Free Masons | 131 |
|     The Toc H | 132 |
| **Youth Activities** | 133 |
|     Scouts | 133 |
|     Boys Brigade | 136 |
|     Girl Guides & Brownies | 137 |
| **The Evils of the Demon Drink** | 139 |
|     The Good Templars | 140 |
| **Taverns of the Times** | 141 |
|     The Strathmore Hotel, or White House | 141 |
|     The Royal Hotel | 141 |
|     The Athole Arms | 142 |
|     The Victoria Inn | 142 |
|     The Red House Hotel | 143 |
|     The Enverdale Hotel | 144 |
| **Their Roots were Here** | 145 |
|     Bill MacIntosh - Mayor of Otago, NZ | 145 |
|     James Craigie | 145 |
|     Jock Sutherland - a Coupar Angus Boy | 146 |
|     Jock Davidson - the Peoples' Provost | 146 |
|     John *(Jack)* Dunbar | 147 |
| **Coupar Angus Fold-Eared Cat** | 148 |
| **Sources** | 149 |
| **Listed Buildings in Coupar Angus and District** | 150 |
| **List of Artefacts from Coupar Angus Museum** | |
| **now in the Perth Museum and Art Gallery** | 151 |
| **General Index** | 153 |
| **Index of Personal Names** | 158 |

## PHOTOGRAPHS

I WISH TO ACKNOWLEDGE THE IMPORTANT CONTRIBUTION TO THE INTEREST OF THIS HISTORY OF PHOTOGRAPHS AND POST CARDS WHICH THE FOLLOWING HAVE KINDLY CONSENTED TO BEING REPRODUCED

Mr Peter Assenti
Mr Norman Bannerman
Mrs Jean Coogan
Mr Albert Croll
Mr Douglas Davidson
Mr & Mrs Jim Dawson
Mr John Dunbar
Mrs Gertie Forbes
Mrs Kathleen Kench
Mrs M. Milne
The late Mr A. McKinlay
Mrs L. Norrie
Mr A. T. Paterson
Dundee Courier & Advertiser
Perthshire Advertiser
Mr Ron Stephen
Mr David Phillips

Everything possible has been done to present all the photographs in as clear a format as possible, within the bounds of computerised help. Many scenes and activities were just not available in their original form, and some had to be resurrected from faded torn prints, and sometimes photocopies of old newspaper clippings with coarse-screen images.

## LIST OF SPONSORS

Coupar Angus, Ardler
and Bendochy Community Council
RW Hynd, Architectural Services, Dundee
The late JN Llewellyn Palmer, Hallyburton
Mr N Bannerman, Red House Hotel
Mrs V McCombes, Dental Surgeon
The Business Centre (Mr Middleton)
Messrs Smith & Sons Coaches
Messrs Robertson, Bookmaker
Mr J Norrie, Hairdresser
Mrs M Scott, East Wood, Blairgowrie
George Husband
Denrosa Apiaries (McGregor)
Mrs Lamb of Lamb & Gardiner Ltd
Elegant Windows
C&W West (M Mathews)
Davidson the Chemist
The Royal Hotel
Victor & Sons (Kusza)
Mrs Hall, Cheshunt, Herts
Donald M Craig, Australia
The Athole Arms
Mr & Mrs J White, Kettins
Mr Murray Gray
The late Mrs Whitelaw, Kirriemuir
Mrs Legge
J Frazer
J Richards
Mrs Pauline Hall
The White House
The Victoria Inn

Published with financial assistance of
Perth and Kinross Heritage Trust

I became interested in Coupar Angus when I came to live in nearby Bendochy which over the centuries has had close connections with Coupar Angus.

I was not the first local historian on my father's side of the family as I am a relative of GEORGE PENNY who wrote a history of Perth in the early 19th century.

This history could never have been so comprehensive without the help of very many people. A few worked very hard, racking their brains, asking their friends, and raking up memories. I owe a very great debt of thanks for this to Charlie Sutherland and the late David Reid of Hay Street who got together, contacted friends and came up with wonderful, long forgotten facts.

Without the assistance of three people - David Apedaile of Coupar Angus, John Dunbar of Johannesburg, South Africa, and Theo Tulley of Hull, this publication would not have seen the light of day.

Theo reprocessed Amstrad tapes to Word, while David retyped some Documents, amended others, scanned photographs then e-mailed them on to John (Jack) Dunbar in South Africa who set up the book ready for printing which was indeed a mammoth task. The words that come to mind are totally inadequate in expressing my thanks and appreciation for their very professional help, given freely so that a record exists of days gone by in the town of Coupar Angus which is very dear to their hearts.

And a word of grateful thanks to Councillor Alan Grant for indexing the book.

In reading this book memories will be jogged again and more facts will emerge. When this happens, pass your memories on to the younger members of the community.

It is my fervent wish that my work will be used by others to write a much better history of the town.

*Margaret Laing*

**DEDICATED TO MY MOTHER MARGARET DONALDSON PANTON BORN IN 1905 AT PRINCELAND FARM COUPAR ANGUS WHERE HER FATHER WAS TENANT FARMER**

## I acknowledge with very many thanks the valuable assistance of the following:

The late Mr Frank Agger - Coupar Angus
Mr David Apedaile - Coupar Angus
Mr J. L. B. Apedaile - Coupar Angus
A. K. Bell Library - Perth
Mrs E. A. Benson - New Zealand
Mr Bob Benzies - Coupar Angus
The late Miss Johan Brodie - Coupar Angus
Mr Alan Cameron, Archivist, Bank of Scotland, Edinburgh
Mrs Ethel Clark - Coupar Angus
Mrs A. Coogan - Woodside
The late Mrs Morag Croll - Coupar Angus
Mr Albert Croll - Coupar Angus
Mr A. G. Currie - Coupar Angus
Mr Douglas Davidson - Blairgowrie
Mr Jock Davidson - Coupar Angus
Mr Jim Dawson - Coupar Angus
Mr John (Jack) Dunbar - Johannesburg, South Africa
Mrs Gertie Forbes - Coupar Angus
Mr D. Gardener - Preston
Mr and Mrs A. Gatt & Wendy Gatt - Coupar Angus
The late Mr Ian Geekie - Banchory
Mr G. Husband - Dundee
Mr J. Kiddie - Abernyte
Prof R. Last - New Alyth
Ex Councillor J. Main - Burrelton
The late Dr Milne & Mrs Milne - Blairgowrie
The late Rev Wm. Macartney - Couttie
Mr Ron McDonald - Coupar Angus
Mr G. McFarlane - Coupar Angus
Mrs Lynda McGregor - Coupar Angus
Mayor Bill McIntosh - Otago, New Zealand
The late Mr M. A. McKinlay - Coupar Angus
Mrs M. Mathews - Coupar Angus
Mr I. Norrie - of Culross, Printers - Coupar Angus
Mrs L. Norrie - Coupar Angus
The late Mr J. Llewelyn Palmer - Hallyburton
Mr A. T. Paterson - Gartlochbank
Mr and Mrs Peter - Keithick Lodge
Mr J. Pitkeathly - Bendochy
The late Mr David Reid - Coupar Angus
Mr J. Richards - Coupar Angus
Mr Jack Scott - Lintrose
The late Mr G. Shepherd - Coupar Angus
Mr J. Smeaton - Coupar Angus
Mr and Mrs Smith - White House, Coupar Angus
Staff of Community Education - Blairgowrie
Mr Ron Stephen - Coupar Angus
Mr Fred Stewart - Coupar Angus
Mr and Mrs Stirling - Keithick
Mr and Mrs C. Sutherland - Coupar Angus
Mrs I. Syme - Coupar Angus
Mr Leo Tulley - Hull
Mrs Flora Whyte - Luton
Mr and Mrs R. Whytock - Coupar Angus
Mr Johan Venter - Pretoria, South Africa
Miss Caroline Young - Coupar Angus
Special thanks to Proof Reader Netta Donaldson

Coupar Angus, in the Valley of Strathmore, is on the fringe of East Perthshire, and approximately 200 feet above sea level. It is bounded to the North by Meigle; to the North West by Bendochy; to the West by Blairgowrie; to the South West by Cargill and to the East by Kettins.

# THE PARISH - and town of Coupar Angus

*Larghan*

It is roughly 6 miles long and 2 miles in breadth at its widest point.

Until 1891, when the boundaries were altered, the oldest part of the town on which the Abbey was built, lay in Angus, hence the name Coupar Angus. It now is entirely in Perthshire.

The town whose oldest buildings were built from Abbey stone, was once known as the Jewel of Strathmore and in the evening light the old red sandstone seems to glow. Although only a fragment of the former Cistercian Abbey remains, there are many fine, historic buildings in the town which are well worth viewing.

Unlike many small towns, Coupar Angus has had little urban development and is, in size and population, almost the same as it was 100 years ago, mostly due to the lack of available building land.

Around the middle of the 19th century, the railway brought prosperity to the town and a certain amount of development took place. A number of fine houses were built and to mark Queen Victoria's Jubilee, a splendid Town Hall, funded by public subscription, was constructed.

Sadly, with the demise of the railway, the town stagnated and took on a forlorn appearance as the once considerable railway property, gradually became an area of industrial dereliction.

In 1996 a Relief Road was constructed along the route of the former main railway line, which has taken through traffic away from the congested town centre from Perth to the South; Dundee to the East; Blairgowrie to the West and Forfar to the North.

Perth & Kinross Council are not unaware of the problems which beset Coupar Angus and they wholeheartedly support plans to give the area a face-lift so that it may once again attract tourists and visitors to its quaint streets.

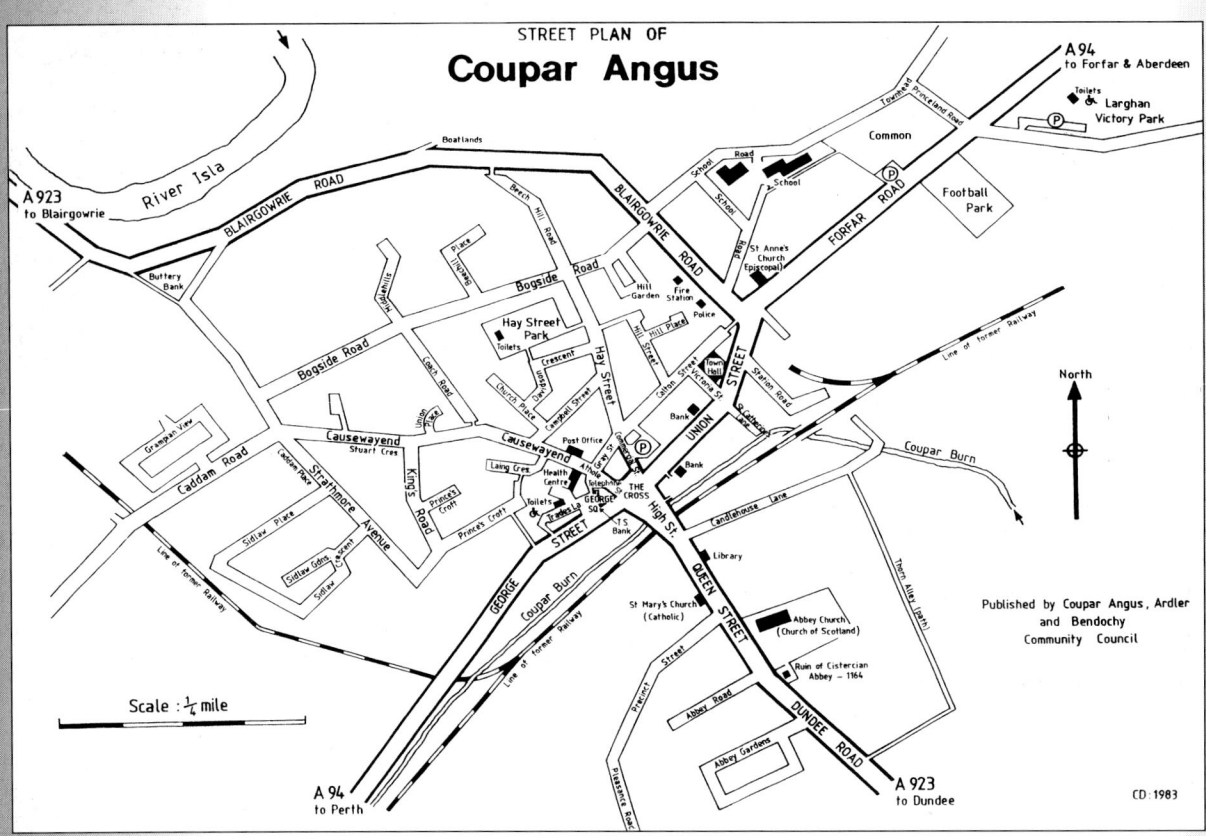

# FROM THE REFORMATION TO THE PRESENT

Due to the lack of records it is unclear whether or not there was a settlement in the immediate area of what is now Coupar Angus before the Cistercian monks arrived in the late l2th century. It is known however that Beechhill, as long as 2000 years ago, had been inhabited for burial relics have been unearthed there.

By the l5th century there were groups of villages or 'ferm touns' scattered throughout the district at Keithick (also known as Cassyend or Causewayend), Balbrogie, Welton, Caddam, Causewayend and Beechhill which would most possibly have sprung up after the arrival of the monks.

The very existence of the abbey and the vast tracts of land it had been given, would have meant protection, security and work for the people of this part of medieval Scotland. Causewayend then would have been surrounded by marsh and bog which would have protected the families there against sudden attack, while the higher ground of Beechhill was more easily defended against all kinds of predators. Up until the l745 Uprising, groups of families lived closely together for protection, as until then they had been subjected to raids by bands of Highlanders who not only terrorised them, but also drove off their livestock upon which their survival depended.

*(Top) What is left of the Abbey.*
*(Above) The little Keithick bridge C1900.*

The 'Union of the Crowns' in l603, is a very important date in Scottish history for it changed the lives of the Scots forever.

Elizabeth of England and Mary Queen of Scots were cousins and on Elizabeth's death, Mary's son to her second husband Lord Darnley, became King James VI of Scotland and I of England. Almost immediately he left for London where he took up residence.

Scotland and England were still two quite separate countries with different people, needs and identities. Democracy was unknown then for the Parliament of this 'unwieldy' United Kingdom represented the land-owning classes only, whose estates and fortunes in many cases, had been built up over the last hundred years or so

Until the Reformation of the l6th century when Roman Catholicism was replaced by Protestantism, Coupar Angus (Cupar until l846) had been an 'Abbot's Burgh'. In l607 it became a 'Burgh of Barony' with Lord Elphinstone becoming Lord Coupar. It is believed that he was chosen to prevent further bloodshed and rivalry between the Ogilvys and the Campbells who had bitterly quarrelled over the possession of the former abbey lands and property.

As the Abbey had declined in power, that of the Ogilvy family increased for they held the office of 'Bailieship' made a hereditary post in l540 by the last Abbot - Donald Campbell, who was a member of the powerful Argyll family.

The Ogilvys continued to dispense justice in the newly created Burgh of Barony until l745 when George II abolished all 'Heritable Jurisdictions'. During the time they held office they built up a considerable fortune for in addition to a salary, all fines were appropriated and should someone die without heirs to the estate, the property also became his. For the loss of this office, the considerable sum for the time of £800, was paid in compensation.

## RELIGION AND WAR

Times in Scotland were to be difficult during the reign of Charles I, for he had made his mind up that Protestant Scotland would become an Episcopalian country like England. He was of the firm belief that by doing this he would unite the two countries once and for all under one religion. The Scots however had other ideas about this and a strong body of devout Presbyterians formed a 'League' and signed a 'Covenant' to oppose the King's plans. They became known as the 'Covenanters'. In Coupar Angus alone, 22 men and 55 women of the Secession or Anti-Burgher Church left it and joined the Covenanting Cause. Covenanters were prepared to die for their faith ...and many of them did.

During the time the Covenanters were suffering persecution in Scotland for their beliefs, so too in England were the Puritans undergoing much hardship for their beliefs. Many of them left the land of their birth and emigrated to the 'New World' known now as the United States of America.

Not only was Charles I hated in Scotland, in England too the people had had enough of his autocratic ways and Civil War broke out there. The end result was that the King was executed and the army commander, Oliver Cromwell, assumed control and became 'Lord Protector'. Much as they had disliked the King, the Scots would not accept Cromwell as their Head of State and instead in l66l proclaimed the executed King's son, Charles II, King of Scotland. Cromwell was very displeased, not only with the Scots, but with Lord Coupar in particular for his support of the Covenanting Cause and ordered that he be fined £3000. Later this was reduced to £750, still a considerable sum of money at the time. Lord Coupar proved himself to be a man of principle for despite being pressurised, he would not change his allegiance to the Covenanters.

In l660 he was fined again - £4800 this time. He died without children and his title and estates went to his nephew the third Lord Balmerino. The family seems to have made a habit of flaunting authority for generations later in l746 Arthur the fourth Lord Coupar and sixth Lord Balmerino, was executed on Tower Hill for the part he played in the Jacobite Uprising.

The title of Lord Coupar became extinct at this time and the Balmerino estates were held by the Barons of Exchequer for a period of ten years before being sold to his nephew - the seventh Earl of Moray. The Moray family still retain the lands of Coupar and are among Scotland's greatest landowners. Darnaway Castle near Forres in Moray, is the family seat.

## THE BURGH OF BARONY

Although there are few records of the Burgh of Barony, it is logical to conclude, that major decisions regarding the town and its inhabitants would have been made by Lord Coupar and/or his deputies. Legal matters as we know, were in the hands of the Ogilvy family whose Courts were held in the open at Beechhill. Later there is reference to those taking place in the 'tollbooth'. The present tollbooth was not built until l762 which is a number of years after the reign of the Ogilvy's had ended, so the possibility exists that there may have been an older 'tollbooth' but its location is as yet, unknown.

## THE TOWN COMMITTEE

From l746 the affairs of the town were in the hands of a Town Committee and, the Minister and Kirk Session of the Parish Church, would have played a major part in the community by seeing that the people were 'God-fearing', 'sober' and 'law-abiding'. From the Minutes of the

*(Right) Bird's eye view of the town.*

Church we have learned that a public pillory was erected at its South door on January 8th 1704. What crime or missdeed warranted such a punishment unfortunately was not recorded. We also know that a minute book of the Church dated 1656 to 1682 still existed in 1740 but sadly since then, has disappeared.

There was a 'Town Committee' Minute Book dated 1826 to 1852 which unfortunately has also gone astray. It was gifted to the Town Council in 1945 by Mr Robert Geekie, a member of a distinguished local family and it is a matter of record that it was still in existence at the changeover from Town Council to District and Regional Councils. The loss of these books has left a lamentable gap in the history of the town.

In 1846 a 'Parochial Board' was formed whose function was to see to the welfare of the poor. A building at the corner of Campbell Street and Causewayend acted as a shelter for the destitute and was known as the Lodging House. Formerly, the care of the poor had been the responsibility of the Church whose resources depended entirely on the generosity, or otherwise of its members, and this new body relieved them of a considerable burden. We have no record of what happened in Coupar Angus but we know that in some areas, vagrants and the destitute on entering a town, were whipped out of it and over the boundary into another county. Then, to be poor or unemployed was looked on as being one's own fault and a disgrace. Even the paltriest amount of aid was given grudgingly, and the recipient was carefully watched to make sure that it went on life's necessities. Many of the elderly lived in constant fear of becoming destitute and the decision made to take them to the Poor House.

This situation improved slowly after World War I, then in 1946 the introduction of the Welfare State ensured that no one should live in dread of becoming destitute. In many of the larger towns throughout Scotland, the former 'Poor Houses' were made into 'Geriatric Hospitals'. For many years a certain amount of dread still existed among the elderly who had memories of their former use.

## FROM CUPAR TO COUPAR

On the 4th July 1846 the spelling of Coupar was changed from CUPAR to the COUPAR of the present day in order to avoid confusion with Cupar in Fife. This year too saw the replacement of the Parochial Board with a Parish Council whose members were known as 'Commissioners'.

They met at monthly intervals in the 'Hay Arms' which is now the Vic.

In 1871 the town became a 'Police Burgh' and a 'Police Commission' was formed with David McFarlane, a local industrialist, as Chief Commissioner. In 1875 the Police Commission gave way to a Town Council and David McFarlane became the first Provost of Coupar Angus.

## THE BURGH BOUNDARIES

In 1891 the Burgh boundaries were changed and the part of the town which lay on the Dundee side of the burn, was transferred from Forfarshire (Angus), to Perthshire.
In 1892 the Burgh Police Act came into

*(Top) Commercial Street c1920. Car park now on left where 3-story building is standing.*

---

BURGH OF COUPAR ANGUS.

A. F. LAING,
TOWN CLERK
AND
BURGH CHAMBERLAIN.
TELEPHONE Nº 4.

Town Clerk's Office,
Coupar Angus 9th January 1945

Dear Mr Geekie,

The Record and Minute Book of the Committee of the town of Coupar Angus commencing 1826 presented by you to the town was handed over to the Town Council for custody by Provost Davidson at the Monthly Meeting held last night and I was instructed to thank you on behalf of the Community in general and the Town Council in particular for your magnanimous and public spirited action in making the gift.

Yours faithfully,

Robert C. Geekie Esq.,
 The Neuk,
  COUPAR ANGUS.

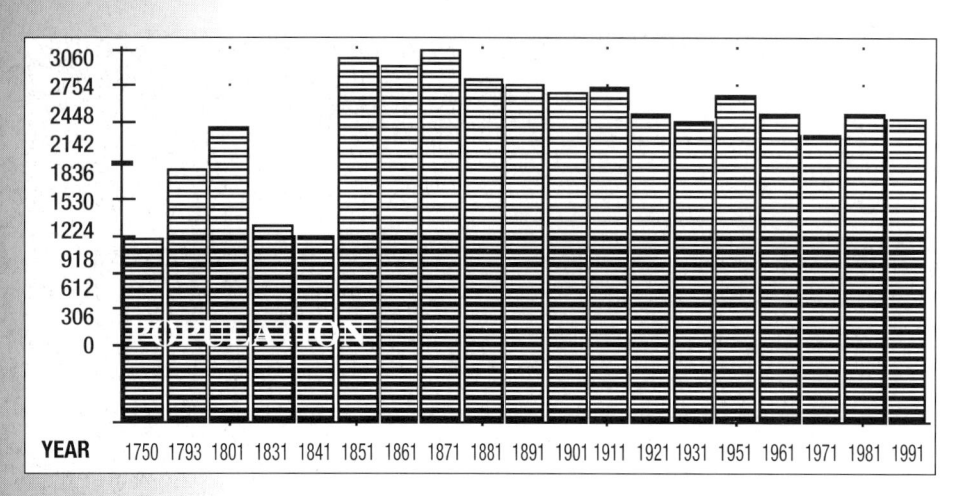

force and the Town Council had a former seal of the abbey altered and adapted to become the official seal of the town. It dates from Abbot Andrew Buchan's period of office (1272 - 1296) the time when Scotland was in the throes of the Wars of Independence.

In 1912 a copy of this seal was to become the centre-piece of the magnificent Provost's Chain of Office of the town of Coupar Angus.

In 1975 Town Councils throughout Scotland were replaced by District and Regional Councils.

Many townspeople regretted and some still do, that local affairs were taken out of the hands of their local officials, for it was strongly believed that they knew the local people, their problems and their needs, much more intimately than the very much larger, newly created authorities.
For the duration of these Councils, Coupar Angus was represented by a District Councillor and a Regional Councillor.

## COMMUNITY COUNCIL

A Community Council was introduced and although this body has no statutory powers, it can play an important part within the town and district and achieve much by members acting together as the eyes and ears of the community and reporting back to the Councillors at the monthly meetings which are held in the Council Chambers of the Town Hall.
In 1995/96 further changes in local government took place and Tayside Regional Council and Perth & Kinross District Council were reorganised. Perth & Kinross Council is now solely responsible for the day to day running of matters within its boundaries.

The function of the Community Council remains unchanged however. It is a non-political body of 9 persons, 7 representing Coupar Angus and one each for Ardler and Bendochy. Although in the district of Coupar Angus, the Parish of Bendochy does not have the same Councillor, as it is in the Rosemount ward. Both Councillors attend the meetings of the Community Council and report to members on the progress made, or otherwise, of matters of local interest and concern.

## THE MINUTES OF THE TOWN COUNCIL STILL IN EXISTENCE.

| | |
|---|---|
| 1912 - 1918 | 1945 - 1947 |
| 1918 - 1925 | 1947 - 1950 |
| 1926 - 1929 | 1950 - 1953 |
| 1929 - 1932 | 1953 - 1957 |
| 1932 - 1934 | 1957 - 1960 |
| 1934 - 1936 | 1960 - 1964 |
| 1936 - 1937 | 1964 - 1969 |
| 1937 - 1938 | 1969 - 1972 |
| 1938 - 1939 | 1972 - 1974 |
| 1939 - 1942 | 1974 - 1975 |
| 1942 - 1944 | |

The above minutes can be viewed in the Archive Department of the A.K. Bell Library, Perth. The Community Council Minutes are available from the Perth & Kinross Council Offices, Perth.

THE MISSING MINUTES ARE:-
1826 - 1852    1852 - 1912

In 2001 the Minute Books for 1891-1911 mysteriously turned up and are now in the A. K. Bell archives where they can be seen by all interested parties during opening hours.

*(L to R back)  D. MacNaughton; J. Coogan, J. D. Bannerman, R. Husband, N. Bannerman, H. Rodger.*
*(L to R front)  J. Fraser, F. Aggar, .L Apedaile (the last provost), G. McFarlane, A. F. Laing.*

# THE HANGING JUDGE

According to old records, in 1645 Bailie John Ogilvy lived in a large house on the east side of the Timber Market which is now George Square. This is the Bailie Ogilvy who in 1699 earned himself the rather dubious title of the 'Hanging Judge', after he had a suspected wrong-doer apprehended and hanged without a trial.

When the dead man's relatives and friends heard the news of the execution, they complained bitterly at the lack of a trial before such drastic action was taken.

When word reached Bailie Ogilvy of their dissatisfaction, he ordered the body to be exhumed, and a Court was convened which found the dead man guilty and sentenced him to be hanged again!

Although these were brutal times, this draconian action seems to have been just too much for the people of Coupar and the saying 'Coupar Justice' was coined - *'First hang a man and then try him'*.

The accuracy of this story may have been open to question, for it could be assumed that over the years it had been altered and added to, but from a newspaper article dated May 1961 comes the following:

**"A COPY OF THE VERDICT OF THAT FAMOUS TRIAL, IN THE HAND-WRITING OF BAILIE JOHN OGILVY HAS ALSO BEEN PRESENTED TO THE COUNCIL".**

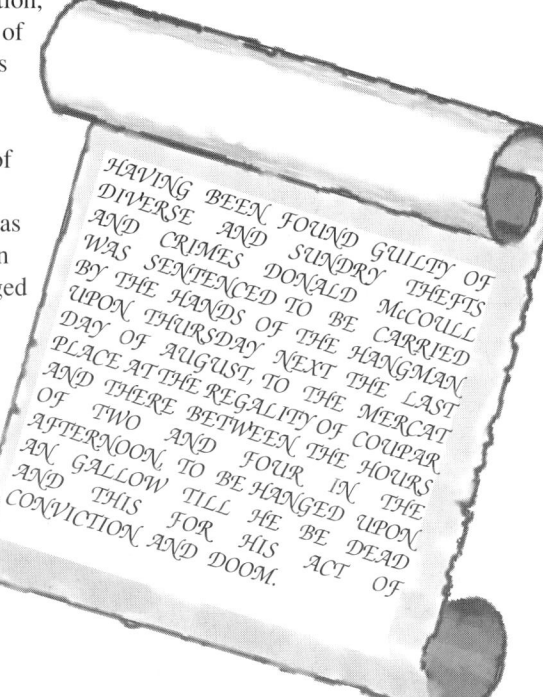

*HAVING BEEN FOUND GUILTY OF DIVERSE AND SUNDRY THEFTS AND CRIMES DONALD McCOULL WAS SENTENCED TO BE CARRIED BY THE HANDS OF THE HANGMAN UPON THURSDAY NEXT THE LAST DAY OF AUGUST, TO THE MERCAT PLACE AT THE REGALITY OF COUPAR AND THERE BETWEEN THE HOURS OF TWO AND FOUR IN THE AFTERNOON, TO BE HANGED UPON AN GALLOW TILL HE BE DEAD AND THIS FOR HIS ACT OF CONVICTION AND DOOM.*

## BAILIE OGILVY'S CHAIR

Bailie Ogilvy's Chair was gifted to the former Town Council of Coupar Angus by the Geekie family. For years it graced the town's Council Chamber in the Town Hall but at the change over from Town Council to District and Regional Councils in 1975 it was decided by the new authority to place it in Perth Museum for safe keeping. Although not on display at present, it can be viewed by arrangement.

Legend has it that this chair was used by the Bailie at trials within the Abbey, but recently experts from the Victoria and Albert Museum in London have dated it as probable 17th century which is after the Reformation. It is described by them as being *"a fairly standard domestic type of the later 17th century"* which would only have been found in the homes of the wealthy of that period, and apparently resembles a set of chairs reputed to have come from Lochleven Castle.

Although it is impossible to be sure that this was the actual chair Bailie Ogilvie sat on during his Courts, some of which were carried out in the open, it is almost without doubt that it did belong to the Ogilvie family who resided in Coupar Angus for many years.

*(Top) George Street with George Square off to the left*

# THE STEEPLE or TOLBOOTH or CLOCKTOWER or TOWNHOUSE

When the Steeple was built in Coupar Angus in 1762 by public subscription, on what is thought to have been the site of the former High Court of Justiciary or Court of Regality, the day to day running of the town was in the hands of a Town Committee, which had taken over some time after Lord Coupar was executed for his part in the 1745 Uprising.

In most Burghs, Townhouses had been built in the 17th century and as no early records exist of Coupar Angus, we must conclude that one had not been necessary during Lord Coupar's lifetime. It is most likely to have been built as the meeting place of the Town Committee, and would also have acted as a secure place for the town's records, and the collection of funds for the taxes which were necessary for the maintenance of what public services were available at that time. The lower part was used as a prison for the part of the town which lay in Angus until the boundaries changed in 1891.

At this time also, Washington became Ardler and Kinloch became part of the Meigle district.

As time passed and Banks were built, there was less need for a secure building and the Tolbooth gradually fell into disrepair. By 1861 the Town Commissioners, who had replaced the Town Committee, were meeting in the Hay Arms *(now the Vic')*, as no doubt it was much more comfortable than the decaying Tolbooth. However, Justice of the Peace and Circuit Small Debt Courts were still held there every few weeks as the necessity arose.

In 1876 Mr Thomson Lowe of Winnipeg, Canada, brother of local G.P. Dr R. Lowe, on a visit to his native town, gifted one hundred pounds (£100) to have the decaying building repaired. In 1912 he offered to provide a new dial for the town clock and to have all the rotten wood in the Steeple replaced. The Advertiser of 24th February of that year stated:

"Mr Lowe's benefactions to his native town have been numerous and handsome"!

Engraved on the Steeple bell is:-

THE GIFT OF THE EARL OF MORRAY

JOHN MILNE AND SON, EDINBURGH

1767

*(Top) The steeple in Queen Street,*
*(Above) The Victoria Inn in Gray Street.*

The steeple bell was tolled regularly - to call townspeople to worship, on joyous occasions, and during the funeral services of prominent people. When Queen Victoria's Consort, Prince Albert died in 1861 from typhoid fever contracted from foul drinking water at Windsor, the pulpits in all of the Churches in the town were draped in black. The steeple bell was rung for the duration of the funeral, and all the shops were closed from eleven until one o'clock.

From an old document we have learned that "until the War the curfew was tolled". Unfortunately it does not state which war and as the date is uncertain it could have been either the Boer War or World War I. Most likely the 'curfew' was not to tell the townspeople to go indoors but rather was a reminder for the shops to cease trading.

The ringing of the bell over the years was not always a straightforward matter, and at times caused quite a bit of controversy. During his ministry, the Reverend F.R. MacDonald of the Parish Church, demanded that the Town Council stop the dissident Churches in town from using the bell to call their respective congregations to worship. Although he threatened them with legal action he did not have his way, for the Councillors decided that the bell belonged to the people of the town, and not to the Parish Kirk. In 1912 another furious row broke out when the Town Councillors decided that the bell would be rung only once on Sundays at 10.00 a.m. They had to change their minds however when presented with a petition from outraged townspeople totally opposed to any change.

In March 1871 Queen Victoria's daughter, the Princess Louise was married to the Marquis of Lorne. This was a time for rejoicing and the event was celebrated in Coupar Angus with the streets and houses decorated with flags and bunting. When darkness fell the Steeple was lit up by gas and candles, which must have been quite an undertaking in those days. There was a torch light procession through the town made up of Police Commissioners, Free Masons, Weavers, Good Templars and many others, all led by the band of the 7th Perthshire Rifle Volunteers. Each group rounded off their evening by having supper at a local hotel. The Police Commisioners ate at Smeaton's Inn (Athole Arms); the Free Masons at the Strathmore Arms (White House); the Weavers at the Hay Arms (the Vic'); and the Volunteers at the Royal Hotel, which formerly had been called the Strathmore, and before that, was known as the Defiant after the horse drawn coach which stopped in Coupar Angus daily, until the middle of the 19th century when the railway rendered it redundant.

The Steeple clock, which is a Victorian addition, has kept good time in the care of Richard Kusza of Victor Watchmakers.

By the early 1990's time had taken its toll on the Steeple, which once again was in need of major repair. Age alone was not the culprit however, for over the decades pigeons had gained access to the roof and upper floors, and the considerable amount of their droppings had acted as a catalyst in the decay of the wood, which resulted in the building having to be completly re-roofed.

Now a Category 'B' Listed Building, the Steeple has lain empty for many years, but this may soon be remedied as plans are in the pipeline to turn it into an up-to-date town museum.

Coupar Angus has many fine old buildings tucked away in its narrow streets, but its Steeple, which stands out against the skyline, is indeed a historic gem, which has survived the rigours of time since its construction in 1762.

# THE AULD STEEPLE BELL

Beneath the steeple roof I've hung
An' every Sunday wagged ma tongue;
But some nae mair wad hae me rung,
The puir auld steeple bell.

The rate-payers they elected men
An' everything some think they ken;
Ane made a motion there an' then
Tae stop the steeple bell.

Ye see it cam' aboot this way,
The scaffies they got up their pay
An' then resolved nae mair tae play
Upon the steeple bell.

Some o' the Cooncil thoucht this richt,
An' voted hard wi' a' their micht
Tae even stop at eight at nicht,
The puir auld steeple bell.

A member o' the Cooncil said
"For lang upon the bell ye've played,
Sae dinna lat us be afraid
Tae stop the steeple bell".

But jist a gawky feckless loon
Wha has nae interest in the Toon;
A blight upon his empty croon,
Says the auld steeple bell.

But some got up - could hardly speak,
An' fairly railed him for his cheek;
They cried "We'll ring it every week"
The puir auld steeple bell.

Some fowk wha hae been born here,
They've heard me ring for mony a year;
Nae doot they'd think it unco queer
Tae stop the steeple bell.

It wis decided aff the reel,
Nae mair on Sunday wad I peel;
The rate-payers they said "Hang the Deil
Wha'd stop the steeple bell".

The rate-payers they've been heard tae say,
The bell will ring, come o't what may;
An' then we'll ken next voting day
Wha'll stop the steeple bell.

Noo a' you fowk wha gang tae kirk,
Or market, or your daily work,
Oh dinna lat the scaffies shirk
The ringin' o' the bell.

It is an auld an' ancient plan
Sae keep it up as lang's ye can
An' dinna fash about the man
Wha'd stop the steeple bell

I've called ye tae the auld kirk door
For mony a year, an' lang afore,
Oh scaffies ring until ye're sore,
The puir auld steeple bell.

I min' the days o' auld gane past,
When tae the kirk fowk hurried fast,
An' some they micht hae been the last
But for the steeple bell.

Noo listen tae the auld bell's plea,
an' dinna lat the custom dee;
The scaffies get a gey guid fee
tae ring the steeple bell.

# THE PROVOST'S ROBES AND CHAIN OF OFFICE

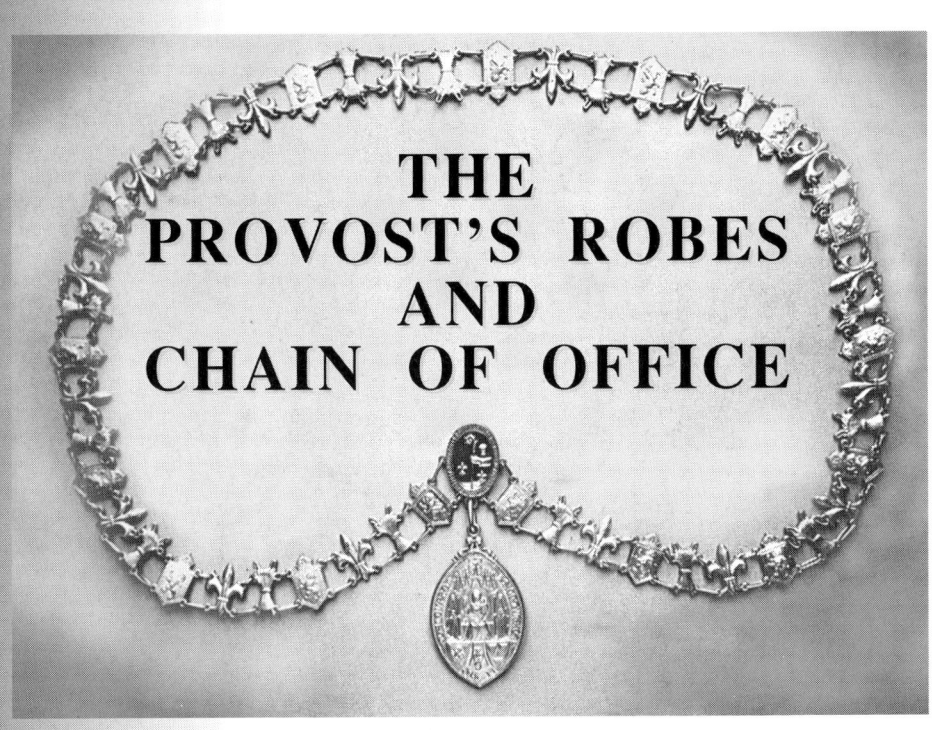

After the Coronation of King George V and Queen Mary on 22nd June 1911 in Westminster Abbey, they paid a state visit to Edinburgh where several functions were held in their honour. Provost Chalmers of Coupar Angus was invited to one of these distinguished gatherings at Holyrood, and fully aware of the importance of the occasion and the honour extended to the town and townspeople by the invitation, purchased splendid scarlet robes trimmed with ermine, which he thought would be worthy of such an auspicious occasion. On his return and at an ordinary meeting of the Town Council, he presented the robes to the Council *"for use by his successors on future occasions"*. A surprised and astounded Baillie Macgregor haltingly accepted them on behalf of the town, for there had been no fore-warning, that such a presentation was to take place.

When word of this reached the ears of the townspeople, they were so delighted by such generosity that they immediately decided that such splendid robes should have a Provost's Chain of Office to accompany them. It was said at the time that, *"A Provost was only half a Provost without a Chain of Office"*.

No time was wasted in forming a committee to see to this, and Mr T. Ferguson, Princeland, became Chairman, with Mr Stuart Geekie, Abbotsville, as Secretary and Treasurer. The committee members were prominent figures in the community of the time - the Rev J. H. Forrest Bell, The Parsonage; Mr. A. Geekie, Abbotsville; Mr D. Murray, Balgersho; Mr C. Boyd, Solicitor; Mr G. Murray, George Street and Mr W. Barnett, Causewayend.

The first step was to decide on the design of the chain, and keeping in mind that Coupar Angus had in the past been one of the principal ecclesiastical sites in Scotland, they felt that this fact must be incorporated in the design. It was decided that the chain was to be made in sets of three links :- the Scottish Lion as a symbol of their patriotism, loyalty and nationality; the second, the fleur-de-lis, as a reminder of the one time alliance with France; and the third, a combination of a sheaf, symbolic of industry, and two pastoral staves, as a reminder of the old Abbey. The centre-piece of the chain was a slightly altered copy of the seal from Abbot Andrew Buchan's period of office (1272-1296).

Estimates from Jewellers capable of making such a chain were then sought and Messrs Elkinton, of Glasgow and London were chosen to carry out the work. The townspeople were then consulted regarding the cash required, and the response was so overwhelming that in a matter of days a firm order was placed for work to commence. In fact, as time went on and the response from the community grew, the length of the chain had to be increased and increased until it was said that it would take a taller man than their present Provost *(Provost Chalmers)* to wear it.

The completed chain measured almost five feet in length, has 52 links and weighs 1 lb. 8 oz. of solid gold. It's quality and design is quite outstanding, and for a small town like Coupar Angus to have such a valuable Chain of Office, is quite exceptional.

*James Chalmers - 1910-1919 who donated the robes of office.*

page 17

## THE PROVOSTS OF COUPAR ANGUS TOWN COUNCIL

| | |
|---|---|
| 1875 - 1895 | David McFarlane |
| 1895 - 1898 | John Adam |
| 1898 - 1901 | Charles E. Anderson |
| 1901 - 1904 | George Ross |
| 1904 - 1910 | James Dron |
| 1910 - 1919 | James Chalmers |
| 1919 - 1922 | Thomas Stuart |
| 1922 - 1928 | James Bruce |
| 1928 - 1931 | William T. Dunbar |
| 1931 - 1934 | David C. Steen |
| 1934 - 1936 | Rev Clark-Barnacle |
| 1936 - 1939 | Annie Robertson |
| 1939 - 1952 | John D. Davidson |
| 1952 - 1955 | David Hume |
| 1955 - 1958 | Charles Heggie |
| 1958 - 1961 | John Tuckwell |
| 1961 - 1970 | John D. Davidson |
| | *Second term of office* |
| 1970 - 1975 | J. Leonard B. Apedaile |

## LIST OF SUSCRIBERS TO CHAIN OF OFFICE

| | | | | | |
|---|---|---|---|---|---|
| W | Aitken | J | Dron | Mr & Mrs W D Graham | Menzies |
| R | Allan | W T | Dunbar | J M | Miller |
| D | Anderson | Mrs E | Duncan MS | Prof G | Moncur |
| L | Anderson | A M | Dundas | The Earl of | Moray, Kinfauns Castle |
| R | Anderson | City of | Dundee | J M | Muir |
| R | Anderson (Jnr) | L R | Falconer | D | Murray |
| W | Anderson | T B | Farquharson | G | Murray |
| | | T | Ferguson | | |
| A | Barnett | T | Ferguson | Dr F | Nicholson |
| W | Barnett | Rev J | Fleming | | |
| Mrs I | Baxter | Rev J | Forrest Bell | J | Paterson |
| Mrs R | Baxter MS | Wm | Fullerton | J | Patrick |
| J McK | Bernard | | | City of | Perth |
| F C | Bishop | J | Galloway | J | Pitkeathly |
| J P | Blyth | C | Gardener | J | Playfair |
| J | Borrie | Mrs H | Gauld | | |
| C | Boyd MS | Alex | Geekie MS | J | Ramsay MS |
| C | Boyd | A | Geekie | L S | Reid |
| E | Brodie | S | Geekie | T | Renton |
| J | Brodie | Messrs | Gilzean | Col S | Richardson |
| J&D | Brodie | Rev T | Goldie | | |
| J | Brodie | Miss B | Gray | C | Robertson |
| R | Brodie | | | J | Robertson |
| J | Brown | J | Halley | W | Robertson |
| J | Bruce | W | Henderson | G | Ross |
| W | Burnett | - | Hill of Hillgarden | | |
| G | Burnett | Miss M | Hill | D | Scott |
| W | Burton | | | W L | Sinclair |
| A | Buttar MS | Miss | Lackie | Rev A | Smith |
| | | Lansdown | Marquis of Meikleour | Mrs | Smoldon |
| J | Campbell | W | Linley | A | Stewart |
| J L | Carmichael | Rev J | Linton | Rev C | Stewart |
| | (Arthurstone) | T | Lowe | D | Stewart |
| H | Chalmers | Dr J | Lowe | D | Stewart |
| J | Chalmers | Misses | Lowe | J | Stephen |
| J | Clark | Misses | Lowe | A W F | Strain |
| W | Clark MRCVS | Mrs | Lowson | T | Stuart Bailie |
| H | Cobb Ex Bailie | | | Miss | Symons |
| E | Cox (Cardean) | H | Mackay | | |
| T | Craig | R | MacIntyre | Major SS | Toyer - The Armoury |
| W | Cumming | J | MacKenzie | | Causewayend |
| | | G | McDonald | | |
| NAC | Davidson | D | McFarlane MS | W N | Walker |
| Miss A | Dobie | W | McGregor Bailie | R | Watson |
| J | Donaldson | J | McInnes | L | Watson |
| P | Donaldson | J | McNeill | D | Welsh |
| J | Douglas | G | Mann | W | Whitson |
| G | Dow | D | Martin | J | Williamson |
| D | Dron | J | Martin | Miss | Wilson |
| | | | | W | Wallace MS |

*(MS - sacred memory of)*

# THE BURGH SEAL

In 1892 the Burgh Police Act came into force and the Town Council had a former seal of the Abbey altered and adapted to become the official seal of the town.

It dates from Abbot Andrew de Buchan's period of office (1272 - 1296) the time when Edward I of England, (the 'Hammer of the Scots') tried in vain to subjugate the Scottish people once and for all.

He marched with his army throughout lowland Scotland, leaving death and destruction in his wake. When he came to the Abbey of Coupar, it too was left very much the worse of his visit for he confiscated most of its treasures.

On his way South from Coupar Angus, Edward's army destroyed Kinclaven Castle whose ruins can still be seen near Meikleour where the river Isla joins the Tay.

From there he went to Scone, where he took the Stone of Destiny back with him to London from its ancient resting place.

It lay in Westminster Abbey until 1996 when it was returned to Scotland.
It did not come back to Scone however, for the Scottish Office decided that it should be kept in Edinburgh Castle. Many Scots are of the opinion that the stone removed by Edward was not the genuine one but a replacement, as the original Stone of Destiny was hidden, when news of Edward's approach reached Scone. Some even claim to know where the genuine stone is.

In 1912 the Abbot's seal from this period in Scottish History, became the centre-piece of the splendid Chain of Office, of the Provost of the Town Council of Coupar Angus.

## THE SEAL OF THE CHAPTER OF THE ABBEY OF COUPAR

In 1902 an antique dealer in Dundee had in his possession a seal which was identified from the description in a "Catalogue of Seals" by Henry Laing, as the "Seal of the Chapter of the Abbey of Coupar".

The seal is made of brass, with the face measuring approximately 13x5 mm. The seal block is surmounted by a figure of the crown. The Virgin is shown holding the infant Jesus in her arms, this figure, in relief also cast in brass, formed the handle.

The Town Hall was built in 1887 of Keithick stone to mark Queen Victoria's Jubilee. The architect was Bailie Smart of Perth, and the cost of construction was £4000 which was raised by public subscription.

## THE TOWN OR VICTORIA HALL

David McFarlane the Industrialist, who was Provost of the Burgh from 1875 to 1895 is reputed to have been the most generous contributor. Like the Chain and the Robes of Office, the Town Hall is quite outstanding for a small Burgh and is testimony to the prosperity of the town then and the public spiritedness of its inhabitants.

Over the decades several internal alterations have been carried out and as we approach the millennium the layout of the building consists of a very fine hall with a stage. There is seating for 154 in the hall itself and 98 in the balcony. The hall is heavily booked by local organisations for events which range from regular Karate Instruction to Bingo Teas. There is a well equipped kitchen, a small assembly room and adequate toilet facilities. The Perth & Kinross Library moved from Queen Street to here on Monday 11th May 1987 and occupies a bright and spacious area in the lower front of the building.

Upstairs is the Community Council Chamber and next to it a small hall. The former more spacious Council Chamber was a number of years ago absorbed into enlarging the caretakers flat which is situated upstairs at the rear of the building looking on to Calton Street.

When in 1975 the Town Council was dissolved everything belonging to Coupar Angus in common with every other Burgh in Scotland, became the property of the new authority which replaced it. What artifacts had survived from the Town Museum and elsewhere were legally transferred to the safe keeping of the new authority to be housed in the Museum or Archives there. Quite a number of articles went missing at this time including Historic Minute Books.

The Council Chambers has still retained some fine pictures and pieces of furniture which legally belong to Perth & Kinross:-

Large oak Victorian board room table.
One handsome Provosts' chair with Town Coat of Arms and upholstered in red leather.
Two matching Baillies chairs upholstered in red leather.
Six smaller councillors chairs upholstered in red leather.
Two Victorian carving chairs upholstered in brown leather
Ten matching hand chairs upholstered in brown leather.
Grandfather clock in oak case with *'Menzies Coupar Angus'* on dial.*
Very fine mahogany oval pedestal table.*
Mahogany side table*
Silver plated ink stand.
* *all the gift of John Davidson.*
Umbrella stand.
Black marble clock with green onyx inlay *(Gifted by Victor Kusza & Sons)*
Portrait of Mrs Charlotte A. Ferguson, donor of Larghan Park and dated 15 May 1945 - artist Arthur Hacker RA.
Presentation portrait of David McFarlane Esq JP - Chief Magistrate and Provost of Coupar Angus - March 1875 to November 1895 - painted by W. S. McGeorge, a local artist and relative of Provost & Mrs John Davidson.
Fine artist's impression in oil of Victoria arriving at the Cross by coach, with the Defiant Inn and ceremonial archway in Queen Street in the background. No artist's name is visible but *'Queen Victoria, Coupar Angus'* can be seen very faintly on the lower right corner of the picture.
There are several photographic portraits by Wilson Laing of Blairgowrie of several Provosts, Councillors, and Provost David Hume JP - 1952 to 1955.
Lady Provost Annie Robertson - 1936 - 1939.
Provost John Davidson MPS, JP - 1939 - 1952.
Provost David Hume JP - 1952 - 1955
Provost J. L. B. Apedaile JP - 1970 - 1975.
Coupar Angus Town Council - 1975.

There are also several pictures *(photographer unknown)* of:-
Frank Agger JP on recognition of his services to the community from 1968 to 1995.
Provost and Baillies *(date unknown)*
Gathering of Provosts from all over Scotland at Glasgow City Chambers 2 September 1915.
Copy of portrait by '*Vendome*' of Dr John Bain Sutherland a native of Coupar Angus, a Dentist who became one of America's most famous football coaches.
Curling match on the river Isla with Farina Mill and stack in background dated 16 February 1895.
Beautifully engraved cup and casket which was presented to William Dudgeon Graham Menzies of Hallyburton in appreciation of his services over many years to the town which included the much needed water supply from his estate. On one side of the casket is an engraving of Hallyburton House and on the other the Town Hall of Coupar Angus.
There is also a Roll of Honour with the names of all the local men who fell in the 1914 - 1918 war.
There are two halberds *(Pike-like objects)* which were carried on ceremonial processions in the town to celebrate the coronation of King Edward VII in 1902, and his son King George V - 22 June 1911.
A framed account of the circumstances which led to the presentation of the official robes and chain of office to the Burgh. All names of donors inscribed on the chain are listed. This record was presented with the chain on 20 December 1911.
The '*Loyal Addresses*' from Provost, Magistrates and Councillors of Coupar Angus to George V and Queen Mary (1910 - 1936) - King George VI (1936 - 1952)
There is a collection of maps from the Town Council period which date back to the early 1900s.

*(Top) The Roll of Honour in the Council Chambers.*

*(Above) Early photograph of the Town Hall with railings intact.*

page 21

In the 19th century most towns in Scotland had three Kirks, each of whom had its own distinctive congregation. These three accounted for the majority of Scottish citizens.

# CHURCH DEVELOPMENT IN SCOTLAND

The first was the Church of Scotland known locally as the Parish Kirk, the Auld Kirk or the Established Kirk. In Coupar Angus it is known as the Abbey Kirk. The history of this church goes back to the Reformation when the Pope and his Bishops were rejected by Scotland. The clear line of descent was interrupted by Cromwell and also by the Stuart Kings who reintroduced Bishops but at the Revolution Settlement of 1690 the matter was settled once and for all when the Church of Scotland was "as law established".

The second of the three Kirks was the Free Church of Scotland whose life and short history are quite clear. In the 18th century there was growing agitation against the Patronage Act of 1712 by which the Laird or the Crown had the right to place a Minister in a Parish whether or not the parishioners wanted him. In 1843 a large group of Church of Scotland Ministers, Elders and People, led by Thomas Chalmers, left the Established Church and formed the Free Church. This historic breakaway is known as the 'Disruption'. In 1900 the Free Church and the United Presbyterians came together, then in 1929 the United Free Church came back into the fold of the Parish Church.

The United Presbyterian Kirk's history is so confused and confusing that Church historians explain it's complexities by means of diagrams, and even they are hard to understand. The whole secessionist movement began in 1733 when Ebenezer Erskine protested against 'Patronage'. Thirty years later Thomas Gillespie, who formed the 'Relief Church', also seceded from the parent Church of Scotland. These were the years of the Auld and New Lichts, the Burgher and Anti Burghers and so on. All the diverse parties finally agreed together in 1847 and the United Presbyterians came into being throughout Scotland. In 1900 they joined with the Free Church and became known as the United Free Church of Scotland.

The "Wee Frees" have no connection with the United Free Church of Scotland, for they were small groups of Highland congregations who would not enter the union.

Descendants from the old Jacobite families, mostly gentry and nobility, formed the Episcopalian Church.

A few families of ancient Roman Catholics - probably from Barra or Banffshire - came to the lowlands, but it was the influx of Irish immigrants that led to the development of the Roman Catholic Church in Scotland that we know today.

*(Top) What remains of the Abbey*
*(Left) The Abbey Church entrance in Queen Street.*

In early times, by order of the King, land owners were obliged to build a Church for their tenants.

## The Early Church

In abbey times, the church within the inner precinct had been used for worship by the monks and a privileged few. Always highly organised and business like, the Cistercians had little chapels built on the abbey Granges Keithick, Balbrogie, Balgersho etc as places of worship for the workers and tenants. The clerics of these were appointed by the abbot and all the money collected in them went to help swell the coffers of the abbey.

A church had existed at Bendochy even before the Cistercians arrived in the area and for many years had been used as a place of worship by the people of Coupar Angus. When the Burgh of Barony was created, Lord Coupar was ordered by the King to build a new church for the townspeople, as the local church was in dangerously poor repair and the journey to Bendochy was considered to be hazardous in bad weather as the Isla had to be crossed by ford or ferry. There is no record of there having been a church in Coupar Angus at this period for worship by the ordinary townspeople and it is possible that the former Monks Church may have been taken over for worship after the Reformation and was the one referred to as being in a dangerous state.

Lord Coupar certainly took his time about having a church built, for it was not until 1686 that the people of Coupar Angus had their own Parish Church. Despite this delay, and the uncertainty regarding location, there was a minister, who, poor soul, was killed along with many townspeople in 1654 defending it when a force of 200 soldiers were sent to the town on the King's orders to point out to Lord Coupar his error in supporting the cause of the Covenanters. This force is thought to have been under the command of General Collisto also known as Alexander Colkitto

MacDonald, who was a close associate of the Duke of Montrose. Lord Coupar was fortunate not to have been in town at the time.

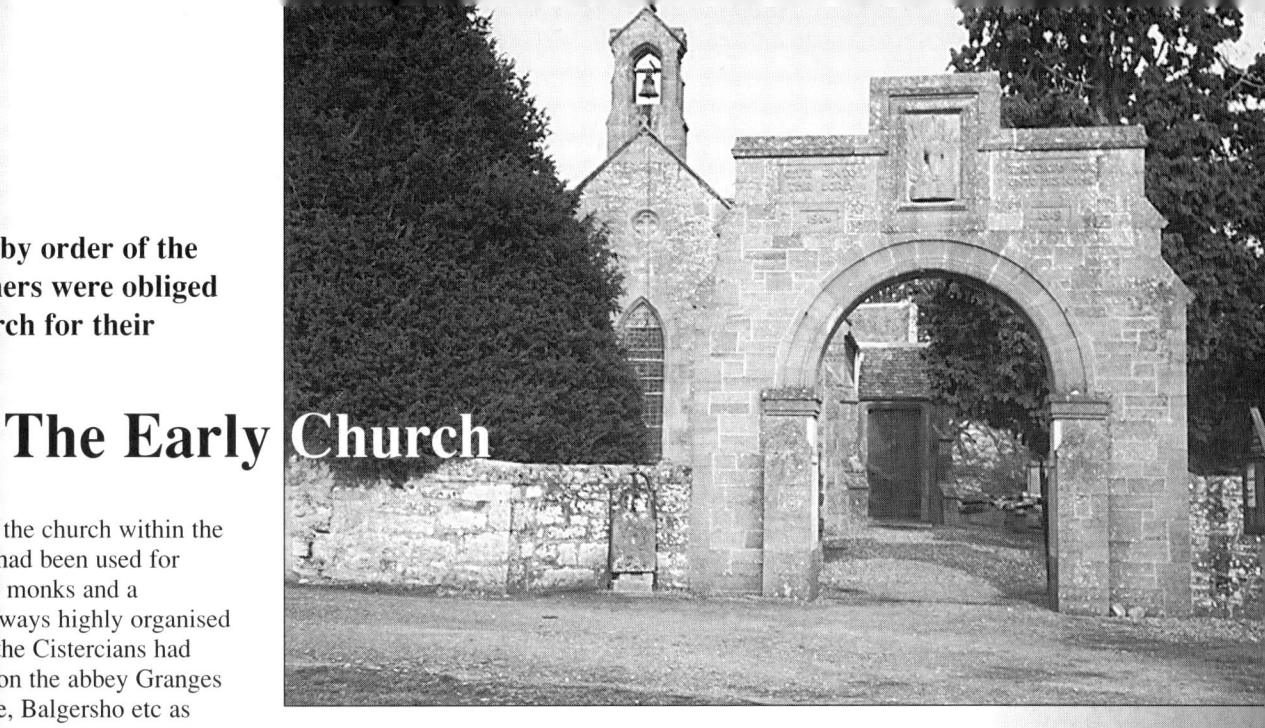

*Present-day Bendochy Church with War Memorial archway.*

## KIRKS IN THE TOWN

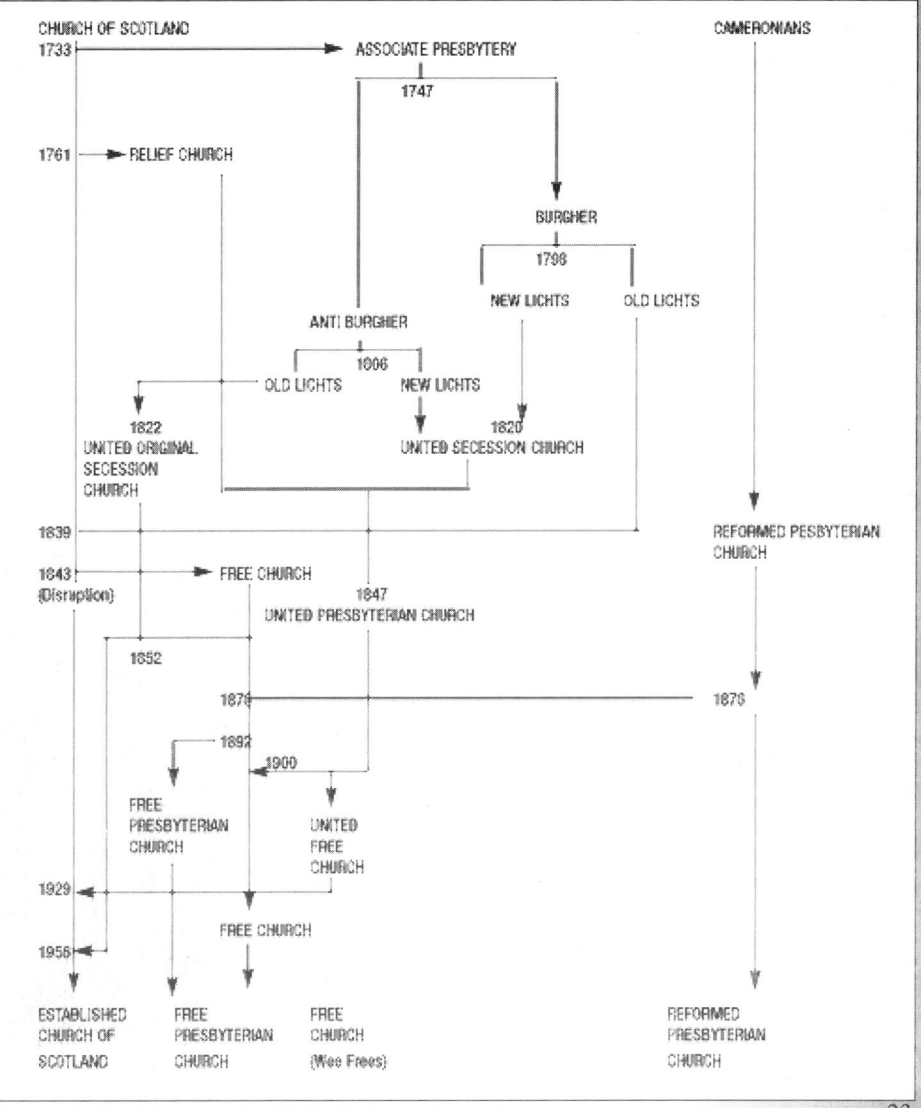

page 23

**The Parish or Established Church in Coupar Angus is better known today as the Abbey Kirk.**

# THE PARISH OR ESTABLISHED CHURCH

Although the King had expressly ordered Lord Coupar to have a new church built for the newly created Burgh in 1607 it was not until 1686 in the second Lord Coupar's time, that the church was built and ready for worship. Where the congregation worshipped until this time is not known but it is unlikely to have been in the former church of the monks, and was most possibly outwith the former abbey precincts.

From Volume ll of the 'Diocese and Presbytery of Dunkeld, 1660 - 1689' by John Hunter, B.D., we know that the Parish Church in 1683 was so dangerous that many of the members of the congregation were afraid to enter it, and that the minister had to resort to preaching "in the abbay vaults". It goes on to say that on 7th February 1686 *"Whilk day, the minister reported that he had now obtayned ane decreet befor the Lords Privie counsel, for building ane new church within the abbey church yeard; and that he was resolved with all diligence to see it made effectual, the present place for divine service being so dangerous and incommodious"*.

On May 7th, *"Alexander Rae, Patrick Brown and William Archer, masons, began to lay the foundation of the new church, being served by two barrowmen; John Barclay, hyred to lead the stones from the old church, James Simson, younger, to throw down the walls, and James Gourlay to digg and carry the morter, and so this work at length after four years obstruction was happily begun"*

It has long been the belief that this church of 1686 was built on the site of the former abbey church, but the above information casts doubt on this theory. We also learn that on December 12th 1686 *"George, Bishop of Aberdeen, preacht Haggaj 2.6,7,8, it being the first sermon that was preacht in the new kirk off Cowpar. Whilk day, collected by James Wightan and James Wilky, collect-ors appoynted thereanent, £14,12s"*

On December 12th the minister proposed to the session *"the buying of ane church byble, since ther was non belonging to the church from former tymes"* He was given permission to do so and on 26th December is written

*This day the new Byble in folio and ane red leather cover produced; payed for it out of the box twelve pounds Scots.*

The minister at this time was George Hay, a graduate of St Leonard's College, St Andrews.

In 1780 repairs to the original church were carried out, then fifty years later in 1831 the building was altered and enlarged to meet the needs of the time. In 1859 work was started on a completely new church which was designed by John Carver, Architect of Kinloch, Meigle, and constructed by local tradesmen William Gow and William Low, Contractors, Muirton; James Anderson, Wright, Coupar Angus; and Andrew Anderson, Slater, Coupar Angus. The work was held up for some time by a legal dispute with the Hill family who objected to part of the new building, the Vestry and Session House, being built over their family burial ground. The original plan was to incorporate the Hill memorials into the new structure but the family won their case and the plans had to be modified and resulted in a much smaller session house and vestry being built than had been originally planned.

(Top pic) The Abbey Church.
(Left) The Abbey Church choir of earlier times c 1900.

The Hill family burial-ground was left undisturbed.
The building stone came from the demolition of the last remaining arch of the former abbey but fortunately a few of the carved stones and tomb slabs from the Cistercian era were saved and brought inside the newly built church where they still remain. A very fine panel of medieval figure sculpture, known as the 'Panel of Weepers' is thought to be from the alter tomb-chest of Sir Thomas Hay, 7th Lord of Errol (1406).

The baptismal font was made from fragments of abbey pillars and holds an ancient bowl which was found in the abbey churchyard, and although its history is unknown, is thought almost certainly to date from the Cistercian period.

The church of 1860 would still have lacked much in the way of ornamentation for this was then considered to be in the Catholic tradition. However a stained glass window was installed in the new church, gifted by Mrs G. Brown of Blairfield.

As time passed the harsh attitudes adopted at the time of the Reformation, began to soften and in 1866 instrumental music was introduced to the services.

This innovation did not please everyone however, and quite a few of the hard-line members left the Parish Church in protest over this. Undeterred the Kirk Session continued with music at the services and in 1892 an organ was installed.

Over the years the church received many gifts which were mostly of communion silver. In 1906 Mrs Macdonald presented a Communion table in memory of her late husband who was Minister of the Parish for over twenty years and a chair to match the table was gifted by the Misses Duncan of Denhead. Two years later the Woman's Guild gifted choir chairs, a brass lectern and had a wooden rail installed round the choir platform.

Over the years the hard working Woman's Guild made many gifts to the church which included paying £310 for the installation of electricity in 1933.

In 1920 the second stained glass window was installed in the Church as the War Memorial for those who lost their lives in the First World War which was known then as the Great War. It was the gift of the congregation and was dedicated on 14th April 1920. The forty names of the fallen are inscribed on a brass tablet below the window which sadly has been joined by another on which the names of those who died in the Second World War are remembered.

This second tablet was unveiled by Provost J. Davidson on 2nd May 1950.

In 1937 Messrs Stewart and Robert Geekie gifted the third stained glass window in memory of their parents, and a year later Miss Lowe of Inglewood presented yet another as a memorial to her parents.

As the 20th century progressed church attendance fell off throughout the country but the Parish Church still had a congregation of over 800 and a Sunday School of 200 children who were taught by the Elders. The Minister's Bible Class numbered over 60 and the Woman's Guild had between 60 and 70 members.

In 1948 the union of St Andrew's Church with the Parish Church, swelled the membership to over 1000 once again.

In 1964 to mark the 800th anniversary of the founding of the Abbey, the Town Council installed an oak pew which was used by the Provost and Councillors on official occasions, until they were replaced by Regional and District Councils in 1975. On the gallery above the pew are the arms of the families who have links with the Abbey and the town. At this time also, an effigy of Sir Thomas, the third Hay to be Constable of Scotland, was brought from the Kirkyard to what the Rev William Cochrane described as "a worthy place in the Abbey Kirk".

The very fine entrance gates to the Kirk-yard were commissioned as part of the celebrations and were designed by the Rev William Cochrane, Minister from 1958 to 1980. Two heraldic shields figure prominently in the design; one bears the Lion Rampant and the other the three Shields and Coat of Arms of the Hays of Errol.

As the 20th century drew to a close and despite prevailing religious apathy, the Parish Church of Coupar Angus or the Abbey Church as it is better known, had a vibrant and dedicated congregation of approximately 500, a well attended Sunday School and an active Woman's Guild.

*(Top) Inside the Abbey Church.*

## THE COMMUNION SILVER

The people of the town had to wait some time for their Church but when it was finally ready for worship it was held in such esteem that its Communion Silver, donated by public subscription, is of exceptionally fine quality and value.

### PARISH CHURCH MINISTERS

1611 Henry Guthrie -
*Also Minister at Bendochy 1595-1631*
1622 David Leitch
1625 Robert Lindsay M.A. -
*Killed defending the Church **
1648 George Haliburton M.A.
1682 George Hay -
*First Parish Church built in 1686*
1699 Thomas Mitchell M.A.
1703 Thomas Ogilvie
1742 Thomas Spankie
1779 Charles Keay
1807 John Halkett
1828 Patrick Stevenson -
*Cholera Epidemic during his ministry*
1881 Finlay Robert MacDonald -
*Founded local company Boys Brigade*
1902 Charles Stewart
1949 John B. Logan
1958 William Cochrane
1981 James Whyte
1987 James Drysdale
1997 Bruce Dempsey

Two cups were made by Perth Silversmith, Robert Gardiner, one of which was presented by the "Inhabitants of Coupar Angus" and the other by "The Yeomanry". They are dated 1687 and are in regular use at present day Communion services. These two cups weigh 27 oz of pure silver and cost £102. 12s. Some indication of their unique importance can be found in that they have been lent to a National Exhibition in Edinburgh on two occasions - in March 1908 and in December 1938.

In 1857 a further two cups were donated by Mrs G. Brown, Blairfield, and in the following year the congregation gifted two more. One can conclude that all these were needed because of the large numbers taking communion.

In 1869 two bread plates and a flagon were purchased by the Kirk Session which cost £9. In 1908 a silver Paten was gifted by Miss Duncan, Denhead in memory of her sister, Jessie.

The communion silver of the Parish Church has been greatly enhanced by the addition of the communion vessels from the former Presbyterian churches in the town - the North United Free Church (St Andrew's), the Relief Church, the Congregational Church and the Original Secession Church.

This quite unique collection of communion plate is of great historic significance.

It has been recorded that in June 1710 the Minister the Rev Thomas Ogilvie had to borrow two cups from the Church at Meigle in order to dispense communion in the Parish Church of Coupar Angus. The reason was that the Rev George Hay who had lost his position as Minister for refusing to take the Episcopalian Oath, had hidden them rather than let them be used for any other than the Presbyterian Communion Service. The cups were duly returned none the worse.

**\* As the Parish Church was not built until 1686, the former Church within the Abbey Precinct may have been used for worship although the latter was in a dangerous state of repair in the years after the Reformation. The matter of where the townspeople worshipped at this point is unclear.**

## PARISH CHURCH MANSES

The first Manse that we have any details of was built in Queen Street in 1781 which was then known as 'Precinct Street'.

In the First Statistical Account which dates from around 1790 the following account is recorded-

*"The Manse was built anew in 1781"*
This would seem to suggest there had been an even older Manse, perhaps on the same site or close-by.

*(Top) The communion silver. The pewter communion collection was gifted to the Perth & Kinross Museum and Art Gallery.*
*(Right) Wedding party on the tennis court of Bogside Road Manse garden c1920.*

The Manse in Queen Street, was added to over the years and in the Second Statistical Account of 1843 we read:

*"The Manse was built in 1781 and has received two additions; rendering it now a comfortable and convenient residence. The Glebe consists of about seven acres".*

It is not quite clear whether or not this Manse was sold by the Church, but we do know when the railway was constructed in Coupar Angus, it ceased to be used as the Parish Church Manse and was divided up into several smaller houses and a shop which over the years has changed from a Butcher's; to an office; to a Tailor's; and to a Restroom or Funeral Parlour.

The former Queen Street Manse is still a handsome building and stands on the west side of the Tolbooth or Clock Tower.

The second Manse was built at the time the railway was being constructed in the town. It was built on an elevated position at the corner of Bogside and Butterybank Road and the cost for this was met by the Railway Company, possibly as part of an agreement for Church land on which to construct the necessary tracks and sidings of what was to become a very important railway station and junction which would bring trade and prosperity to Coupar Angus.

This fine Manse was home to several Parish Ministers then in 1950 the North United Free Church *(St Andrew's)* came back into the fold of the Parish Church and it was decided that their manse in Dundee Road, would become the third manse of the Parish Church. The one in Bogside Road was sold and became a private residence.

When the Rev William Cochrane came to the Parish in 1958 he moved into the centrally situated Manse in Dundee Road, which was smaller and more easily managed than the former in Bogside Road.

The history of this Manse is quite interesting, for before becoming the manse of the United Presbyterian or North Free Church *(St Andrew's)* it had been the Manse of the South Free Church in Queen Street *(now St Mary's R.C. Church)*.

In the 1980's to meet changing needs this manse was sold and one of modern proportions and design was acquired in Caddam Road and is known as the Abbey Manse.

*(Top) The Abbey Churchyard C1900.*
*(Above) The Watch, or Guard House in the churchyard C1900.*
*(Right) Receipt for renting Pew No 48*

page 27

# THE ABBEY KIRKYARD

The Parish Church stands within the ancient kirkyard of the town. A number of years ago many of the old broken stones were removed and placed in what was then thought to be a safe place. Unfortunately, no trace can now be found of them, which is regrettable, but many interesting memorials have survived intact.

Near the fragment of abbey ruin are several ancient stone coffins and a number of interesting carved stones which sadly are now showing the ravages of time.

In the centre of the burial ground is a reminder of the era of the body-snatchers, men like Burke and Hare who would stop at nothing to obtain fresh corpses to sell for medical dissection.

The small octagonal building - the Watch or Guard House - was built in 1822 of abbey stone as the shelter for the watchmen who guarded the burial ground from grave robbers. At that period it had glazed windows, shutters and observation ports. The stonework forming the fireplace is part of the Tomb-slab of Abbot Allan (1296-1335).

In a corner of the kirkyard, near the fragment of abbey ruin, is a further stone building, once known as the Arthurstone Mausoleum, which houses a memorial tablet. It has had a variety of uses in more recent years and it is believed that when the Carmichael family built the Church in Ardler, in memory of their dead children, it was no longer required and so became a 'Rest Room' for the town where coffins could lie before burial.

The former glebe alongside the church was also a burial ground for in 1994 when it was proposed that houses be built here, investigations on behalf of Historic Scotland showed that the area was a medieval burial ground. The plans for house-building were abandoned.

*(Above) The remains of the Abbey C1900, accessible from the Churchyard.*
*(Right) Engraving on Charles Muirhead's tombstone.*

## THE SECESSION OR ANTI-BURGHER CHURCH

On 14th March 1740 a group of Presbyterians from Coupar Angus and the surrounding Parishes who had become dissatisfied with the Parish or Established Church, put the wheels in motion for the formation of another. Initially they were joined with the seceders of Dundee whose Minister held a service every third week in Coupar Angus. In 1747 the Coupar Angus congregation came out on the side of the Anti burghers and the union with Dundee was severed.

The first Minister of the Coupar Angus Church was Robert Carmichael who was ordained on 21st August 1751. There seems to have been a large congregation then, and in 1757 it is recorded that the session consisted of at least eleven elders. The numbers dropped however when the people of Rattray set up their own church four and a half miles away, and those who lived nearer attended there rather than travel to Coupar Angus. Before this time, the nearest sister church had been at Kinclaven.

> " THE COURSE OF HIS MINISTRY WAS BRIEF, BUT THE EXTENT OF HIS GREAT LITERARY ACQUIREMENTS, THE MATURITY OF HIS JUDGEMENT AS A THEOLOGIAN, THE ENLIGHTENED FIDELITY OF HIS OFFICIAL LABOURS, THE SANCTIFIED SWEETNESS OF HIS DISPOSITION, AND THE HEAVENLY SERENITY OF HIS DYING HOUR WILL BE LONG REMEMBERED BY THE SURVIVING FEW WHO HAD THE HAPPINESS OF KNOWING HIS WORTH"

Thomas Small from Abernethy was the second Minister and was ordained on 18th November 1767 but died aged twenty-nine after only five years in the town.

During his ministry a very strange thing happened, for despite nearly all the inhabitants of the town being ardent church-goers, some seem to have believed in the supernatural. It has been recorded that all the fires in the town were extinguished, then broom and whins were lit by friction - possibly by using a wheel - then wood was piled on and allowed to burn to ash. When this had cooled, the Coupar cattle were driven through the ashes to the nearest water as a protection against all kind of diseases and ill-luck. When word of this reached the Kirk Session they reacted swiftly and decided that, as there was no medical proof that this was in any way beneficial, the perpetrators were guilty of meddling with the *"works of darkness"*. The participants were severely rebuked and made a spectacle of after public worship. Unfortunately no details have been given as to what form this took.

James Bishop became the third Minister in 1774 and although the congregation increased during his ministry, he resigned after being 'censured' by the Presbytery in Perth for drunkenness.

In 1781 Alexander Allan took over as fourth minister. During his ministry twenty two men and fifty five women became Covenanters. When he died in 1824 the congregation numbered approximately three hundred.

Charles Muirhead arrived in 1825 as fifth Minister but he died in 1830. A tribute to his memory is engraved on his tombstone.

In 1830 Dr William Marshall was ordained as sixth Minister. He was an author and Historian of acclaim who left a legacy of important books. Among them are 'Historic Scenes in Forfarshire'; Historic Scenes in Perthshire'; and 'Men of Mark in British Churches'

In 1865 a new Church was built at a cost of £1250 *(now the YWCA and known as* the former Original Secession Church) most possibly on the site of the original building of 1751. The original manse *(It is not known where the first manse stood or still stands)* was sold in 1867 and money from its sale, and a further £430 which was raised locally, plus a grant of £250 from the Church Board, went to building another. This manse stands close to the former Church and has been a private residence for many years.

At the time the new Church was built there was a congregation of two hundred and eighty but it was in debt to the tune of £212. Not all the members were Coupar folk however, for we know that quite a number came to worship here from the Parish of Bendochy.

The last Minister was Thomas Granger from Hamilton who was ordained on 28 October 1873. Unfortunately he died suddenly on a visit to Dysart on 23 August 1880 aged seventy-four.

After his death the roll of the Church dwindled and soon what was left of the congregation, joined the Free Church of Scotland who then had two Churches in the town - the South Free Church in Queen Street and the North Free Church in Union Street *(St Andrew's)*.

Since the 1930's the former Church has been the meeting place of the local Young Women's Christian Association (YWCA). The building stands back from the main road opposite the Bank of Scotland and is almost hidden from view by buildings in front of it.

Although no longer a place of worship it is used by a very dedicated group of women whose motto is *'By love serve one another'*.

## THE MINISTERS

1751 Robert Carmichael
1767 Thomas Small
1774 James Bishop
1781 Alexander Allan
1825 Charles Muirhead
1830 William Marshall
1873 Thomas Granger

## THE RELIEF/ ECUMENICAL UNION/ CONGREGATIONAL CHURCH

The Relief Church in Coupar Angus was formed by several incidents which occurred over a period of time within the Secession or Anti Burgher Church. The first step taken by those who broke away was to buy land in Campbell Street, then build a Church capable of seating seven hundred people which was ready for worship by 1790. Its manse was built close beside the Church.

The first Minister of the Relief Church was James Grimond from Kinclaven who was paid a stipend of £75 per annum.

The Minister's father was still an elder in Kinclaven Church and when he and his two daughters visited the Relief Church to hear his son/brother preach, all three were severely reprimanded by the Session of Kinclaven and banned from worship there.

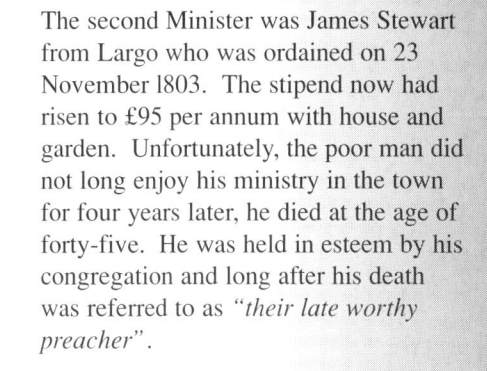

The second Minister was James Stewart from Largo who was ordained on 23 November 1803. The stipend now had risen to £95 per annum with house and garden. Unfortunately, the poor man did not long enjoy his ministry in the town for four years later, he died at the age of forty-five. He was held in esteem by his congregation and long after his death was referred to as *"their late worthy preacher"*.

William Dun from Dennyloanhead followed Mr Stewart and was ordained on 30 November 1808. By now the stipend was £130, but dissent had set in within the church which had an adverse affect on the number of the congregation. David Reston was ordained on 15 March 1826 as the fourth Minister at a reduced stipend of £100, but dissatisfaction still rumbled on. In 1836 there were 450 Communicants on the roll but 85 families from that number lived outwith the town. Mr Reston does not seem to have been happy in Coupar Angus and asked that his resignation be accepted because of differences which had arisen within the congregation.

These problems however seem to have been resolved in 1850 when the congregation announced to the Presbytery that they wished to be joined to the Evangelical Unionists which later would come to be known as the Congregationalists. For many years after this, the church still was referred to as the Relief Church.

After 1850 the Ministers were as follows:

James Frame 1850-1854
Robert Wallace 1855-1876
James John Brown 1876-1881
John D. Brown 1882
David Stevenson McLachlan 1883-1889
William Tiplady 1890-1891
David Zerubabel Haig Forson 1892-1910
Magnus Sinclair 1910-1917
A. W. Groundwater 1921-1952

In November 1954 the Church, and shortly afterwards the Manse, were demolished to make way for housing, the area later being renamed 'Church Place', which is all we have to remind us of the Church which stood here for over one hundred and sixty years.

The Communion Plate is now part of the unique Abbey Church's collection.

## THE BURGHER CHURCH
## 1810 to 1827

The Burgher Church in Coupar Angus was formed as the result of a number of incidents which had caused unrest among the members of the other churches in the town. The matter came to a head when the congregation of the Relief church called William Dun from Dennyloanhead to be their Minister. This was so strongly opposed by some that when Mr Dun was appointed, they broke away from the Relief Church, and a petition containing fifty-two names was handed to the Burgher Presbytery in Perth which requested that a **BURGHER CHURCH** be formed in Coupar Angus.

Permission was given for this on 1st October 1811 and in September 1812 a grant of £20 was received from the Synod to help build a meeting house which could seat four hundred. The minister's stipend was to be £100 per annum with an extra £5 for each Communion.

The Presbytery recommended that the new congregation should "let their seats" in order to raise the money required for the Church's upkeep. Two hundred and thirty two seats were let which realised an income of £29 per half-year. In April 1813 four Elders were ordained but difficulties arose when attempting to call a minister.

Their first choice was a Mr Andrew Young, but the Synod whose decision it was, sent him instead to Lochmaben. The Rev William Proudfoot of Pitrodie was the next choice, and although his congregation was much smaller than that of Coupar Angus, the Presbytery decided against transferring him to the town.

page 30

Finally on 28th June 1815 Mr Daniel McLean from Mauchline in Ayrshire was ordained. At this time the Church had forty seven members and three hundred and thirty three adherents which surely must be an indication that not everyone attending the Church was quite convinced that it was following the right lines. Mr McLean was to be the first and last Minister of the Burgher Church in Coupar Angus. For the next five years all seems to have gone smoothly but in April 1820 the Session had to approach the Burgher Presbytery in Perth for financial advice. Advice may have been given but financial help was not, then three years later the Minister left to take up a charge in Largs.

Several attempts were made to call another minister but all were unsuccessful. For a time the congregation bravely struggled to keep going but in 1827 had to face the inevitable and the affairs of the Church were wound up.

The Burgher Church now deeply in debt, was sold and converted to a weaving shed for hand-looms and most probably was the first small factory or mill in the town. *(More is written about this in the chapter on 'Industry')*

Some years ago, the area where the Burgher Church stood was entirely cleared to make way for housing and renamed 'Laing Crescent'. Some of the older residents of Coupar Angus however still refer to it as the 'Burghers'.

*(Top) The St Andrews Church Womens Guild c 1900.*
*(Right) "Now showing" at the new cinema c 1930.*

## THE UNITED PRESBYTERIAN OR SOUTH UNITED FREE CHURCH

It is on record that this Church in Queen Street was built in 1863. Its former Manse was in Dundee Road almost opposite the fraction of ruin of the Cistercian Abbey.

The first Minister, Thomas Granger was ordained on 28th October 1873 and he ministered in the town for thirty-seven years. He died in 1919, 9 years after his retiral.

Thomas Goldie from Kilwinning was his successor and was inducted on 21 September 1910. For a time he did War Service with the Y.M.C.A. in France but no details have come to hand of who attended to the needs of the congregation during his absence. Mr Goldie retired in December 1927 and the congregation then joined with that of the North United Free Church.

The desanctified building became a Cinema in 1929 replacing the old very basic wooden Picture House which stood back from the road in Hay Street. In the early 1990's it was demolished and a new housing complex was built on the site. The introduction of television was the death-knell of the Playhouse Cinema and it closed down in the 1950's and became a store.

In 1966 the Roman Catholic community in the town bought the building and converted it once more to a Church. It is known now as St Mary's Roman Catholic Church.

### THE MINISTERS
Thomas Grainger    1873 - 1910
Thomas Goldie      1910 - 1927

---

"The Rendevous of the Services"
# THE PLAYHOUSE
**Queen Street : Coupar Angus**
Monday to Friday each evening at 7.15.
Saturdays - 6 and 8.30.
recently equipped with the most
Modern Sound Reproducing System
**NOW and always Presenting
PROGRAMMES OF
UNEXAMPLED EXCELLENCE**
Open very Sunday at 7.15

## THE MINISTERS

James Masson 1884 - 1898
John Linton 1898 - 1917
John Walker 1918 - 1927

### AFTER THE UNION

John Ewing Adam 1928 - 1940
Fred. Levison 1940 - 1949

*\* Pupil teacher's were trained in the class-room situation under the supervision of a qualified teacher.*

## THE NORTH UNITED FREE CHURCH (ST ANDREW'S)

It has been recorded over the years that this church in Union Street was built in 1843 and that its Manse was built two years later in 1845.

The first Minister on record however was inducted in 1884 and was James Masson. Mr Masson retired in 1898 and died six years later in 1904.

The Free Church in Scotland held very strong views on every aspect of life and had their own colleges for training ministers and school teachers. The Free Church School in Coupar Angus was in the building at the corner of Union Street and Blairgowrie Road *(now a private residence)* near the Town Hall. It had two class-rooms which held one hundred and twenty seven pupils although no doubt such numbers would be frowned upon nowadays.

The Free Church teachers were highly respected and it was generally accepted that they were very well trained. When the new Burgh School was built in 1886 the head-teacher of the Free Church school was appointed as its head-teacher and he, and his staff of "pupil teachers"* transferred to the new school. Shortly afterwards the former Free Church School was sold and money from the sale was used to build the very fine hall behind the church.

On 14th December 1927 the North United Free Church was joined by the congregation of the South. The new joint congregation decided to worship in the North Church and the former South Church Manse became the Manse of the new congregation. In 1929 the name of the church was changed to St Andrew's. The North Church Manse was let for a number of years until sold in 1952.

In 1949 St Andrew's Church decided to rejoin the Parish or Abbey Church. In 1951 the empty building was converted and made into a large hall for the Abbey Church which has proved to be a boon, not only to church-members and the organisations who use it, but to the townspeople in general.

*(Top) Union Street with St Andrew's Church on the left*

## A DEED OF SETTLEMENT THE NORTH FREE CHURCH (ST ANDREW'S)

From a Deed of Settlement dated 7th November 1851 which belonged to Mr David Reid, Hay Street, the following interesting facts have emerged.

As we already know, the Free Church was built in 1843 and its Manse two years later. Very little was known about the

---

### OLD CHURCH IS NOW NEW CHURCH HALL

**£3000 Reconstruction Scheme at Coupar Declared Open.**

In the presence of a large and representative gathering, the Earl of Mansfield performed the opening ceremony at Coupar Angus Abbey Church's new hall on Wednesday.

The hall is the former St Andrew's Church, and has been completely renovated at a cost of nearly £3000. A service of re-dedication was conducted by Rev. J. B. Logan, minister of the Abbey Church; Rev. R Henderson, Glenisla, Moderator of Meigle Presbytery; and Rev. J Sibbald Clark, Alyth, Presbytery Clerk. The service opened with the National Anthem; the Moderator conveyed the Presbytery's best wishes to the congregation.

Rev. Mr Logan introduced Lord Mansfield who, in an inspiring address, said that grand hall had been reconstructed with faith and prayer, which meant far more than money.

The thousand communicants formed by the union of the two churches had all worked, under Mr Logan, towards the achievement.

Lord Mansfield remarked he was well acquainted with Coupar Angus, and knew the late Rev. Charles Stewart, a former minister of the Abbey Church, very well. He took a great interest in the burgh, and was proud to think the congregation had that beautiful hall as a centre of religious work. Before Britain could solve the present problems facing her, Christianity would have to be brought more into the lives of the people.

**A Dream Come True**

Declaring the completion of their new hall was a dream come true. Mr Logan said that, last February, it had been decided by the Reconstruction Committee to proceed with the work. Plans had been drawn up and a representative Hall Fund Committee had launched an appeal for money. Various efforts had been organised, and, with the aid of money from the sale of property, the total sum required had been obtained.

They now had an outstanding suite of modern halls, including a large hall seating 350, provided with comfortable chairs and an up-to-date fitted stage with curtains. There were also a smaller kitchen, and cloakrooms.

Mr Logan hoped the halls would be fully used as a centre of Christian community life. He was sure they would b a great asset to the church and its members, both old and young,

Letters of best wishes were read from the former minister of St Andrew's Church and his wife, Rev. and Mrs F. Levison, who were unable to be present, and from Mr and Mrs Frank Benzies, who were on holiday.

Tea was served by the Woman's Guild and the Hall Fund Committee.

**Enjoyable Concert**

The platform party included Rev. J. B. and Mrs Logan, Rev. R. Henderson, Rev. J, Sibbald Clark, the Earl of Mansfield, Messrs A. Watson, J. M. Bowie, W. Crerar, A. MacKay, and Provost Davidson. Miss V. Allison accompanied the praise. Mr J. M. Bowie, Session Clerk, proposed a hearty vote of thanks to Lord Mansfield.

A first-class concert followed by talented members of the congregation:- Miss C. Bruce (soprano); Misses M. Duff, V. Allison, Messrs R. G. King, G. Petrie (vocal quartette); Mr Wm Gilzean (readings); and Mr Adam Rennie (violinist). Mr G. C. M. Robertson was accompanist.

Votes of thanks were proposed by Mr Logan.

Free Church School however but from a study of the Deed, we learn that it was purpose built at the same time as the Church and Manse. The Free Church placed great emphasis on good education and had its own teacher training college. The Church, Manse and School were built on what was then part of St Catherine's Croft. They had right of access to the Coupar burn through the Croft, as had the other feu holders there, which shows how important it was then as a source of water supply. Access to the burn was "by the road leading to the burn", and the older residents of the town to whom I have spoken, feel sure this could only be St Catherines Lane which runs between the old Malt Barns and Lamb & Gardiners. At one time this lane was an important route with a ford across the burn.

Shortly after the Parish School was built in 1877 the Free Church School was sold and the money went towards building a new hall behind their Church. I had concluded, wrongly, that the sale had realised a considerable sum of money, for the hall, which is used to the present day, is of very fine construction. Mr Reid put me right however when he told me that his Great Grandfather - Mr David Reid of Elmsley, Dundee Road, who had a building firm in the town then, had constructed it for the cost of the materials only.

Before his death Mr Reid had the marble clock which was presented to his great grandfather by the Church at that time, as a token of appreciation.

On a silver plate, much worn by years of polishing, the following is inscribed:

**PRESENTED TO
DAVID REID ESQ
BY THE DEACONS COURT AND
CONGREGATION OF THE FREE
CHURCH OF COUPAR ANGUS AS
AN ACKNOWLEDGE-MENT OF
HIS SERVICES IN BUILDING
THEIR HALL
DECEMBER 7TH, 1880**

*(Top) Belmont Castle Eventide Home, Meigle.*

## BELMONT ESTATE

Mr Reid's firm also built the extension to the mansion house at Belmont, for Prime Minister Sir Henry Campbell Bannerman, which is an indication to the size and prestige of the firm and to the skill of its workforce, for Belmont is a quite outstanding edifice. Mr Reid also leased the Leys quarry near Meigle which, no doubt, was the source of the stone.

Initially Belmont was a small fortalice consisting of a small, very plain square tower rising three stories to a parapet. It belonged to the Nairns of Dunsinane then in the 17th century it passed to lawyer, Sir George Mackenzie of Rosehaugh. He was known as Bloody Mackenzie for his relentless persecution of the Covenanters. Later, through marriage, the estate came into the possession of the Wharncliffe family from whom Sir Henry Campbell Bannerman acquired it.

The Airlie family owned quarries in nearby Auchterhouse. The stone was transported by the Dundee and Newtyle Railway* to the Airlie Stone Yard in Dundee where it was dressed and sold on to building firms. Many of the tenements which still survive to the present day, were built of Airlie stone. Some was also transported by ship to London and was used as paving slabs. Of a quite distinctive blue/grey colour, the Airlie Stone was in great demand at a period when country houses were being rebuilt and extended.

*The Airlies were amongst the biggest shareholders in the railway company.*

## THE SCOTTISH EPISCOPAL CHURCH

The Episcopal Church in Scotland has been non-established and independent since 1690. It is part of the world-wide Anglican Communion whose origins are believed to date from the time St Ninian arrived in Scotland around 400 AD.

In Roman Catholic medieval times, it was formed into thirteen Sees with Archbishoprics at Glasgow and St Andrews, but after the Reformation their Bishops lost their power.

In a futile attempt to retain power over the Scottish Presbyterian Church, James VI restored episcopal jurisdiction on two occasions by reforming it in the style of the Church of England. This course of action led to disaster and much conflict. In 1592 the Presbyterians overthrew the King's "tulchan bishops" whom they suspected were supplying the Scottish nobility with funds.

Episcopacy was restored in 1610 and an uneasy period of peace followed until in 1637 there was a riot in St Giles Cathedral, Edinburgh, when Charles I attempted to introduce a Scottish Prayer Book and episcopacy was condemned at the Church of Scotland General Assembly the following year.

Undeterred by past events Charles II re-introduced episcopacy and created new bishops, among whom were the moderate thinking Leighton and the more extreme

Sharp who would become Bishop of St Andrews. Once more a period of unrest followed this action and conflict broke out in which Sharp was murdered and Leighton resigned.

During the Jacobite uprisings of the 18th century, the Episcopal Clergy were very greatly persecuted. The 1712 Act of Toleration had allowed Episcopalians to use their Church of England Prayer Book, but some still preferred the 1637 Scottish Prayer Book and refused to pray for the King.

An Act of 1719 made it illegal for more than nine people to worship together and although very few Episcopalians actually had supported the Jacobites, two of their Clergy were hanged and many of their meeting houses were destroyed.

In 1746 a further Act restricted worship to gatherings of only five persons. After the death of Bonnie Price Charlie in 1788 the penal laws were repealed, but it was not until 1830 that Scottish Episcopalianism began to develop and strengthen. New churches started to be built then, and in 1851 the first cathedral in Britain since the middle ages, was built in Perth, and dedicated to St Ninian. The Scottish Episcopal Church still remains an independent and disestablished church in communion with the Church of England.

## ST ANNE'S SCOTTISH EPISCOPAL CHURCH

As long ago as 1790 the Scottish Episcopalians of Coupar Angus and district were meeting together for worship. Around 1824 the Rev J. Torry who was rector at Meigle, began to hold services regularly in the town, firstly in a room in Gray Street and later in premises in Reid's Close where there was also an Episcopal school-room which was known as the 'Girls' or 'Industrial' school.

In 1846 several of the leading members of the church including Edward Collingswood of Keithick and Mungo Murray of Lintrose*, decided to have a church of their own and set about looking for a site.

These two gentlemen worked hard at finding finance for the project and donations were given by friends all over the country. From an old Minute Book we see that William Ewart Gladstone and the Dowager Queen Adelaide, widow of William IV, were among the subscribers.

The church, which was ready for worship in 1848 is of simple English architecture, and stands a short way back from the Coupar Angus to Forfar Road.

Inside the church are five stained-glass windows manufactured by Clutterbuck of London, and installed in 1890 in memory of various members of the Graham Menzies family of Hallyburton. Two smaller windows in the chancel are in memory of Canon A. Clark-Barnacle who after twenty-two years at St Anne's, died in 1951.**

When General Sir Basil Hill retired to Coupar Angus, it was to be a blessing for St Anne's which was experiencing grave financial difficulties at the time, for he took it upon himself to put the Church finances on a sound footing. Apart from giving substantial sums personally to the endowment fund, he persuaded many of his friends to grant covenants in favour of St Anne's which resulted in £5000 being added to the endowment fund.

St Anne's and the Abbey Church work closely together, and for a good many years now have combined to hold a joint service on Remembrance Sunday in the Abbey Church. A joint service of evening worship is held on Good Friday each year in St. Anne's.

### THE MINISTERS

| | |
|---|---|
| Dean J. Torry | 1822 - 1879 |
| Rev Robert Ritchie | 1880 - 1887 |
| Rev E. Sugden | 1887 - 1901 |
| Rev Dr E. W. Sutton | 1901 - 1902 |
| Rev Forrest Bell | 1902 - 1914 |
| Rev H. Boys | 1914 - 1919 |
| Rev S. Deuchar | 1919 - 1927 |
| Canon A. Clark-Barnacle | 1929 - 1951 |
| Rev N. M. Gordon-Kerr | 1952 - 1954 |
| Rev W.M. Girdwood | 1954 - 1967 |
| Rev Canon C. Glennie | 1967 - 1973 |
| Rev A.A. Conn | 1973 - 1979 |
| Rev D. Roberts | 1979 - 1984 |

St. Ninian's and St. Catherine's were linked in 1970 under Rev D. Grant. Rev Roberts was first Rector of the three charges.

| | |
|---|---|
| Rev A. Gray | 1984 - 1990 |
| Rev H.M.D. Petzsch | 1990 - 1991 |
| Rev K.W. Rathband | 1991 - |

St Anne's has a very well equipped, comfortably heated Church Hall which was built in 1966 on land gifted by Miss C. Clark of Gowan Bank. It is used mainly for Church purposes - meetings of the Congregation and the Vestry, the Women's Guild, the Lunch Club and Sunday School. Some other organisations outwith St Anne's are also allowed to use it e.g. the Mother's Union, Bendochy W.R.I. and the Bible Society of Scotland.

*(Left) St Annes Episcopal Church at the start of the Forfar Road C1900.*

## THE RECTORY

The Rectory was built in Forfar Road in 1866 and was described at the time as a 'Mansion House'. The cost of this very fine house was met by Mungo Murray of Lintrose.

It remained as the residence of the Rectors until 1982 when it was sold to a private bidder. The Rector at that time was the Rev. David Roberts who was the first joint Rector of St Ninian's, Alyth, St Catherine's, Blairgowrie and St Anne's, Coupar Angus. He then re-located to the newly built, more easily managed, Rectory in Rosemount Park, Blairgowrie, which is jointly owned by the three charges.

*I am deeply indebted to Mr John Kiddie who was Secretary to the Vestry for over forty years until 1992, for his help in supplying the information which filled the gaps in my research. My thanks are also extended to Mrs Averil Valentine for her assistance.*

\* *Mungo Murray had travelled with David Livingstone in Africa*

\*\* *Canon Clark-Barnacle was Provost from 1934 to 1936, a County Councillor and a member of the Eastern District Licensing Court.*

## THE ROMAN CATHOLIC RELIGION

It was Rome educated St Ninian who brought Roman Catholicism to Scotland around the year 397.

Scotland was very isolated from Europe at that time, and there were great differences between Catholicism and the Celtic Church. Gradually however it bowed to the power of Rome.

By early medieval times the Roman Catholic Church in Scotland was very powerful and directed by the Pope in Rome, with whom close links were kept. As time passed it became more and more corrupt and those of the Protestant faith, were often cruelly treated.

Over the years distrust and dissatisfaction had grown steadily, and matters finally culminated with the Reformation of 1560 when Roman Catholicism was well and truly overthrown, and the land and wealth of its abbeys which was considerable, was distributed amongst the nobility and the powerful families in Scotland. The former Abbeys through lack of use, fell into decay many having been seriously damaged by the rampaging Protestant mobs who had been influenced by the hard line John Knox.

There was no organised Catholic opposition to the Reformation although many groups and individual Catholics continued to worship in secret. A few Bishops made unsuccessful attempts to reform but these came to nothing and in 1571 John Hamilton, the Archbishop of St Andrews, was hanged as a traitor which ended all opposition.

There were scattered groups of Catholics in small communities in the Highlands and Islands who were served by travelling Priests, one of whom John Ogilvie a Jesuit, was hanged in 1615. Three hundred and sixty one years later he was canonised.

Anti-catholic feelings ran high for many years and in 1688 a mob damaged James VII Chapel in Holyrood Palace. None-the-less Priests were still being trained in Scots Colleges in Paris and many ministered in secret under great difficulties until 1878 when freedom of worship was restored. It had been estimated that by 1800 there were thirty thousand Catholics in Scotland.

1829 saw the removal of all restrictions regarding worship with the passing of the Catholic Emacipation Act, and the first publication of the Catholic Directory took place that year. Blairs Seminary in Aberdeenshire was also refounded at this time.

It was the influx of Irish immigrants to Scotland in the mid 19th century however which swelled Catholic numbers dramatically. As a result of this, rivalry erupted especially in the world of football which had become a very popular spectator sport with the very large working class who had been lured to the towns and cities by the Industrial Revolution and the work and wealth it created.

## ST MARY'S ROMAN CATHOLIC CHURCH

From the time of the Reformation until 1829 it was illegal to practice the Roman Catholic faith. After Roman Catholic emancipation, the Catholic community of Coupar Angus had no church within the town in which to worship, and it was not until 1966 that the disused cinema *(formerly a Church)* was bought, and planning permission obtained to re-convert the building to a Church once more.

The original church had been built by the United Presbyterians in 1863 but later they changed the name and became known as the South United Free Church.

*(Top)_ Happy faces at the Gospel Hall which visited Coupar Angus after World War II C1976.*

It closed in 1927 and the dwindling congregation joined with the North United Free Church. In 1929 the North United Free Church became known as St Andrew's.

The conversion from cinema to church was not an easy one, but through hard work and perseverance the volunteer work-force by October 1966 had the church ready for worship.

Clergy from both the Church of Scotland and the Scottish Episcopal Church attended the Service of Dedication as did the Provosts of Coupar Angus, Blairgowrie and Alyth. It was a momentous and moving occasion and would long be remembered.

Four hundred years had passed since Catholics in Coupar Angus had their own place of Worship. After the Reformation when catholicism was banned, those in the town who still clung to the old faith, had risked their lives to meet and worship, secretly, in the ruined vaults of the former Cistercian Abbey of St Mary's.

The present day church is also dedicated to St Mary and strangely, the first priest of the new Catholic Church, Father McNamara, had formerly been a Cistercian monk until ill-health had forced him to seek a less demanding roll in the Church.

The link with the past was complete.

*(Top) The story of the Cameronians.*

### THE CAMERONIANS

was the name of a regiment which was raised in 1689 by the Earl of Angus, made up of devout Covenanters, the followers of Richard Cameron, one of the most zealous in condemning Ministers who accepted the "Indulgences".

Cameron was sent off to Holland in an attempt to teach him "to hold in check the ardencies of his heart and tongue", but on his return to Scotland he was as inflexible as when he had left. He formed an extremist 'army', the Cameronians, and in June 1690, he published the 'Declaration of Sanquhar' then fled to the hills. A month later at Airds of Moss, near Auchinleck in Ayrshire, he, his brother, and nine followers, were killed after a fierce struggle with dragoons under Bruce of Earlshall.

His head and hands were cut off and taken to Edinburgh where they were presented to the Privy Council who had them displayed at the 'Netherbow'.

## COUPAR ANGUS NEWSLETTER

The Winter 2000 Coupar Angus Newsletter (CAN) featured an attractive sketch of Bendochy Church by Roland Portchmouth. Bendochy is an unusual little Parish in that it has no village, no school now and no hall except a very small Church Hall. Long ago it was a very busy agricultural area but modern farming methods have decimated the population. Many of the former farm houses and cottages are now homes of business and professional people.

Before the 18th century, farm land throughout Scotland was divided into small sections which one family could cultivate with the few implements available then.

# AGRICULTURE - the legacy of the Monks

## CHANGES AND GROWTH

A narrow uncultivated ridge called the 'run-rig', divided one person's holding from his neighbour, and these small farmers virtually scratched out an existence, hardly producing enough to feed themselves and their livestock, never mind having a surplus to sell or barter at local markets for other essentials.

During the 18th century however, great changes occurred in agricultural methods which altered forever the lives of country people throughout lowland Scotland.

After laws were passed by Parliament, laws which made the enclosure of land compulsory, those who could afford to do so (the big landowners), fenced or walled, not only the arable land, but also much of the common grazing on which country people had depended for grazing their livestock, without which they could not exist. Farm-touns or villages like Caddam, Welton, Balbrogie and Keithick, were virtually decimated, for many young people were forced to leave the land and their homes, and make for the nearest town or city where they hoped to find work. Some were employed on the now much larger farms and 'Trysts' or 'Feeing Markets' were held in Coupar Angus and district, where those seeking farm-work, or a change to another farm, could meet prospective employers and strike a deal. Some young men joined the armed forces while others emigrated with their families, to parts of the then British Empire - Canada, Australia, New Zealand and South Africa, in the hope of a better life. Those who went abroad, often retained a deep love for the land of their birth, and the many Scottish place-names, scattered throughout these countries, bear testimony to this.

In South Africa there are suburbs of Johannesburg called Blairgowrie and Dunkeld, and rural towns such as Dundee.

Quite a few people however, seem to have settled in the town of Coupar Angus itself for in 1755 the population of the Burgh was 1,491 and by 1793 when almost all the land had been enclosed, it had risen to 2,076. The enclosure of agricultural land was not all bad news however, for it coincided with several other changes in farming methods. One was the introduction from Holland, of root crops such as turnips, and these and potatoes, could now be grown economically in the larger fields. Previously the peasant farmer had ploughed with cumbersome oxen but these were now replaced with horses, which were much more easily managed, and Smiddies sprang up like mushrooms in country towns and their surroundings.

Another very important result of growing turnips was that cattle could be kept inside over the winter months and fed on them. Formerly, most of the cattle had either to be slaughtered or sold off to drovers who took them to the cattle market in Falkirk where a ready market was found in English buyers who came north specially for this event. In 1781 a Tannery or Tan-Yard was built in Pleasance Road in the area of the town which then lay in Forfarshire. It has been well recorded over the years that 2,600 hides of different kinds were dressed annually - 50 per week. Hides could possibly have been brought to the Tannery from the surrounding district as it is unlikely that this number of animals would have been slaughtered each week from the immediate area of Coupar Angus. The leather produced however, would have found a ready market, for there would have been a great demand for it by the 15 Master-shoemakers and 2 Saddle-makers in town, to make into boots, shoes, harnessing etc.

The ability to over-winter cattle also meant that the accumulated manure from them could be spread on the land to improve its fertility and crops such as wheat could now be grown on land where previously it had not been possible. Flax, linseed, barley and peas were replaced by potatoes, turnips and wheat. Barley would of course, continue to be grown to fill local needs - to be milled down into meal - the staple diet of many. It served brewing purposes too for as well as the several Inns in the town, over 40 houses were licenced to brew ale, an art which was a legacy from the Cistercian monks who had excelled at this.

The quality and size of livestock also improved around 1800 and an Agricultural Association was formed and most local farmers were among the fifty strong membership.

In 1808 Hugh Watson the tenant of Keillor, started to gather high quality stock and produced cattle of outstanding quality. He is credited with being one of the three outstanding farmers whose cattle breeding eventually led to the Aberdeen-Angus breed of cattle which is acclaimed throughout the world.

The drainage of low-lying land also began and in 1830 embankments were built along the river Isla to prevent the low-lying land from the regular flooding it had been subjected to over the centuries. In 1831 Lord Douglas Hallyburton devised an ingenious drainage scheme for the time, by having a massive soak-away constructed, which allowed flood water from a burn, to seep away instead of inundating the land.

Although the Enclosure Act had resulted in many country people leaving the land the larger fields with their increased crop yield, meant there was a better supply of food for the ever increasing population of the towns and cities. A great many people were now living there, attracted by the prospect of the work the Industrial Revolution had created.

Potatoes had been introduced to the area in the 18th century and this crop proved to be a boon as the staple diet of many of the poorer folk whose diet until then had consisted of the by-product of corn - porridge, oat- bannocks and gruel. The work-horses were fed on corn which stored well over the winter months.

In 1840 a Farina Mill was built at Couttie *(in earlier times Couparmaculty)* by a Mr Archer. This mill turned surplus potatoes into flour and was a great asset to local farmers when crops were heavy and supply outstripped demand. The cultivation of potatoes carried on over the years and by the end of the 19th century large quantities were being transported by rail, to buyers all over the country. There was a flourishing trade in seed potatoes which were taken by rail to Montrose and Dundee then shipped to buyers on the Continent of Europe. This new market unfortunately rendered the Farina Mill obsolete and it closed down. In February 1912 it was demolished by Mr Hugh Swanson, a mason from Coupar Angus. The felling of the chimney, or 'stalk', which was over 80 feet in height apparently presented no problem.

The railway closed in 1982 but the trade in potatoes still flourishes, only now they are transported by road.

The arrival of a railway had meant that coal could be transported to hitherto fuel-starved Coupar Angus quickly and cheaply, and coal fired factories sprang up which employed large numbers of townspeople. There was a down side to this however, for it also meant that cheap imports of farm products could also be transported throughout the country, which had a disastrous effect on farming generally, and many small farmers had no alternative but to give up.

As the 19th century drew to a close the economy of the area was given a massive boost when soft fruit growing was introduced. Not until World War I, when the country once more relied on home produced food, did the farming economy improve.

Conditions in the Valley of Strathmore proved ideal for raspberry growing and many farmers diversified to them, and to a lesser degree, strawberries. Each summer berry-pickers flocked to the area on foot, by bus and by train from as far afield as Glasgow. Blairgowrie in particular attracted large numbers of Tinkers, now called Travelling People, who not only met there for an annual get-together of friends and relations but in order to make money by fruit-picking.

In the early days the pickers brought along their own tents, then later dormitories were constructed as living quarters on the larger farms, for berry-farmers were aware that they were totally dependent on the pickers to harvest the crop. Many of the local school children along with their mothers, spent the entire summer holidays fruit picking and what they earned, most often paid for their winter school-wear. From 1989 to 1991 due to cheap imports of soft fruit from the former Eastern Block countries at the end of the Cold War, the price of home produced raspberries dropped by 45%. The berry-farmers however worked together and met this new and disturbing challenge to their livelihood.

In recent years fruit-picking has become less popular and fewer berry- pickers now come to the area. Berry-farmers have had to look further afield and many bring pickers in by bus from towns such as Kirkcaldy, Dundee and Perth. Quite a number of students come here now from the former Eastern Block countries, not only for the money they can earn, but to see as much of Western Europe as they can at the same time. In the past twenty years or so blackcurrants have been successfully grown here in ever increasing acreages and are harvested successfully by machine. Over 40% of the raspberry crop is now harvested mechanically by machine, but demand for top quality hand-picked berries is still very strong. This means that berry-pickers are still required if this sector of the industry is to survive.

After World War I, much of Lintrose Estate was purchased by the government, and many small-holdings created for returning soldiers, which was a departure from the usual policy of absorbing small farms into large ones. These thrived for many years before some amalgamated, and several of the houses were sold. All are now in private ownership.

*(Left) Couttie bridge over the river Isla with the chimney of the Farina Mill in the background C1900.*

Until the 1960's there was a Preserve Works in the town where a great deal of locally produced soft fruit was made into jam. It was known locally as the 'Jeelyworks' and was located where the Chicken Processing Plant is now.

Since the beginning of the 20 century, there has been a steady improvement in agricultural equipment. More and more machines have been introduced, machines which are capable of doing every possible task imaginable. This has led to a further depopulation of the countryside. A good example of this can be seen in figures from the nearby Parish of Bendochy which is totally agricultural. In 1811 the population there was 748; by 1951 it had dropped to 462; and in 1981 it was 177.

Earlier this century the tractor had replaced the horse and the many Blacksmiths whose livliehood had depended on them had either to diversify or give up.

Now almost every small country school has closed and many of them have been sold and are now private residences. With fewer farm workers employed, their former cottages have been sold or rented out as self-catering holiday accommodation.

Most of the farms in the area are 'mixed' farms, where cereals, potatoes and berries are grown. Some also keep cattle while on the dairy farms grass crops are grown as silage for winter feeding. Carrots are also cultivated in some places and they can be successfully harvested by machine. Fields of cabbages, cauliflowers and brussel-sprouts still need a sizeable workforce to harvest them, although they can be planted out by mechanical means.

A comparatively new crop is Oilseed Rape which, as its name suggests, produces oil for culinary purposes. There are Spring and Winter varieties and the fields of bright yellow flowers quite transforms the countryside. Winter barley is also grown in quantity and often the countryside is green all winter through. At one time there was an auld-wives saying - *'A green February fills the kirk-yard'* which was thought to be caused by a mild winter leading to unseasonal growth in February, and not killing off germs. Now-a-days, unless the countryside is covered in snow, every February is a green one and has little to do with mild weather and everything to do with the hardier varieties of crops which grow throughout the winter.

Coupar Angus and the Valley of Strathmore is one of the finest farming areas not only in Scotland, but in the United Kingdom. Much of the excellence for this is due to the Cistercian monks who, so many centuries ago, came here and taught the people of that time the fine agricultural skills upon which to-day's farming excellence is founded.

## AGRICULTURAL LEASES OR TACKS

The Cistercian Monks were the first to devise leases when their land holdings became so large that they could no longer manage them personally. These 'Tacks' were very carefully thought out with provision made for every possible eventuality. One such example was that should the out-going tenant be old and infirm, the new lease-holder had to see that he was cared for.

A Bailie was appointed to see that all the details in the leases, which were always very much in favour of the land-owner, were strictly adhered to.

In the 20th century the laws regarding rented land have eased and are much more in favour of the tenant than of the landowner, but it took a long time to change to this and from a Lease dated 1842 some very interesting facts have

*(Top) The former Bendochy school, now a private residence.*
*(Left) Farm workers houses at Coupar Grange, now private residences.*

emerged. Very few of these documents have survived in private hands and this one was lent me by the late Mr David Reid of Hay Street, Coupar Angus whose ancestors farmed at Myreridge *(Myreriggs)*, in the nearby Parish of Bendochy.

The Lease *(agreement)* between Patrick Murray Esquire of Simprim *(near Meigle)* and William West described Myreridge *(Myreriggs)* as a 'Pendicle' of about 79 Imperial Acres. William West and all other tenants of pendicles on this land had the privilege of grazing the pasture and cutting the reeds at nearby Monkmyre. It is thought that the loch then was mostly marsh and bog and could have been flooded peat diggings. Modern drainage of the surrounding fields may possibly have created the large expanse of water we see there today. There are certainly few reeds in evidence there now and what they had been used for in the past is matter of speculation - for roofing the cotter houses - for strewing on the floors or perhaps as bedding for the livestock? The farm was let for a period of 19 years and should the tenant die during this period his heir, be they male or female, could take over the lease for the remainder of the time.

The proprietor reserved the exclusive right to hunt and shoot or to fish the running streams on the farm at any time he or his friends wished. Should they want to quarry or excavate for minerals they could do that too. Marches *(boundaries)*, could be altered and roads could be put through the property and the landowner could cut down and carry off timber growing there. Should crops be damaged by any of these activities, the tenant could deduct a small percentage from the rent in compensation.

This was fixed at "Seventy pounds of clear money" per annum which had to be paid at two terms - Candlemas and Lammas. In addition, the tenant had to "drive yearly to the house of Arthurstone, five Bolls of coals or any article of similar weight, from the Shore of Dundee or a proportionally greater number of carriages a shorter distance". He had also to "perform his proportion, along with the other tenants, of all carriages necessary in the repairing or the rebuilding of the Church, Manse and Offices, School and Schoolhouse and other Parish Buildings in which the lands lie and to abide by and implement regularly and without delay, the calls made on him by the Ground Officer".

There was the right of appeal should the tenant think the demands made by the Ground Officer to be excessive. The tenant had also to agree to live on the farm permanently and stock it properly and cultivate and manure the fields in the manner laid down by the proprietor. In addition to keeping the farm-house and steading in good repair, the five pendicle houses on the land were also his responsibility in matters of maintenance. Other conditions in the lease were that the tenant had to reclaim, at his own expense, the moor ground on adjoining Southfield which would have been a formidable task then, and to "protect and preserve" the hedges. Insurance on the property had to be met by the tenant and the corn which was to be made into meal, had to be ground at the Mill of Coupar Grange where the "accustomed dues" were to be paid. Should the tenant "bankrupt himself" he was not to be allowed to remain in the farm and his Creditors were banned from interfering in any way with the land, its crops and livestock.

Should the lease not be renewed at the end of the 19 years, the tenant had to "flit and remove himself, his family, servants and dependents, goods and gear furth and from the lands hereby let at the termination of this lease".

Not a lot was left to chance as you can see and the lease was very much in favour of the land-owner. In 1861 a new one was drawn up for Mr West but now the land belonged to Mrs Morrison of "Wester Errol and Cupar Grange Heiress of Entail", who is believed to be the daughter of Patrick Murray Esquire.

By then a new farm house and steading had been built and not surprisingly the rent had gone up accordingly. These buildings are still there today and the property is known now as Easter Myreriggs - a small soft fruit farm of about two acres.

William West died in 1868 some years before this lease expired. He and his family are interred in Bendochy Kirkyard where the headstone can still be seen.

*(Left) Lintrose House.*

## COUPAR ANGUS FARMERS SHOW OR THE HORSE SOCIETY

Country people have always had a great interest in heavy horses which dates from the time they were used for all the heavy work on farms. Life on the farms then could be very lonely for the unmarried workers who lived in bothies, and the plough-lads who looked after the horses. In grooming and feeding their horses a bond akin to friendship was forged between man and beast.

It was because of the love and interest in these majestic animals that the Horse Society was formed in Coupar Angus by Mr R. G. Halley *(Bob)* of Glenesk, Coupar Angus and Mr Pat Thomson, after World War II, at a time when people were searching for new interests which the war had for so long denied them.

Bob Halley was to become the Secretary and Treasurer for the duration of the Society.

Similar shows were held in Alyth, Blairgowrie, Bridge of Earn and further afield but it was generally accepted that the Coupar Angus show was the most outstanding with the greatest exhibition of Clydesdale horses in Scotland. The horses mostly belonged to the farmers, but they had no objection to the men who worked them, taking them along to the shows. A few had special show harnesses which would also be worn when they went into town. Mostly however it was the every day working harness that was worn after having been polished with loving care until it looked like new. Decorations made by the handlers from cotton, wool or straw added a festive touch to show occasions.

The first Coupar Angus Farmers or Horse Society Show was held on Saturday 14th July 1945 in Foxhall Park with £200 and five cups to be competed for. Such was the popularity of this event that over one hundred horses took part. They were all lined up on the Common waiting to be led across the road to Foxhall. When the first horses arrived back at the Common there were still horses waiting to take part in the parade. There were also classes for ponies and a tug-of-war with a prize of £20 for the winning team.

In 1946 the show was held in a field where Larghan Park is now, and the prize money on offer had risen to £500. Meals were available there but in the newspaper advertising the show, those planning to attend were advised to bring their own 'lunch baskets' with them.

Corston was the venue in 1947 when the prize money had risen to £800. On 10th July 1948 it was again held at Corston. This year also saw the North East Scotland Jumping Championships as an added attraction. Refreshments, lunches, high teas and snacks were on offer, and the Dundee Police Pipe Band played to the crowds. There is mention for the first time of a car park which cost five shillings per car, and buses ran regularly to and from the show ground. Admission was two shillings and six pence for adults ($12^1/_2$p) and one shilling and three pence for children.

The following year, 1949 Corston Farm was still the venue but now the prize money was £1000. 1950 however was the last time the event was held at Corston.

Sadly the Horse Society was the victim of its own success for as each year it had grown bigger and more popular, so too had it become much more difficult to organise and run.

Although there was great enthusiasm and support for the show to continue as an annual event, volunteers to help with the organising and running of it were so thin on the ground, that the decision was reluctantly taken to discontinue it. On 14th July 1951 the last show was held at Knollhead Farm, Kettins not far from the sites of the previous shows.

The Society had made quite a bit of money during the few short years of its existence and this was now divided amongst various organisations and charities in the town.

The gate pillars at the entrance to Larghan Victory Park were paid for by the funds of the Horse Society.

The Industrial Revolution which had roughly coincided with the enclosure of farming land, had forced many displaced country dwellers to leave their former homes and way of life.

# THE COUNTRY ESTATE - AS A SOURCE OF EMPLOYMENT

Very many headed for the cities where they joined disaffected townspeople, as they felt a better living could be had in the mills, shipyards, steelworks etc. Most only exchanged one miserable existence for an even worse one, but some managed to better themselves by becoming skilled in one of the many new technologies of the times.

Although the average worker lived in miserably poor accommodation, massive fortunes were accumulated by the businessmen and share-holders of the industries which were first in the field of mass-production techniques, for the British Empire at that time was crying out for all manner of goods which they could supply. This new-found wealth created a fashion, for many of the 'nouveau riche' wished to raise their social position and splendid houses were built, surrounded by formal gardens and parkland befitting their wealth. In England, Manor houses were built by the moderately rich, while the very wealthy merchants and industrialists bought land to create large estates, then built a fine mansion house set in beautifully landscaped gardens.

In Scotland however, the impact of the Industrial Revolution was not so great as in England, but fine country estates began to emerge none-the-less, although possibly to a lesser degree in opulence to those in the south. The nobility and old established landed gentry who also had business interests, followed the trend and their estates underwent radical changes with large comfortable houses being constructed, or the smaller original ones extended. In carrying out these improvements - the building of stately homes; the laying out of landscaped gardens and policies; and the construction of workers houses, boundary walls etc., a great deal of work was created for tradespeople, and an army of masons, carpenters, slaters, plasterers, labourers and gardeners was required. Once the house was built and ready for occupation, a large staff of domestic servants was needed to see to the smooth running of the 'big house', and to the care and welfare of its occupants in the days before central heating and the labour saving devices we have today. A large staff also was kept busy in the gardens and grounds all year round, keeping paths, flowerbeds and shrubberies in perfect order. The hot-houses were tended with care to ensure there was a plentiful supply of flowers, fruits and vegetables for the mansion house.

## THE HALLYBURTON ESTATE

A good example of an old and long established family estate in the local area is Hallyburton. The present day mansion house dates from 1680 and replaced the fortified tower at Pitcur which had been the family home for centuries in the days when security was paramount. In 1432 Walter, second son of the 1st Lord Hallyburton of Dirleton, married the co-heiress of Alexander de Chisholm, the result of which was that Pitcur became his. Although it is now in a ruinous state, it is still apparent that the castle conformed to a T-plan with the main block lying east and west, with a wing projecting northwards from the centre.

The walls were built of red-brown coursed rubble four storeys high, and the

*(Top) Hallyburton House*
*(Left) Coupar Grange mansion house.*

main block has two vaulted chambers with a kitchen in the basement. The sleeping accommodation was situated on the higher floors. Due to its dangerously ruinous state, the building can now only be viewed externally. Quite close to the Castle is one of the finest souterrains in Scotland. This tunnel-like underground structure of several interconected passageways, as long ago as in Roman times, was used when danger threatened, to hide the people who lived there and to store the grain and animals, for once inside no trace of the entrances could be seen. Sadly since its discovery in the late 19th century, a fair bit of deterioration has taken place and the remaining passage is in danger of collapse. In order to view the Souterrain, permission must first be obtained from Hallyburton Estate Office before proceeding to the site.

As the 17th century progressed and times became more settled, the Hallyburton family, and others like them, left the secure but comfortless Pitcur Castle and moved to a spacious country house at Hallyburton. The last Hallyburton daughter married the Earl of Huntly and around 1820 they made their home here. It was the Countess of Huntly who planted the majority of the trees on the estate and the arboretum adjacent to the west end of the house. The tradition of planting trees carried on through the generations and the woods around Hallyburton contain many which were pioneers of their time - Douglas Fir, Wellingtonias and Western Hemlocks. These trees were introduced to Great Britain in the 18th and 19th centuries by Scottish Landowners who first tested their viability in this country. On the death of the Countess, the estate passed to her youngest son, Lord Frederick Gordon who, in later life, married Lady Augusta Kennedy Erskine, a widow living at the House of Dun in Angus. After their marriage they divided their time between Hallyburton and the House of Dun. Lady Augusta was the natural daughter of William IV by Mrs Fitzherbert. When Lord Herbert died Hallyburton Estate was bought in 1880 by Graham Menzies, the founder of the Distillers Company Ltd. At this time the house was altered and extended, a new front was constructed and a wing added. On the death of his father, W. D. Graham Menzies inherited the estate and in 1890 on his marriage, took up residence. The present owner Julian Llewellen Palmer is his great grandson. In 1903 W. D. Graham Menzies added to the house and considerable renovations and improvements were carried out. These were designed by Sir Robert Lorimer, one of the foremost architects of the period. The lodge and lodge gates

*(Top) The gardens at Hallyburton in their heyday.*
*(Centre) The Isla in flood at Coupar Grange.*
*(Left) Pitcur Souterrain.*

were built at this time to make an impressive main entrance to the now magnificent house set in its seven acres of splendid gardens.

In 1912 Hallyburton House achieved acclaim when it was featured in an article in the March edition of the 'Scottish Field'. The estate at this time had a very large domestic and outdoor staff which consisted of butler; housekeeper; lady's maid; seamstress; upstairs, downstairs, kitchen and nursery maids; nannies; a dozen gardeners; foresters and estate handymen; grooms; and coachmen. The outdoor workers were housed within the grounds. Long before education became compulsory for all five to thirteen year olds, the Laird made sure the children of the estate workers were taught the three R's - Reading, Writing and Reckoning (Arithmetic).

Consecutive owners of Hallyburton have always maintained close links with the town of Coupar Angus, and in the days of the more personal Town Council, took an active part in the town's affairs. Their generosity to the town in general, and its poor in particular, is a matter of record, while their reputation as employers is one of excellence. From a newspaper of January 1871 comes the following:

"Admiral Lord J. F. G. Hallyburton gave an annual fete for his servants at the Mansion House".

This event carried on until the outbreak of World War I. The Hallyburton name comes up time and time again in Newspapers, Log Books and Minutes of the various meetings of activities and events in the town.

World War I changed forever the way of life of every man, woman and child in the land. Women in particular had been given a new taste of freedom when they had been accepted into the workplace which until then had been the sole province of the male. This was not a freedom they would give up without a struggle and even when men returned from the war, many women retained their war time jobs. Domestic service, which had at one time been the only option for women of refinement, was now less attractive. As time went on fewer and fewer women entered service, and by World War II good domestic servants were increasingly scarce. Hallyburton Estate suffered from the lack of domestic and outside help as did all other large houses. Labour costs were high which along with increased taxation, made anything but minimal help simply unaffordable.

During the wars many mansion houses were abandoned, while some had their roofs removed in order to avoid paying what had become crippling taxes. Others were sold for very little and turned into country house hotels. The present Laird's grandmother Mrs M. J. Lindsay however managed to keep Hallyburton Estate intact and from 1946 to 1989 and endeavoured as far as possible, to run it in a traditional way. In 1988 however the house was considered to be too big and too difficult to keep, so the east wing was demolished, making a more compact and easily run home.

Thanks to the forward planning of the present Laird - Julian Llewellen Palmer, in the early 1990's a large area of Community Woodland was planted at Tullybacart, with well signposted walks which are in constant use by many walkers and hikers. This far sighted project not only utilises unproductive hill land, but gives pleasure to those who value our countryside.

Time cannot stand still! Hallyburton may not be the big employer of former times, but it has changed and adapted to meet present day needs. The smaller house still remains an architectural gem. The grounds, although less formal, are still attractive, and the farm land reflects the excellent husbandry lavished upon it.
*Julian Llewellyn Palmer died on Easter Sunday 2002 whilst on Safari in South Africa.*

### KEITHICK ESTATE

Over the centuries the spelling of Keithick has altered dramatically -

KATHICK: KATHIK: KATHYK: KETHEG: KETHEK: KEITHOCK: KETHET: KETHICK: KETHILK: KETHYK AND KEYTHYK
The Barony of Keithick existed long before the Cistercian Monks arrived in

(Top) Keithick House
(Left) Fishing in the burn that runs through Keithick den.

page 43

the area in the 12th century. In two Charters drawn up at Perth, William the Lion (1165-1214), brother of Malcolm IV the founder of the Abbey of Cupar *(now Coupar Angus)*, gifted the lands of Keithick and Aberbothry to the Monks. The Cistercian Abbey was almost certainly built of stone quarried on Keithick Estate. The quarries there produced very fine stone for centuries and when exhausted were used as infill sites in the 1960's by the former Town Council of Coupar Angus. In the closing chapter of the Abbey, the last Abbot, Donald Campbell of the powerful Argyle family, divided the finest Abbey lands amongst his five natural sons and Nicol Campbell became owner of Keithick. Keithick remained in the Campbell family until 1750 when due to financial difficulties, it was sold.

From 1750 until 1800 Keithick's owner was James Stewart Mackenzie *(sometimes Stuart)*, the Lord Privy Seal who also had the estate of Kirkhill near Meigle which was bounded by Camda Estate *(Camno)*; Lord Eilbank's Estate of Fullerton and Newtyle Estate. From this the conclusion is reached that Kirkhill stood where Belmont Estate is now. The first Wood - James - became owner of Keithick in 1800 after the death of the Lord Privy Seal.

The Woods of Keithick are descendants of the famous Admiral Sir Andrew Wood of Largo (1455-1515). He was a wealthy merchant and one of James III's most loyal and trusted supporters, who in 1487 saved the King's life by ferrying him across the Forth in one of his ships, in order that he escape from his enemies who supported his son James Duke of Rothesay, who coveted the throne. Matters came to a head in 1488 at the Battle of Sauchieburn with the fifteen year old son victor. Attempting to escape from the battlefield, James III was ambushed and killed, fulfilling the prophesy that he would be betrayed by his nearest of kin.

Admiral Andrew Wood quickly transferred his allegiance to the new King James IV, and undertook to defend the Firth of Forth against attempts by the English to invade Scotland. So successful was he that he has been called the 'Scottish Nelson'. He was rewarded with a knighthood, the custody of Dunbar, the right to build a 'fortalice' *(small fort)*, and to erect a Burgh of Barony at Largo. Largo Tower now stands on the site of the Admiral's fortalice.

Sir Andrew Wood was quite a character and had a canal excavated from his home to the Church at Upper Largo so that he could be rowed to worship.

*(Top) Another view of Keithick House.*
*(Centre) Keithick den.*
*(Above) Balgersho den.*
*- all C1900.*

The exact date when William Edward Collins Wood became owner of Keithick after James is not known but it was sometime before 1835. In the Statistical Account of that date he is described as being a very public spirited gentleman and prominent member of the Scottish Episcopal community in Coupar Angus. The Episcopal Meeting Place in Reid's Close which doubled as a Girls School, was owned by him. He was sympathetic to the plight of the poor and under-privileged of the district, and when handloom weaving was at an all time low in the town, and weaving families were suffering severe hardship, he donated large quantities of foodstuffs to the 'Soup Kitchen' set up in Coupar Angus to save the destitute from starvation.

Keithick Estate is unusual in that ownership has been passed on through the female line of the family on several occasions.

Not long after Miss Brodie Wood became the Laird of Keithick, a meteorite crashed through the roof of the South Lodge. The actual meteor, which was estimated to be one metre across, entered the atmosphere on 3rd December 1917 at 1.15 p.m. It was reported as having been seen as far north as Aboyne in Aberdeenshire, and to the south at Hexam in Northumberland, as it travelled over north west Fife and the Carse of Gowrie. When it reached the Sidlaw Hills it stopped glowing and what sounded like an explosion occurred but this was possibly a sonic boom as the meteor broke through the sound barrier. The Curator of Perth Museum at the time - Mr Henry Coates was so intrigued by such a rare happening that he set about collecting evidence and even found an eye-witness in Mrs Welsh of Carsie Farm, who had seen one of the fragments hit the ground.

Four of the fragments which landed locally were recovered. One had dug itself into the lawn at South Corston Farm while another landed in a field at Carsie just south of Blairgowrie.

Fortunately for the inhabitants of South Keithick Lodge, the piece which hit the roof was not as large as that at Essendy which weighed over 22 lbs. Casts were made of the smaller meteorites and taken to Perth Museum and the larger piece was sent to the Royal Scottish Museum in Edinburgh.

Although of rather severe demeanour, Miss Brodie Wood was a generous benefactor and gave handsomely to many charitable causes as well as to those in need. She was Guide Commissioner for many years and a wide range of activities took place in the grounds of Keithick House which are still remembered by the older generation of former Guides in Coupar Angus. It is rather sad therefore that she is best remembered for the acrimonious legal action over a 'Right of Way' at the river Isla, when Mrs Barnett of Coupar Angus took her to court. Miss Brodie Wood defended the action successfully but feelings ran high in Coupar Angus and those who had supported Mrs Barnett made an effigy of poor Miss Brodie Wood and paraded it through the town before burning it on a ceremonial bonfire.

In retrospect it can be concluded that Miss Brodie Wood had no personal objection to people walking along the river banks in a law abiding fashion, but was placed in an untenable position when her tenant at Boatlands Farm complained of damage to fences and trespass over his fields.
There is still no Right of Way at Boatlands but that does not seem to deter present day Coupar Angus folk from walking there.

When Mr Douglas Wood Parker died at the early age of 56 Mrs Wood Parker lived on at Keithick. She was the Perthshire County Commissioner of the Girl Guides from 1956-1966. She took an active part in many local activities and especially in St Anne's Church and fund raising events were often held in the grounds of Keithick. Mrs Wood Parker died in January 1984, and on her death the estate passed into the hands of Trustees on behalf of the children of her eldest daughter Mrs Stirling who continues to farm there. Her husband Mr James Stirling has looked after the estate since the death of Mrs Wood Parker.
The very fine 'B' listed Mansion House which was designed by Architect D. A. Whyte-Templeton of Newtyle, was built in 1825 of stone from the Keithick quarries. It stands on the site of the ancient village of Keithick which also was known as Cassyend *(Causewayend)*.

As Keithick is not Mr & Mrs Stirling's main residence, the Mansion House has been divided in such a manner as to be easily reinstated to its original. Part is rented and the other is retained by the Stirlings for use on family occasions. The North and South 'B' Listed Lodges and Farm Steadings were built in 1850. All the formerly tenanted farms, apart from the Mill of Keithick, are now farmed by Keithick Farms Limited.

### KEITHICK ESTATE OWNERS FROM THE REFORMATION TO THE PRESENT

|  |  |
|---|---|
| 1560-1800 (approx) | Nicol Campbell and his descendants. |
| 1750-1800 | James Stewart McKenzie |
| 1800-18?? | James Wood |
| 18??-1911 | Edward Collins Wood (Born 1841) |
| 1912-1915 | Miss Collins Wood |
| 1916-1952 | Miss Brodie Wood |
| 1952-1967 | Douglas Wood-Parker |
| 1967-1984 | Mrs Janetta Verona Wood-Parker |
| 1984 | Trustees on behalf of Mrs Stirling's children |

*(Top) Balgersho House C1900.*

Between 1830 - 1850, and despite great difficulties, most of Scotland's railway lines were laid. It was an immense achievement for tunnels had to be blasted through hillsides, and bridges, embankments and viaducts had to be constructed.

# RAILWAYS - forerunner of industry

Marsh and bog-land presented problems but finally these were overcome, and lastly stations with raised platforms were built so that passengers could board and alight from trains in safety. In the early days, many people did not appreciate the danger of crossing the new railway lines and were killed. At the local village of Ardler, then Washington, an eighteen month old youngster was very seriously injured by a passing train, when crawling on to the line through a gate which had been left open.

By 1850 over 1000 miles of railway had been laid in Scotland. The Glasgow to Aberdeen lines were operating, and for the first time ever the ordinary people of Coupar Angus could travel widely from their own doorstep.

Until 1840 rail travel had been very costly. In 1844 a law was passed which made it mandatory for each new line to have at least one train a day travelling in each direction. The trains had to have carriages with seating which was protected from the elements, and the fare was not to be more that one old penny per mile in the third class coaches. As trains stopped at every station, many people now were able to travel to work by train.

The railway made a tremendous difference to the townspeople of Coupar Angus, for fuel had been scarce as the peat diggings had all been worked out for some years, and now coal could be transported quickly and cheaply to the heart of the town. Factories were built which were powered by coal, and businesses gradually sprang up in the healthier economic climate.

Not everyone was happy about the success of the railways however, for the companies who owned the Turnpike roads and the horse driven coaches saw their income gradually draining away. Some farmers complained that the smoke from the engines would damage their crops, while others thought that travelling by rail would cause heart attacks. A few complained that *"the working classes now had too much freedom of movement"*.

(Top) The station in 1968.
(Centre) The Railway Hotel, or "Red Hoose" as it was known as C1900.
(Right) The railway level crossing near The Cross C1900.

page 46

# COAL SUPPLIES AND THE RAILWAY

Coal arrived at both Dundee and Perth harbour by ship and was collected at the above mentioned places for delivery by horse haulage to the various towns, villages and estates in the district.

Completion of the Dundee & Newtyle Railway in 1832 meant that coal could now be collected locally by Merchants and Hauliers at the Railway Company's Newtyle Rail terminus. This arrangement existed until 1837 by which time the Newtyle and Coupar Angus Railway Company had been formed and had extended the railway to Coupar Angus.

For the next eighteen years, coal and other goods would be handled at Coupar Angus Station, both for the town, the landward area and for Blairgowrie until the opening of the Blairgowrie branch line in August, 1855.

The Newtyle & Coupar Angus Railway Company was purchased in January, 1846 by the Scottish Midland Junction Railway Company to become part of the railway under construction between Perth and Forfar. In time this line would extend from Perth to Kinnaber Junction *(a junction at Montrose)* where it met the East Coast line, forming a rail link between the cities of Perth and Aberdeen and would be the property of other railway companies before 1860 when it became part of the Caledonian Railway.

Coal supplies would also have been available via the Scottish Midland Junction Railway on the completion of the Perth- Forfar line.

As time passed, railway carriages became quite luxurious. As more and more people travelled by rail, hotels were built, some of them quite splendid, *(Gleneagles)* to cater for the new mobile public. In Coupar Angus the Railway Hotel *(now the Red House)* was built by a Banker in 1849, who no doubt was long sighted enough to see that his investment would pay handsome dividends.

The Tannery or Tan Yard in Coupar Angus was built in 1781 in keeping with most small towns for leather was an essential commodity for boots and shoes and harnessing for horses which were the only means of transport then. Soon after the Tannery came a Sawmill then in 1835 William Culross set up a Printing Business in the Victoria Buildings where the Co-op Supermarket was untill 2001. William Culross was a man with more than one iron in the fire however for the Post Office and the first Savings Bank were also run by him.

*(Top) Speedy coal deliveries from three old friends.*
*(Centre) The level crossng seen from the Cross*
*(Right) The Coupar/Blairgowrie railway bridge over the river Isla.*
*- all C1900.*

page 47

From medieval times in Scotland flax had been woven into linen and was a small but important home industry which was mostly concentrated in Fife, Angus and East Perthshire, although throughout the country cloth would have been produced in smaller quantities for local needs.

# INDUSTRY - Linen and Jute

## THE COUPAR ANGUS LINEN AND JUTE INDUSTRY

In the early days linen was required by religious establishments - abbeys, priories etc., and for use in the homes of the wealthy classes, while coarser linen was woven for the needs of humbler folk. In Alex J. Warden's book 'The Linen Trade' mention is made of the carters, wainmen, lackeys and women in 1314 at the Battle of Bannockburn, "putting on shirts, smocks and other white linens".

Over the years the industry suffered many fluctuations and set-backs and in an attempt to boost trade in 1686 an Act was passed, which made it mandatory for all corpses to be wrapped in Scots linen grave-cloths.

In the 18th century a flourishing home-weaving industry was concentrated in Causewayend. At this time the weavers were mostly men, while the women and girls of the household were kept busy spinning flax into yarn, for it took five or six spinners to keep one loom going. Nearly all the women and girls did nothing but spin and this is where the legal term of 'Spinster', for an unmarried woman, was derived.

In Coupar Angus however, at the season of planting and harvesting, all indoor work was abandoned and people took to the fields. Although farm work was just as hard if not harder than that of spinning and weaving indoors, the towns-people could work alongside their friends and neighbours and catch up on local gossip and events. To help relieve the back-breaking toil of harvesting a piper was employed by the farmer to keep the labourers happy.

After the Jacobite Risings in the late 17th and early 18th centuries, a "Board of Trustees for Manufacture" was set up to try to stimulate the trade and improve the quality of linen, for it was believed that this would lead to weavers earning more money, which in turn would ease the unrest throughout the country. To achieve this, money was made available to reward those who could devise new methods of weaving or improve existing looms. Those who could produce extra fine quality linen were also rewarded. Foreign manufacturers were brought in to teach the Scots better spinning and weaving skills, and many poorer people were given flax, hemp seed, and in some cases spinning wheels, in an attempt to produce cloth of a higher quality, which hopefully, would lead to increased earnings and a better standard of living.

In 1763 a Spinning School was set up in the town where girls between the ages of 8 and 14 were taught. There is no mention however, of where this school was. To make sure quality remained high, Inspectors and Stamp Masters were appointed by the Board of Trustees, and those who flaunted the rules and regulations were prosecuted.

After the Treaty of Union (1706/7) there was a dramatic increase in the export of linen from Scotland to the southern part of America.

In the reign of Queen Elizabeth of England, land in the southern states of what is now the United States of America was colonised by the English who named it Virginia after their Queen.

In 1619 the first Negro slaves were brought to America from Africa, first of all to clear the land which would eventually yield excellent crops of sugar, cotton and tobacco upon which massive fortunes for the owners would be based. The coarser type of linen known as harn was shipped to Virginia from Dundee to be made into clothing for the slaves on

*(Top and above)*
*Jack Oldings third factory C1900.*

these estates. It is quite possible that some of this harn could have been produced in Coupar Angus.

Salted herring also, was exported from Scotland to feed the Slaves until the Plantations produced crops for their own needs.

History has recorded that every attempt to avert trouble in the Highlands was unsuccessful but the increase in Linen production was. Much of the cloth woven locally was taken to Balgersho. There was a well and bleaching green at Bogside, on land owned by Mr McLaren of Beechhill. Although it had always been a traditional bleachfield, in 1861 he barred the weavers from using it but relented, after public outrage was graphically reported in the local 'Advertiser' Newspaper.

At this time the Bleachfield at Balgersho was owned by John Ross, but later it would be in the hands of the Geekie family. As well as owning the bleachfield, Ross was also a linen merchant who bought from local weavers then sold the linen on, most often to merchants in England. Then, men known as 'Hawkers' were employed by merchants and they travelled the countryside buying linen direct from the weavers there.

**By 1780 water-powered Mills were being built in many parts of the country and in 1798 the first mill of several, was built in Blairgowrie on the banks of the river Ericht. The Coupar burn however did not have enough water to power a mill so none was built here until much later when coal, transported by the railway, became available.**

By a complicated system there was enough water however to supply the Waulkmill in Precinct Street where woollen cloth for local needs - coats, blankets and plaids - was washed and worked to make it more compact *(known as fulling)* and sometimes was dyed. Mr George Young, has been given a lot of credit for the success of the linen industry in Coupar Angus in the early 18th century. He has been described as *"a very able and astute business man who started off penniless and by the age of forty had accumulated a fortune"*. At this time to take goods from place to place was difficult and costly, for roads were poor and transport was horse-drawn. Young proposed that a canal between Perth and Forfar would solve the problem, but although a survey was done the scheme did not go ahead because of the high cost of construction.

It has been recorded that Mr Young *"applied harsh and parsimonious methods"* in all his business dealings for he and his agents *(Hawkers)* scoured the countryside for the cheapest yarn which he then supplied or sold to weavers. As there was no fixed rate then, terms for cloth were agreed between him and the individual weaver, and were always to his advantage. He extended credit to those who could not make ends meet and by deducting small amounts from the price of the finished cloth in repayment, effectively tied the weaver to him, for it was unlikely the man would ever be able to pay off the debt. This was called being 'thirled' - an old word meaning 'enslaved'.

By 1747 despite his penny-pinching ways Mr Young was insolvent, which was most likely caused by a prolonged period of depression in the trade.

As the century drew to a close, the trade once more picked up and in 1792 - 97,810 yards of brown linen and 116,793 yards of harn were produced locally for the English market.

## THE BUCKY

The first mill or weaving shed we know of in the town was a manually operated one in what had formerly been the Burgher Church in what is now Laing Crescent and still known as the 'Burghers' to many of the older generation. It was called the 'Bucky', which is possibly an indication of its size, and the tale has been passed down that at break-times the workers sat outside on a wall and discussed all manner of things in such detail that they became known as the 'Coupar Parliament'

*(Top) George Street with the second power loom factory chimney in the background.*
*(Left) Causewayend with Campbell Street going off to the left.*
*- all C1900.*

# THE MANUFACTURY

The second mill was still a manually operated one, and stood at Middlehills. In the Valuation Roll of 1855 it is described as a 'Manufactury' owned by the Myles family who rented it to Mr John Robertson. Mr Robertson employed three hundred workers, three quarters of whom were women. As it is difficult to visualise from what is left of this building that so many people could have worked there, it can be concluded that the spinners and weavers probably worked from home and that the 'Manufactury' was used for finishing and storing the cloth. Hessians, sackings, sheetings and drills were produced by John Robertson and there is evidence that the business had been operating for quite some time before 1855 when the first Valuation Roll was introduced. In 1861 things were not going well for the weavers however and from the 'Advertiser' of the period comes the following -

"THE DISRUPTION OF THE AMERICAN UNION IS SAID TO BE THE CAUSE OF THE VERY DEPRESSED CONDITION OF THE HAND LOOM WEAVER AND SO WHILE YANKEES ARE FIGHTING ABOUT THE "BLACK SLAVES" OF AMERICA THE REBOUND OF THEIR WHIPS IS LASHING SEVERELY SOME OF THE "WHITE SLAVES" OF BRITAIN" and again - "WEAVERS WAGES REDUCED _ OUR PRINCIPAL MANUFACTURER HAS SEEN FIT TO STINT STILL FARTHER THE MISERABLE PITTANCE ALLOWED TO THEM FOR THEIR WORK. HANDLOOM WEAVING IS NO DOUBT A DECAYING TRADE!"

A charity Soup Kitchen was set up in town during the winter of 1860/61 to alleviate the suffering of the poor. It was supplied with greens and vegetables from the leading farmers of the area while the ladies of the town supplied bread on a regular basis. The Manufactury closed in 1868 as it was unable to compete against the three power-loom factories which had sprung up in 1866. It lay empty until 1873 when it was leased as a warehouse to Messrs Geekie and Black who had built the second power loom factory in the town. Ten years later it again became vacant but was never re-let. This co-incided with the premature closure of Messrs Geekie and Black's Linen Works.

As we already know, the first mill to be built on the river Ericht at Blairgowrie was in 1798 and was called the Meikle or Blairgowrie Mill. By 1864 there were eleven water-powered mills on the banks of the Ericht but it was not until 1866 that Power Loom Mills were built in Coupar Angus. It was only when the Caledonian Railway was built and coal could be transported here cheaply and efficiently, that mills for the production of linen and jute became economically viable.

In 1866 three power loom factories were built and this would change the town dramatically, for house and shop building increased rapidly with the new found prosperity with the many jobs the mills created.

New roads were constructed and old ones upgraded while some had a change of name. What had formerly been referred to as the 'New Road' was now Union Street, Barlatch Street became George Street, the Timber Market became George Square and the Wynd was changed to Trades Lane. Most houses in town had gaslight for a gasometer had been built in Campbell Street as early as the 1830's and streets too were now lit by gas.

## GUTTED MILL MAY BE CLOSED EIGHT MONTHS
### £15,000 BLAZE AT COUPAR ANGUS

Fifty-five Coupar Angus juteworkers were thrown out of employment yesterday by a fire that gutted Durie & Miller's jute mill, and did £15,000 damage. Blaze robbed the burgh of its main industry.
Mr David Turner, manager, told a "Courier and Advertiser" reported that it was not possible to state when work might be resumed at the mill.
It is understood, however, that there is little likelihood of the mill resuming for about eight months.
The place has been completely gutted, though it is thought some of the machinery may be again fit for use. Fire started in the black-out about seven o'clock yesterday morning. It is believed to have had its origin in the engine-room. Workers coming along the street saw the sky lit by the glare and found on arrival that their place of employment was blazing.
So fierce was the heat that telephone wires near the building, which is situated close to Coupar Angus Station, were melted.
About ten feet from the blazing building was a power sub-station belonging to the Grampian Electricity Co., Ltd.
It was thought for a time that the station with its 11,000-volt cable might become involved, and workers stood by ready to shut off the power. Luckily the work of Perth Fire Brigade, under Depute Firemaster Duncan, averted this danger.

### All-Day Battle
The fire had a firm hold and part of the roof had fallen in by the time the brigade arrived, after a record-making run
From the entrances at the railway siding they poured in water while burning rafters crashed among the ruined machinery. Jute cloth bags, machinery, and bobbins were a blazing mass, with which the firemen were busy for most of the day.
The building, a single storeyed structure, has for years been the centre of Coupar Angus's only industry. During the past few months the workers have been busy carrying out Government contracts, providing sand-bags, &c.
Auxiliary firemen helped the Perth brigade and assisted in retrieving from the office the petty cash and a number of books and papers. Employees' gas masks, left overnight, went up in smoke.

*(Top) Jack Olding's third power loom factory.*
*(Left) Cutting from Courier & Advertiser 26.1.40*

## THE FIRST POWER LOOM FACTORY

In the Valuation Roll (1866) the first power-loom factory is described as being 'near the Railway Station'. This rather sketchy address was later changed to Union Street. This factory was built by Peter, William and John Ferguson and run by them until 1880 when it was bought by James Campbell and John Smith. It then became the Coupar Angus Linen Works.

In 1882 Mitchell and Morrison were the registered owners, then two years later in 1884 the name was changed to Coupar Angus Jute Works, which is an indication that jute production had started here. In 1895 it was sold again, this time to Alfred Wigglesworth. In 1910 Mrs Selina Wigglesworth of Bournemouth, was the registered owner of the mill which was now rented to Messrs Durie and Miller. In 1915 Durie and Miller were still the tenants and the owner Mrs Wigglesworth had changed her address to London.

In 1920 Durie and Miller were the owners of the factory which continued to operate under their management until on 25th January 1940 fire gutted the building which resulted in fifty-five workers losing their jobs. The mill which stood on the land now owned by Messrs Lamb and Gardiner, was never rebuilt.

## THE SECOND POWER LOOM FACTORY

The second mill was also built in 1866 by Mr Alex Geekie of Baldowrie in partnership with Mr Andrew Black. It stood where the Grampian Country Food Group's Processing plant is now in George Street. It was called the 'Strathmore Works' and was described as 'Flax Spinners and Linen Manufacturers'. Five hundred local people were employed here but its success into linen manufacture was to prove short lived, for it it was unable to recover from a severe blow which was dealt to the finances of the Company.

*(Top) Opening of the refurbished chicken factory - (L to R) Wilson Marshall and Lord Gray of Conton.*
*(Right) An advertisement showing the second factory, which became the chicken plant.*

In order that the factory should be run as cost-effectively as possible, the decision was taken to send an Agent to India to buy the necessary raw materials direct. Unfortunately the Agent entrusted with the very large sum of money for the transaction disappeared with the cash.

The factory had to close and five hundred local people were thrown out of work.

In 1885 part of the former Linen Works was turned into an Agricultural Engineering Works by a consortium of the following business men - Joseph Lindsay, Engineer, Dundee, David McFarlane, Manufacturer, Coupar Angus, Charles Boyd, Solicitor, Coupar Angus, Alexander Geekie, Baldowrie, Robert Grant, Surveyor, Coupar Angus, and John Smith, Manufacturer, Alyth. Misfortune was to dog this venture also, for although two hundred workers were employed, by 1895 the Agricultural Engineering Works was no more and the building had been taken over by John Fleming and Son who would run it as a Fruit Preserving Works. With ever increasing amounts of soft-fruit being grown in the area, John Fleming's business flourished until in 1940 it was sold to Harry Truscott. In 1945 Walter Brown of Reading was the registered owner, then in 1950 it changed hands again this time to Messrs Smedley. In 1955 the owner was the National Canning Company of London then in 1961 an entirely new type of industry arrived in the town.

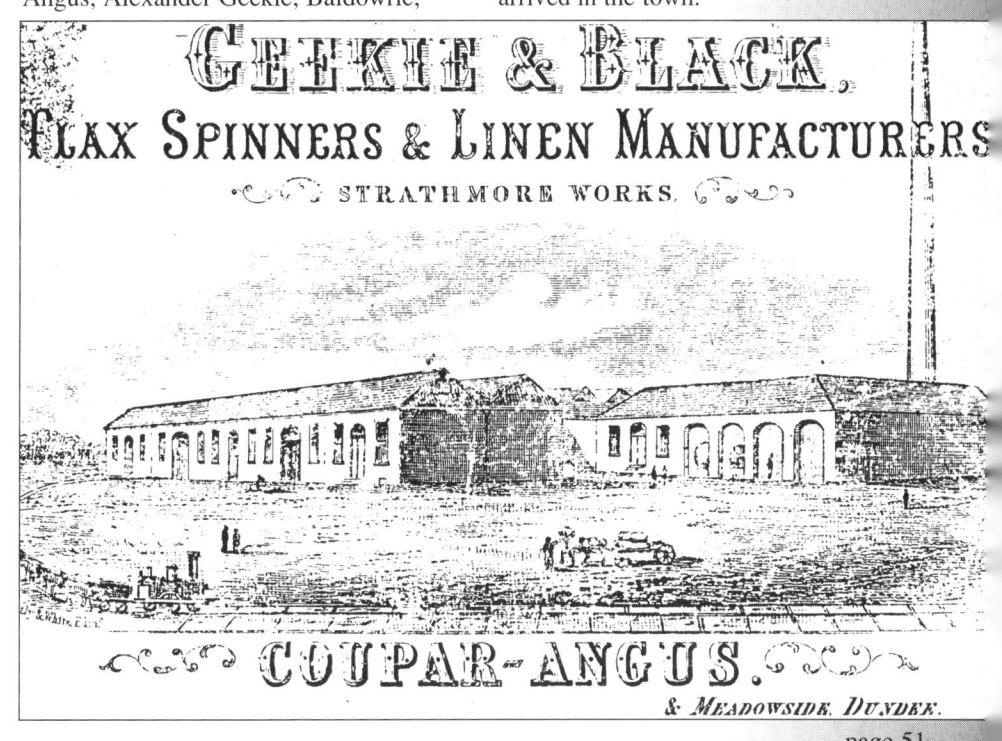

At this period, Mr Daniel Marshall, purchased from Lord Airlie of Cortachy a business called the Caledonian Barbecue Company. At the same time he bought the former Canning factory from which to run this new business. The processing of chickens began on 6th November 1961 with J. L. B. Apedaile, trained in these skills in the United States, as manager of the plant. The staff training in the entirely new methods of chicken processing proved to be so successful that soon 5,000 to 6,000 birds per day were handled from live-bird to pre-packed and frozen.

Even a serious fire in 1962 did not halt production, for cold stores were found in Perth and Dundee where the frozen products could be stored before dispatch to retail outlets.

It is ironic that on the evening before the fire, the Coupar Angus Fire Station had been officially opened. After the fire, the factory was redesigned to achieve greater output which was crucial if the firm was to survive the cut-throat competition from home and abroad. The target was quickly achieved and soon 100,000 birds a week were being processed. As this number rose steadily to 150,000, then to 200,000, per week, the staff numbers, which were originally around sixty, rose steadily too.

D. B. Marshall supplied retailers all over the country - Marks and Spencer, Safeway, Littlewoods etc and in 1997 approximately five hundred workers were employed on a two shift system. While the bulk of employees are from Coupar Angus, others come from the Perth area, Blairgowrie, Alyth. Forfar, Kirriemuir and Dundee.

The firm became known as the Marshall Food Group Ltd and was the largest employer in Coupar Angus and its surrounding area.

In September 1998 Aberdeen-based Grampian Food Group acquired the whole share capital of Marshall's Food Group, including the Coupar Angus factory. The Grampian Food Group is the U.K.'s leading independent food and drink company with strong links with farmers, suppliers and customers. Among their quality products are white and red meat, chicken, pork, beef and lamb.

## THE THIRD POWER LOOM FACTORY

Again in 1866 the third power loom factory in the town was built by George and David McFarlane. David McFarlane was a very public spirited gentleman and the first Provost of the Town Council of Coupar Angus, who worked ceaselessly throughout his life for the betterment of the town and its inhabitants.

The well-designed factory was called the Strathmore Linen Works. Built of dressed sand-stone externally it was rather similar to that of Messrs Geekie and Black although much smaller in size, and when in full production around 200 people were employed. It was to achieve considerably more success than its unfortunate neighbour however, for it continued to operate profitably in McFarlane ownership until 1905 when it was sold to William Inglis Rodger. The factory survived in his ownership until in 1935 the effects of a nation-wide recession forced it to close down, but by that time it had been operating with a much smaller work-force due to the introduction of improved mechanisation.

The building lay empty for three years, then in 1938 the Eassie and Balkeerie Supply Company moved in and started trading as the Coronation Works Store. Not a great deal is known about this business which was owned by Sir Thomas Wedderspoon of Castleton of Eassie. It was known as E.B.S.C.O. and part of the business was located in the former Malt Barns, also called Victoria Mills.

In 1942 Messrs Levrington and Olding became the owners with the intention of converting the building for the sale of John Deere and Caterpillar Tractors. The firm was called L.O. Tractors and their plans were dealt something of a set-back when shortly after their arrival the War Department requisitioned the building. Everything had to be put on hold until the War ended.

L.O. tractors became Jack Oldings in 1955 and for many years traded successfully until the mid-eighties, when amid much dismay it closed down. This was a severe blow to the town not only for the loss of what was believed to be a well-established, thriving company, but during the time of Jack Olding's ownership, the building had been very well maintained and attractively decorated each summer with beautiful hanging baskets of flowers, which made an attractive landmark for those entering the town from the south.

Marshall Food Group then bought the building to provide extra space for their ever expanding operation.

In 1994 the building was demolished and at present *(2000)* the former factory site

*(Top) Aerial view of the second power loom factory, now Grampian Country Foods.*

page 52

The Cistercian Monks were the first to introduce market trading as a way of disposing of the extra commodities, butter, cheese, chickens, bees-wax (for candles) etc., which were paid as rents by the tenants of their vast lands.

# COMMERCE - from street markets to super markets

As a way of making even more money, they also encouraged people to come and trade, and charged them for doing so. The present day Cross was where the market was held, and people came quite a distance to buy and sell goods. From time to time Highlanders, who were looked on then as wild people, made the long journey in order to sell wool, coarse hand woven blankets, and spokes of ash for making cart wheels.

After the Reformation of the 16th century market trading continued, but now the rents or tolls from the stalls went to Lord Coupar.

As time passed, traders set up little covered booths on market days to protect their stock from the elements. On days when there were no markets, they travelled the countryside, some on horseback, selling all types of commodities - needles, pins, laces etc., to people in the farm-towns and villages. Sometimes goods were exchanged, for money was scarce. These traders were known as 'Chapmen' or 'Packmen', and as time went on the more business like among them, became the first shop-keepers and merchants.

In the 18th century a great Mid-summer Fair and Feeing Market was held in Coupar Angus. This was very well supported, for the many farm-workers in the area had a rare day off work, and turned out in force. The Chapmen assembled in large numbers at these fairs, and it became a tradition that a young 'lad' would buy his 'lass' a present at the 'fairing'.

In the mid 19th century many changes took place in agriculture, which meant that people had to leave the country areas in large numbers and seek work in the towns and cities. Some went overseas, but as a result of this exodus farm produce became scarce, and the markets and fairs suffered accordingly.

In the town in the early 19th century, the annual horse and cattle markets were attracting fewer people than in earlier days. The weekly market was suffering in popularity also, for Meigle and Blairgowrie now had their own. The famous Horse Market which was held on the third Thursday in March and often carried on into Friday, attracted traders from all over the country in its heyday. It survived until the late 19th century, although as the century progressed, was reported to be 'dwindling down'. Cattle and farm machinery were also sold at the Horse market in its later years, for as time passed, horses of quality became increasingly scarce. In the mid 19th century a good working horse could make as much as £50 or £60, which was a great deal of money then. Sadly all we have to remind us now of these colourful days are the Gingerbread Horses which are still produced by the local baker, but the Horse Market Candy which was also looked forward to with relish, is no longer made.

Before the railway made its impact felt in the town, there were twenty shops, two weavers shops, one coal shed and one wrights shop. The railway stimulated trade enormously and by 1900 there were eighty five shops, three stores, two bakehouses, seven workshops, three factories, a steelyard (public weighing system) and at the railway depot, a granary, maltbarns, yards, sheds and stances. There was a byre complete with dairy cattle in Union Street.

### LIST OF THE PROFESSIONS in 1794

Apprentice & Journeymen . n/a
Bakers . . . . . . . . . . . . . . . . . . 7
Barbers . . . . . . . . . . . . . . . 3
Brewers . . . . . . . . . . . . . . . . 9
Butchers . . . . . . . . . . . . . . . 9
Carriers to Dundee & Perth 9
Carriers to Edinburgh . . . . . 1
Coopers . . . . . . . . . . . . . . . . 3
Day Labourers . . . . . . . . . 57
Drovers . . . . . . . . . . . . . . . 2
Dyers . . . . . . . . . . . . . . . . . 2
Excise Officers . . . . . . . . . . 3
Farmers . . . . . . . . . . . . . . . 43
Fiddlers . . . . . . . . . . . . . . . 3
Flax Dressers . . . . . . . . . . . 11
Gardeners . . . . . . . . . . . . . . 3
Manservants . . . . . . . . . . 94
Masons . . . . . . . . . . . . . . . 23
Master Shoemakers . . . . . . 15
Merchants . . . . . . . . . . . . . 25
Midwives . . . . . . . . . . . . . . 3
Milliners & Seamstresses . . . 7
Minister . . . . . . . . . . . . . . . 1
Plasterers . . . . . . . . . . . . . . 1
Public House Keepers . . . . 45
Saddlers . . . . . . . . . . . . . . . 2
Shoemakers . . . . . . . . . . . . 15
Smiths . . . . . . . . . . . . . . . . 8
Staymaker . . . . . . . . . . . . . 1
Stocking Makers . . . . . . . . 2
Surgeons . . . . . . . . . . . . . . 3
Tailors . . . . . . . . . . . . . . . 22
Teachers . . . . . . . . . . . . . . 5
Watchmakers . . . . . . . . . . . 3
Weavers . . . . . . . . . . . . . . 101
Wheelwrights . . . . . . . . . . . 5
Womenservants . . . . . . . . 126
Wrights . . . . . . . . . . . . . . 20

*(Top) The Cross - the focal point of commerce in Coupar Angus.*

page 53

# BUSINESS DIRECTORY 1906

### Advertising Agents
Wm. Culross & Son, The Cross

### Bakers
T. B. Gray, Union Street
John Mackie, George Street
J. B. Ramsay, Causewayend and Commercial Street
James Turpie, Athole Street

### Billposter
John R. Brown, Commercial Street

### Blacksmiths
J. Campbell, Trades Lane
Charles Crichton, Causewayend

### Bookbinder
Wm. Culross & Son, The Cross

### Booksellers, Stationers, &c.
Wm. Culross & Son, The Cross
D. Stewart, George Street
Miss Wilson, Commercial Street

### Boot and Shoemakers
D. Dron, George Street
Colin McArthur, Hay Street
Stuart McFarlane, Gray Street
James Slidders, Commercial Street
John Stephen, Queen Street

### Butchers
W. Barnett, Causewayend
J. Dow, Queen Street
A, Forsyth, Commercial Street
D. Welsh & Co., Athole Street

### Builders
J. Bruce, Causewayend
J. Pitkeathly, Precinct Street
David Reid, Elmslie

### Cabinetmakers and Upholsterers
James Forrester, Gray Street
John Sinclair, Athole Street

### Carting Contractors
D Borrie, Campbell Street
J. & D. Brodie, Queen Street
J. M. Shepherd & Co., Princes Croft
Wordie & Co., Railway Station

### Chimney-Sweepers
A. C. Black, Hay Street
George S. Mann, slater

### Chemists and Druggists
James Gow, George Street
David McGeorge, The Cross

### China Merchants
Mrs Burnett, George Square
D. Sutherland, Athole Street

### Coal Merchants
C. E. Anderson & Son, Ltd., Old Station Road
George Bannerman, Causewayend
A. C. Black, Hay Street
J. & D. Brodie, Queen Street
J. B. Osler, Railway Station

### Confectioners
J. K. Black, Queen Street
Mrs Graham, Causewayend
T. B. Gray, Union Street
John Mackie, George Street
Miss McIntosh, George Square
J. B. Ramsay, Commercial Street
Miss Spiers, Union Street
Miss Tasker, George Street
Mrs Whittet, Queen Street

### Coach and Cab Proprietors
James Patrick, Queen Street
William Robertson, Royal Hotel

### Corn Merchants
C. E. Anderson & Son, Limited
W. Fullerton, Railway Station
T. Martin & Son, Keithick Mills
J. B. Osler, Railway Station

### Cycle Agents
C. Gardiner & Co., Union Street
Irving Bros., Commercial Street

### Dairy Keepers
J. Anderson, Causewayend
J. Dick, Union Street
R. L. Shepherd, Commercial Street
J. Whytock, Peattie Farm

### Dealers - Horses, Cattle, Pigs etc
J. Lamond, George Street
James Patrick, Queen Street
David Peebles, George Street
Jas. Stewart, Woodside Farm

### Drapers
David Anderson, Cash Stores
James Brodie, High Street
James Chalmers, The Cross
Mrs McFarlane, Causewayend
J. T. Paterson, The Cross
Charles Stewart, George Street
Thos. Stuart, Commercial Street

### Dressmakers.
James Brodie, High Street
Miss Bruce, Queen Street
James Chalmers, The Cross
Miss Forster, Hay Street
Miss Hill, George Street
Mrs Lowson, George Street
Miss McArthur, Commercial Street
Mrs McFarlane, Causewayend
J. T. Paterson, The Cross
Miss Stewart, Calton Street

### Engravers and Lithographers
Wm. Culross & Son, The Cross

### Fancy Drapers
Mrs Lowson, George Street
Miss Symons, George Street

### Fancy Goods & Toy Merchants
Miss Crichton, George Street
Miss McArthur, Commercial Street
Miss Wilson, Commercial Street

### Feeding Stuff Merchants
C. E. Anderson & Son, Ltd., Railway Station
J. B. Osler, Railway Station

### Fish Merchants
John Brown, Commercial Street
George Murray, George Street
Thomas Robertson, Calton Street

### Fishing Tackle Dealers
T. B. Farquharson, Union Steet
J. M. Muir, The Cross

### Fruiterers and Greengrocers
J. K. Black, Queen Street
Couttie Bros., Athole Street
Mrs Graham, Causewayend
David Mitchell, Hay Street
George Murray, George Street

### Funeral Undertakers
John Adam, Hay Street
James Forrester, Gray Street
G. McDonald & Son, Trades Lane
Ross & Wallace, Queen Street

### Gamedealer and Poulterers
A. Forsyth, Commercial Street
David Mitchell, Hay Street

### Gardeners (Jobbing)
J. Geekie, Causewayend
James Gibb, Commercial Street

### Government Washing Contractor
William Linley, Precinct Street

### Grocers
John Baxter, George Street
George Dow, Commecial Street
*James Dron, George Street
James Gray, Union Street
*Wm. McGregor, George Street
*Jas. McNeill, The Cross
*J. M. Moncur, Causewayend
David Peebles, George Street
Mrs Saunders, George Square
(* Licensed)

### Hairdressers
D. F. Forbes, The Cross
John M. Gow, Commercial Street

### Ironmongers, Oil Merchants, &c.
T. B. Farquharson, Union Street
J. M. Muir, The Cross

### Joiners and Carpenters
John Adam, Hay Street
James Forrester, Gray Street
G. McDonald & Son, Trades Lane
John Sinclair, Athole Street
Ross & Wallace, Queen Street

### Maltster
William Panton, Union Street

### Manure Merchants
C. E. Anderson & Son, Ltd., Old Station Road
J. B. Osler, Railway Station

### Millers (Meal and Barley)
T. Martin & Son, Keithick Mills

### Milliners
D. Anderson, Athole Street
James Brodie, The Cross
James Chalmers, The Cross
Miss Forster, Hay Street
Mrs Lowson, George Street
Mrs McFarlane, George Street
J. T. Paterson, The Cross
C. Stewart, George Street

### Millwright and Cartwright
David Murray, Balgersho

### Teachers of Music
J. C. Johnstone, Beechhill
Miss Lyon, The Cross
Miss MacCulloch, Blairgowrie Rd.
Miss Watson, Victoria Place

### Nurseryman and Florist
John Russell, Causewayend

### Painters and Paperhangers
W. Gilzean & Son, Gray Street
Charles Gowrie, George Square
James Irvine, George Street
Charles Robertson, The Cross

### Plasterers
Peter Donaldson, Craigvaar

### Plumbers, Tinsmiths, &c.
James Clark, Union Street
John Doig & Sons, Commercial St.
John Galloway, George Street
A. Laing, Hill Street

### Potato Merchants
C. E. Anderson & Son, Ltd.
John Lyburn, Kinnochtry
John Mosson, Station Road
J. B. Osler, Railway Station

### Printers and Publishers
Wm. Culross & Son, The Cross

### Private School
Miss MacCulloch, Blairgowrie Rd.

### Quarry Masters
James Bruce, Causewayend
David Reid, Elmslie

### Saddler
C. B. Paterson, The Cross

### Seed Merchants
C. E. Anderson & Son, Ltd., Old Station Road
T. B. Farquharson, Union Street
J. M. Muir, The Cross
J. B. Osler, Railway Station
John Russell, Causewayend

### Shopkeepers, General
Miss Crichton, George Street
John Geekie, Causewayend
Miss Geekie, Causewayend
Mrs Graham, Causewayend
Mrs McArthur, Commercial Street
Mrs Robertson, Causewayend
Miss Spiers, Union Street
Miss Stewart, Calton Street
Mrs West, George Street
Mrs Whittet, Queen Street
Mrs Wilson, Causewayend

### Slater
Geo. S. Mann, Gartmorn Cottage

### Solicitors
C. & C. Boyd, National Bank
Robert Watson, The Cross

### Stationers (Manufacturing)
Wm. Culross & Son, The Cross

### Tailors and Clothiers
James Brodie, High Sreet
James Chalmers, The Cross
James Keay, Calton Street
John T. Paterson, The Cross
C Stewart, George Street
Thomas Stuart, Commercial Street

### Tanners and Curriers
George Honeyman & Son

### Turners and Bobbin-Makers
P. Carr & Son, Brunty Mills

### Tea and Refreshment Rooms
J. K. Black, Queen Street
T. B. Gray, Union Street
Miss McIntosh, George Square
J. B. Ramsay, Commercial Street
Miss Speirs, Union Street
C. Zucconi & Co., The Cross and Causewayend

### Watchmakers and Jewellers
David Marshall, Athole Street
Alex. Sutherland, Union Street

## SHOPS AND BUSINESSES FROM APPROX 1914 into the 1960'S

**George Street**
| | | |
|---|---|---|
| Gardener, | Jeweller | Now a house |
| Dron, | Grocer | |
| Campbell, | Sweets, etc | |
| Richards, | Fishmonger | |
| Anderson, | Sweets | Now Itani |
| Smarts, | Grocer | |
| Keay, | Grocer | Now Robertson & Black |
| Storrar, | Butcher | Now Morrison, Butcher |
| Kermath, | Newsagent | Now Newsbox |
| Bradley, | Tailor | Now Furniture Place |
| Bannerman, | Painter, The Ironmonger | Now Lindsay Ironmonger |
| Gatt, | Footwear | Now Stephen, Photographer |

**George Square**
| | | |
|---|---|---|
| Buttercup, | Dairy | Now Barber |
| McIntosh, | Sweets | Now a house |
| C & W West, | Electrician | Now Chip Shop |
| | Store | Now a house |
| Burnett | China | Now Lloyds TSB |

**The Cross and High Street**
| | | |
|---|---|---|
| Mrs Tarbet, | Sweets | Was Meg's Cafe - now empty |
| Muir, | Ironmonger | Now baker |
| Old Post Office | | Part of Co'Op but Post Office is again in Co'Op |
| Whyte, | Grocer | Now part of Co'Op |
| Co'Op | Grocery Store | Still there but plans to relocate |
| Brown | Printer | Upstairs at Co'Op Building |
| Hume | Draper | Now Abbey Tabet |
| Cocker, | Electrician | Norrie, Hairdresser |
| McNeil, | Grocer | Now Elegant Windows |
| Agger, | Fruit and Veg | Now Fred Stewart |
| Patterson/Victor | Sadler/Jeweller, | Now business centre |
| Dow, | Grocer | Now Athole Bakery |
| Mortali/Pacitto | Cafe | Now video outlet |
| Adam RennieE/Banneman | Newsagent/ Decorator | Now Morning Noon and Night |
| Husband, | Electrician | Now a house |
| Davidson, | Chemist | Still Davidson but formerly McGeorge |

**Athole Street**
| | | |
|---|---|---|
| Welsh, | Butcher | Now a house |
| Dunbar, | Baker | Now a Take-Away |

**Commercial Street**
| | | |
|---|---|---|
| Chip Shop | | Now closed |
| Doig, | Plumber | Now a house |
| Stuart | Draper | Now Murray Gray |
| Blyth, | Chemist | Was Cheers - now closed |
| McArthur, | Sweets | Now a house |
| Sutherland, | Newsagent | Now car park |
| Brown, | Fish Shop | Was Brown, Painter - now car park |
| Gow, | Barber | Now car park |
| Wilson, | Hats | Now plumber's store |
| Gardener, | Bootmaker | Now back part of Morning Noon and Night |

**Union Street**
| | | |
|---|---|---|
| McNeil, | Fishmonger | Now Plumber |
| Sutherland, | Watchmaker | Now a house |
| Stewart, Ltd | Grocer | Now part of Davidson Chemist |
| Grayburn, | Bakery/Tearoom | Now dental surgery |

**Queen Street**
| | | |
|---|---|---|
| Kenny, | Barber | Now house opposite steeple |
| Munn, | Tearoom | Now house opposite Culross |
| Thomson | Sweets | Now house next to Culross |
| Culross | Printers | Still Culross |
| Playhouse | Cinema | Now St. Mary's R.C. Church |
| Adamson | Tailor | Now part of a house |
| Brodie, | Sawmill | Now housing complex - Brodie's Yard |
| Whitelaw, | Joiner | Was P Gibb Joiner and Undertaker |

**Gray Street**
| | | |
|---|---|---|
| McFarlane, | Footwear | Now Gray's store |
| Donalsdon, | Ironmonger | Now store under Masonic Lodge |

**Calton Street**
| | | |
|---|---|---|
| Eva Clark | Sweets | Now a house |

**Hay Street**
| | | |
|---|---|---|
| Doig, | Sweets | Now office - Eddington & Neave |

# BUSINESS DIRECTORY 2000

### Candlehouse Lane
| | |
|---|---|
| Ellis & Everard | Agricultural Contractor |
| James Gow | Blacksmith - now Signwriting Firm |
| Delta Services (Security) | Now Murray Antiques |

### Causewayend
| | |
|---|---|
| G Meldrum & Son | Builders |
| Kumfir Kut | Hairdresser |
| Langs Catering Services | Grocer |
| Winter's Wool Shop | Now Closed |

### Commercial Street
| | | |
|---|---|---|
| Chip Shop | Now Closed | |
| Cheers | Off Sales & Video | Now Closed |
| Grays | Carpets & Furnishing | |

### Athole Street
| | |
|---|---|
| Chinese Take Away | Formerly Dunbar the Baker |

### George Square
| | |
|---|---|
| Mr Snip | Barbers |
| Brodie's Chip Shop | Take Away |
| R Stephen | Photographer |

### George Street
| | | |
|---|---|---|
| Sidlaw Hardware | Ironmonger | |
| Pypers | Now in Burrelton. | |
| C & W West | Electricians | |
| The Furniture Place | Nearly New and Antiques | |
| The News Box | Papers & Confectionery | Closed |
| A & A Morison | Butcher | |
| Robertson & Black | Property Shop | |
| Itani | Outfitter | |
| Smith & Sons | Bus Company | Now relocated out of town |
| Rosemount Homes | Workshop | |
| W Robertson | Bookmaker | |
| Grampian Country Foods | Formerly D B Marshall | |
| Coupar Angus Co'op | Grocer and Post Office | |
| Coupar Angus Repair Service | Auto Repaairs | |

### Union Street
| | |
|---|---|
| Lamb & Gardiner | Car & Petrol Sales |
| J G Middleton | Office Management |
| Crighton | Plumber |
| Kinloch Hair Salon | Hairdresser |
| Denrosa Apiaries | Honey Producer |

### High Street
| | |
|---|---|
| Abbey Tablet | Confectioner |
| A G Norrie | Hairdresser |
| F Stewart | Fruiterer |
| Elegant Windows | Soft Furnishings |
| R Clark | Electrical Contractor |

### Precinct Street
| | |
|---|---|
| D Malloch & Co | Road Haulage |
| J S Rodger | Joiners |
| Smiddy Garage | Auto Repairs |
| A McAllan | Building Contractors |

### Pleasance Road
| | |
|---|---|
| Henderson | Furniture Outlet |

### Queen Street
| | |
|---|---|
| Nicol Whitelaw | Joiners |
| Culross | Printer |
| Strathmore Melamine | Workshop & Shop |
| Smiths Taxis | Taxi Service |

### The Cross
| | | |
|---|---|---|
| Victor & Sons | now Business Centre | Closed |
| Athole Bakery | Baker | |
| Ollies Cafe | now Video Outlet | |
| Davidson & Sons Ltd | Chemist | |
| Morning Noon & Night | General Merchant | |
| W McCombe | Dental Surgeon | |

### Calton Street
| | |
|---|---|
| Watson & Lyall Bowie | Solicitors |

### Blairgowrie Road
| | |
|---|---|
| M Coull | Chiropodist |

### Hay Street
| | |
|---|---|
| Edington & Neave | Slaters & Plasterers |
| W G McNaughton | Joiners & Undertakers |

### Grampian View
| | |
|---|---|
| S Irving | Architect |
| R Murray | Plumber |

### Campbell Street
| | |
|---|---|
| D Brown | Driving School |

### Princes Croft
| | |
|---|---|
| M Proudfoot | Elect Contractor |

### School Road
| | |
|---|---|
| D Reid | Plasterer/Slater |
| Bryan & Carrick | Agric Implements |
| Ritchies Taxis | Taxi Service |
| Thermalec | Heating Engineer |

### Forfar Road
| | |
|---|---|
| East of Scotland Farmers | Agricultural Supplies |

### HOTELS
Enverdale Hotel - Royal Hotel - Red House Hotel

### PUBLIC HOUSES
White House *(Strathmore Hotel)* - Athole Arms - The Victoria Inn - The Nortel Bar

### LEISURE COMPLEX
The Nortel Leisure Complex

### BANKS
The Bank of Scotland - The Royal Bank - Lloyds T S B

---

The firm of Lamb & Gardiner is one of the oldest businesses in Coupar Angus. It started as Gardiners Bicycle Shop at the Cross in the late 19th century. The father of the late Thomas Lamb, joined the firm after the first World War and the firm diversified into motor cars and went from strength to strength. The late Tommy Lamb was a quiet, retiring gentleman, who unbeknown to many, was extremely generous to the disadvantaged in the local society. A very public spirited gentleman, he did not wish a full account of his business to be published in the History of Coupar Angus and naturally his wishes have been respected.

The story covers 160 years of Culross the printers. No one knows why a printing works was started here in Coupar Angus, but one theory is that the Cistercian monks of the Abbey left a heritage of the written word which enabled William Culross to set up business in 1835.

# CULROSS - printing arrives in Coupar Angus

His first premises were in Victoria Buildings, on the corner of the Cross, between Athole and George streets. *(See heading pic)*

William Culross seems to have been an imposing figure and a drawing exists of him sitting in the woods accompanied by his Cairn Terrier, with an axe nearby. He was an astute business man, for as well as his printing business which was housed in the upper part of the building, he was Postmaster and Agent for the Savings Bank. Around 1906 in addition to his other business interests, he started the 'Strathmore Library' where popular books and magazines were loaned out for a small fee.

William Culross was followed in business by his son David who was known to have lived in Woodside and is buried in Cargill. David's reputed bad temper was perhaps caused by ill-health and there is a story of him throwing one of his crutches at someone in displeasure.

The first Culross fire occurred in 1911 and resulted in a move from the Cross up Queen Street into the yard next to Nick Whitelaw, previously occupied by Charlie Gardner, the Blacksmith.

With no children to inherit, David Culross sold the business in 1922 to a young man from Glasgow, Frank Benzies. Frank had a World War 1 legacy of a stiff leg, injured in a flying crash with the Royal Naval Air Service. Because of this disability, the family wish for him was a quiet life in the country, but Frank proved to be a bombshell! From Dundee and Glasgow, craftsmen like James McDonald, Bob Doig and John Cameron were recruited, and together they trained a first-class workforce for Culross the printers.

This all happened when Scotland was administered from Edinburgh. In those days, all towns and cities employed Parish Clerks who carried out their duties using forms printed by Culross. The sole suppliers of these forms in Scotland, Culross, were known as "Poor Law Publishers".

When the early 1930's brought the Depression at the same time as the demise of the Parish Councils, Frank Benzies quickly diversified to become a commercial printer, ruler, bookbinder and typecaster, winning custom all over Scotland.

The Print Works was also proving to be a marriage bureau, with the likes of John Donaldson, Bill Robertson, Frank Cobb and Alex Arneil taking brides from the staff.

The second disastrous fire in 1938 meant that Culross crossed the road to premises formerly owned as a garage by Mr Brough. Production was started there within a few weeks, with the firm of J. B. Stewart Builders effectively doubling the size of the new factory and taking over the old site for a builder's yard.

*(Top) The first Culross premises on the Cross C1900.*
*(Right) Frank Benzies in his office, in the late '40s.*

page 57

During the paper rationing times of World War II, staffing levels at Culross had to be reduced, but amongst the stalwarts were Georgie *(Mrs Arneil)*, composing type, and Bob Doig who turned his hand to everything.

Frank Benzies divided his war effort between Culross and the Air Training Corps and, while holding the rank of Wing Commander, was awarded an MBE for his services.

The present Chairman, Bob Benzies, joined his father in the Company, commencing training in 1948.

After the war, stationery shops in Perth, Inverness and Forfar were added to the business. These have since been sold and since 1950 Culross has seen three completely new changes of technology taking place.

A Melamine Department making table mats and coasters has been in production since 1990 is now well established, and achieving sales all over the world.

The third fire was in the Melamine Department on an October night in 1993 when the roof came off the workshop which long ago had been the house of Jim Whittet the postman. Reconstruction of the building provided a perfect Melamine workshop and a seconds outlet where visitors are welcome.

In 1993 management of Culross fell to the grandsons of Frank Benzies. Frank S. Benzies is in charge of the production side of the business and Douglas Benzies directs the Sales effort.

Together with a versatile staff, they look forward to the future - and the continuing story of Culross the printers.

In May 2001, tragically Mr Douglas Benzies lost his life in a road accident.

We wish to thank Mr R. Benzies for this contribution which appeared in the 1996 Spring edition No 45 of the Coupar Angus Newsletter (C A N).

*(Top) Queen Street, the present-day location of Culross.*
*(Above) The Culross crew in 1966 with Bob Benzies centre, in white coat.*
*(Right) One of the early printing presses in the late '40s.*

The firm was founded in 1897 in Blairgowrie by Walter Davidson who had come to the area from Hawick. He had three sons all of whom became Pharmacists - John, Norman, and Walter Jnr. John qualified in Edinburgh and joined his father in the business.

## DAVIDSON - chemist and councillor

When Norman qualified it was time to expand so a suitable branch was sought.

In 1926 the Coupar Angus shop was purchased from David McGeorge who had been in business in the town since the 1890's.

John took over the management of this branch and shortly afterwards he and Helen McGeorge were married. John and Helen had one son Douglas and a daughter Jean. When Walter Senior died in 1942 John became Company Chairman. Douglas also followed in the family tradition and became a pharmacist. He joined the management of the Company in 1953 when it became a Limited Company. Douglas is now the Chairman of the Company which has expanded steadily over the years and now has nineteen Pharmacies, six Veterinary branches, and one Drug Store.

Those who can still remember the caring helpful attention they received from John (Jock) Davidson, will be pleased to know that in each and every one of the branch shops, none of this has been lost, for the wellbeing of the customer and friendly and efficient service is as important today as when the firm was founded over one hundred years ago.

*(Top) Davidsons the Chemist on the Cross.*
*(Above) Davidson the Provost.*
*(Right) The Chemist shop as it used to be.*

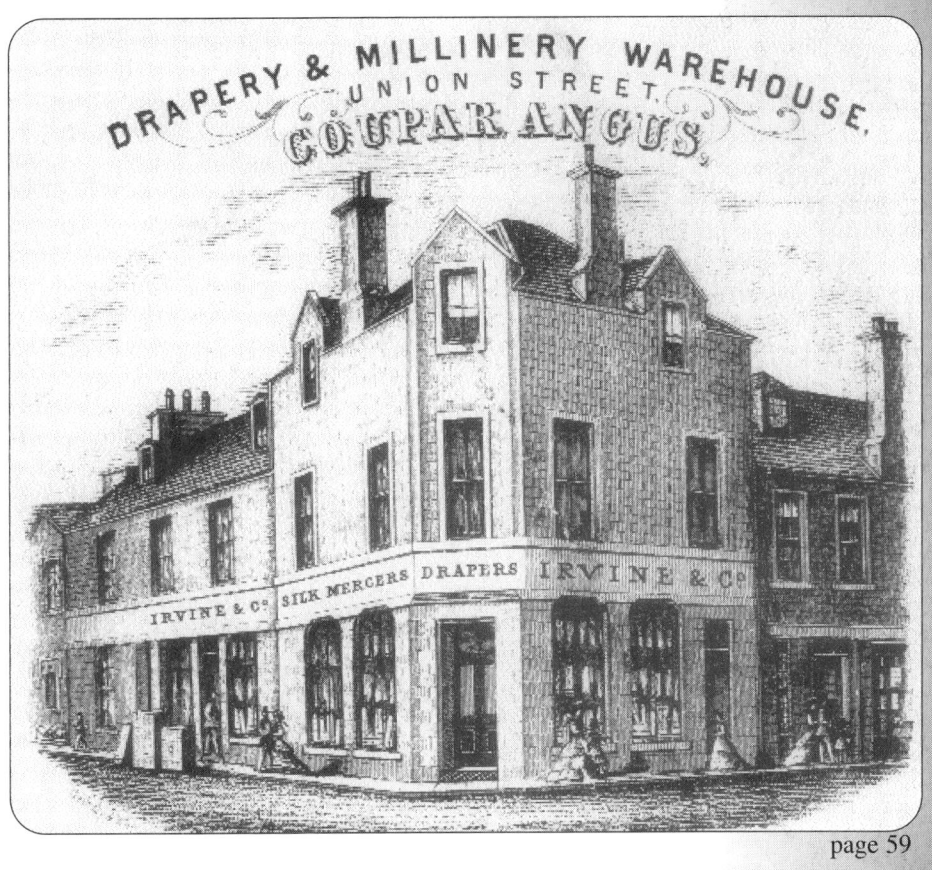

A Tannery or 'Tan-Yard' was built in 1781 where 2600 hides were dressed each year using 9000 stone of bark in the process. The leather from here was supplied to the saddlers and shoemakers in town.

In 1796 there were 4 Whisky Stills - 3 of 40 gallons and 1 of 30 gallons which may give a clue as to why there were 3 Excise Officers and 45 Pubs' in the town.

By 1833 there was a Farina Works at Couttie which turned potatoes into flour. Most possibly, it was not in operation all year round but only after the harvest and until all the available potatoes had been processed.

This year too saw the advent of a Steam Saw Mill in Coupar Angus which would remain on the same spot until the early 1990's - almost 110 years. The Sawmill site was purchased by Perthshire Housing Association and is known as 'Brodies Yard'.

At the end of the 18th century, a Man-Servant's annual wage was between £9 and £11 while a Woman-Servant was paid between £3 and £4. Then butter cost nine old pence per pound *(approx 4p)* but a pound then was made up of 22 oz.

A hen cost one shilling to one shilling and six pence (7$\frac{1}{2}$p).

A Mason's wage was one shilling and six pence (7$\frac{1}{2}$p) per day and a Tailor was paid ten pence *(approx 4p)*. A Labourer was paid one shilling per day (5p) but he also got his meals.

**The Population in Coupar Angus in 1755 was 1491 by 1793 it had risen to 2076**

(Top) Paterson the Saddler C1900.
(Centre) The Athole Street Bakery with Mr W. T. Dunbar extreme right C1930.
(Right) The Grayburn Bakery in Union Street C1900.

Education in Scotland dates from the 4th century when St Ninian built his 'Candida Casa' at Whithorn. In the 6th century, St Columbas' followers travelled from Iona throughout much of Scotland, not only spreading the word of God, but teaching those who wished to learn.

# SCOTTISH EDUCATION - in the beginning

By the 15th century Scotland had three fine universities - St Andrews 1411 - Glasgow 1451 and Aberdeen 1494 which followed the pattern of those in Europe rather than of England.

In 1496 an Act of Parliament called for the compulsory education of the eldest sons of all ruling barons, the strategy being that they would be the future holders of the important posts in commerce, law and government.
In the 17th and 18th centuries, a modest expansion in education for the lower classes took place, when Parish and Burgh schools were built. From the Old Parish Records, we know that as far back as 1694 Coupar Angus had a schoolmaster, Mr John Ramsay, so it is safe to conclude that there was a school in the town then, or perhaps even earlier. The heritors *(land-owners)* were responsible for providing and maintaining schools in their areas, and in many cases were very unwilling to spend the money needed for either suitable buildings, or well-educated schoolmasters.

A further Act of Parliament in 1696 was devised to pressurise them even more to face up to their responsibilities, and provide schools for the children who lived in the districts of their estates. About the same time, the Reformed Kirk began to take an interest in Scottish education by insisting that they be given the right to approve or reject the appointment of teachers in both Burgh and Parish schools. Their strong belief was that the three R's (Reading, Writing, Reckoning) were the first principles on which education, should be based. An Act of 1803 is looked on now as the start of State controlled education for pressure was once more applied on land-owners, who after employing all manner of delaying tactics to try to avoid the extra expenditure, eventually capitulated and standards in education generally did improve.

This 'dragging of feet' however, caused friction with the Churches in Scotland, who were anxious to see progress and improvement carried out much more rapidly. The result was that the Scottish Episcopal Church, the Free Church of Scotland and the Roman Catholic Church, formed their own schools for the children of their respective congregations.

After 1843 quite a number of 'Private' or 'Dames' schools sprang up but many were of poor educational standards and did not survive for any length of time. Undoubtedly, the greatest change of all came in 1872 when School Boards were formed. In Coupar Angus, as elsewhere in the country, the elected members of the School Board were all 'Pillars of Society' - business men who took the responsibility for the education of the children of their town very seriously indeed.

The Education Act of 1872 also made education compulsory for all five to thirteen year olds. This did not please everyone however, for many children aged eight and sometimes younger, were employed in local factories. These young 'wage-earners' were now obliged by law to attend school on a part-time basis. They were known as 'half-timers' and often many of them fell asleep in class since they had worked as many as six hours before attending school.

Schools were now funded by parliamentary grants and school rates but those who were too poor to pay the rates or fees, or to buy books, were given financial help from the parish rates.

All matters pertaining to education was in the hands of the **SCOTCH EDUCATION DEPARTMENT** (1872-1918) which set out to ensure that a well balanced nation-wide system of education was available to every pupil. Inspectors were appointed to visit schools twice yearly to see this was achieved. Should any aspect of education not come up to the expected standard, a warning was first issued and if matters did not quickly improve, part of the school grant would be withheld until an acceptable level was reached.

In 1883 the school leaving age was raised to fourteen, then in 1891 all fees in elementary schools were abolished. 1888 saw the introduction of a Leaving Certificate for those pupils who achieved good results in their final examinations. In 1918 elected Local Education Authorities and School Management Boards replaced the School Boards. Also at this time, Roman Catholic Schools came into the State system but were allowed to retain their religious distinction.

In 1929 a Local Government *(Scotland)* Act, introduced County Councils with their own Local Education Committees. In 1946 the power of the Education Committees was increased and Libraries

*(Top) Post-war view of Coupar Angus school - note, no railings.*

and Further Education also came under their jurisdiction. At this time also the school leaving age was raised to fifteen years, which put immense pressure on space in schools. Teaching staff also were in short supply and a special recruitment scheme was speedily introduced to remedy this.

The following decades saw a great deal of new school building and in the late 1960's early 1970's reorganisation began along comprehensive lines of education in State schools.

In 1972 the school leaving age was raised to sixteen.

## THE COUPAR ANGUS SCHOOL BOARD

On 5th April 1873 the members elected to the School Board met for the first time - The Rev Patrick James Stevenson D.D. of the Parish Church - The Very Rev. John Torry of the Episcopal Church - Rev Thomas Bain of the Free Church - James Whitson, Isla Park - James Paton, Banker - John Ferguson, Manufacturer and James C. Lawson, Builder.

Dr Stevenson was the unanimous choice for Chairman and Mr Charles Boyd, Solicitor was appointed as Clerk to the Board.

No time was lost in getting down to the responsible task of seeing that all the children of the Burgh between the ages of five and thirteen, attended school.

One of the first decisions of the Board was that a 'suitable person' be employed to ascertain the number of children who were now legally obliged to attend school. The School Board members met in the Parish Church Manse and at their second meeting, Mr Andrew Allan was appointed to carry out this exacting task. He was instructed to 'proceed without delay' and issued with forms on which to record all the relevant details 'of the children for whom education

must be provided'. This was quite an undertaking, for the population of the town at this time was around 2300. In a very short space of time he found there were 797 children of school age in the area, 469 of whom attended one school or another, and 61 in employment who received tuition on a part-time basis.

At this period in the town's history, children aged eight and sometimes even younger, worked part time in local factories. When legally obliged to go to school, their attendance has been recorded as being 'very poor' and often they fell asleep at their desks. The Board wrote to all factory owners asking that proof of age be sought before children were employed, in an attempt to stop children under eight working there. This did not go down well with some parents who had relied hitherto on the extra cash these youngsters earned. Mr Allan would continue in the service of the Board as Attendance Officer, for as government grants were linked to the number of attendances, it was critical that as few as possible absences occurred.

There were three schools in Coupar Angus at this time - the Burgh, or Parochial School as it was called, stood roughly to the east of the Nortel Leisure Complex, next to the Red House Hotel. Its Headmaster was a Mr Logan who lived in a school-house *(no longer standing)* in St Catherine's Lane.

The Second School was the Free Church School which was located in the building at the corner of Union Street and Blairgowrie Road *(Now private dwellings)* and its Headmaster was Mr Loutet.

The third was known as the Girls or Industrial School and stood in Reid's Close whose teacher or instructress

*(Top)* 1935 glamorous line-up at Coupar Angus school. *(Left) From the school log book of 1873.*

page 62

was Miss Reid. It was run by a Board of 'Managers' one of whom was Dean Torry. It has often been referred to as the Episcopal School, but the reason for this may have been that it was run by a committee of Episcopalian gentlemen and the building had been their Meeting House for religious services before St Anne's Church was built. There is no evidence that tuition was restricted to the daughters of members of the Episcopalian congregation. In some areas, Industrial Schools had been introduced to train delinquent children in useful skills for worthwhile work in adulthood, and by strict discipline to show them the error of their ways. No evidence exists however, that the purpose of the Coupar Angus school was anything other than to train girls for work in domestic service.

The Free Church and the Industrial school decided to 'come under the wing' of the School Board who straight away visited them and recorded in their Minutes - "there are three schools in the Burgh all giving efficient education". *(The third was the Parochial School).* The education may have been efficient but the state of the buildings was far from satisfactory. From the Second Statistical Account the following description of the Parish school and school-house gives a graphic picture of how bad they were —

*(Top) 1910 glamorous line-up at Coupar Angus school.*

"HE *(the schoolmaster)* HAS LEGAL ACCOMMODATION, UNDOUBTEDLY viz TWO ROOMS, INCLUDING A KITCHEN BUT LITTLE MORE. THE SCHOOL-ROOM ALSO IS BAD, IN POINT OF SIZE, SITUATION, VENTILATION AND REPAIR. A MAJORITY OF THE HERITORS *(Land- owners)* ARE AT PRESENT DESIROUS OF BUILDING A NEW ONE".

This school of 112 pupils, had two class rooms in an area of 14,148 cubic feet. The Free Church School too was in poor condition and the Board decided that the rooms be white-washed, the windows and water-closet repaired and the drains cleaned out. 127 pupils were being taught in this two room school of 15,960 cubic feet.

The Girls or Industrial School also had two rooms and a roll of 64 pupils. Its area was 8,103 cubic feet and it is thought to have stood where the present day Joinery Workshop is now in Reid's Close, for by 1880 it is described as a workshop.

Later all three schools would be sold, but in the meantime, the Free Church and Industrial Schools were rented from their Trustees by the School Board until such time as a modern school was built. There were also several smaller Private or Dames schools in the area but these were not deemed worthy of mention in the records of the time. Jointly, these three schools catered for 303 children who must have been packed into them like sardines. Now that education was compulsory the question was where were all these children who had not previously attended school to be taught?.

The Managers of the Masonic Lodge were approached with a view to renting their premises to the Board on a temporary basis for a period of perhaps two years but no longer than three. Agreement was reached and an annual rent of £7 decided upon. At the same time negotiations were entered into with Mr McLaggan, the proprietor of an adjacent Inn *(now called the Vic')* for the use by pupils of a water closet in his back-yard, and a rent of £1 per annum was agreed. A blackboard, desks and maps were purchased and speedily installed in this makeshift class-room which would be in the charge of a newly appointed teacher - Mr George Watson from the Parish of Abbey St Bathans - who had been carefully selected from as many as sixteen applicants and a short-leet of five.

Hand Bills were distributed throughout the area and an announcement was placed in the Peoples Journal and Dundee Advertiser stating that school for all children between the ages of five and thirteen would commence on Monday 13th October, 1873. The number of children attending school was checked against the Census return by Mr Allan, to make sure that no child had slipped through the educational net so carefully put in place by the Coupar Angus School Board members. Mr Allan had his work cut out for there were quite a number of 'defaulters' from families who had not realised the awesome power of the School Board.

In 1874 a 'Tinsmith' who was ordered to appear before the School Board to explain the non-attendance of his son at school, refused to comply to this request and instead wrote notifying them of his intention to educate his child himself. He was threatened with prosecution in no uncertain terms so straight away he wrote another letter, this time one of abject apology with a promise to see 'that his child faithfully attended school in future'.

The wives of the School Board members also felt it their duty to take an interest in their husbands' educational responsibilities and when it was suspected that the sewing tuition was not quite up to standard they, as a body, visited the school in Reid's Close and inspected the pupils work which they pronounced 'unsatisfactory'. The teacher resigned!.

The members seem to have been an autocratic bunch for they decided that Members of the Press would be excluded from their meetings and instead, they would submit a report to the Press. The first to express disquiet with this was Mr Logan the Schoolmaster. His complaint however was brushed aside by the Board but this was not to be the end of the matter. Whether or not Mr Logan had stirred things up a bit in town we do not know, but what is known is that a deputation of business men, which included Mr David McFarlane, Messrs Peter and William Ferguson, Mr James Robertson, Mr James Cromb and the Rev. Mr Wallace of the Relief Church turned up at the next meeting of the Board, and so strongly did they express their objections that not only was the Press to be allowed to attend School Board Meetings in future, but members of the Public also, could be present if they wished.

A committee had been formed early on by the School Board to investigate every possible aspect of the building of a new school, and in double quick time they had compiled a comprehensive report. A site upon which to build the school was of paramount importance and their first choice was a field called 'Playfair Park'.

Unfortunately the owner was not in a position to 'comply with their request', but undeterred by this set back, they forged ahead and found an area of land in Union Place *(now School Road)* which belonged to a Mr Gentle who was willing to feu it to them. It consisted of an area of 134 poles, the feu duty of which was three shillings (15p) per pole.

Application was made to the 'Scotch Education Department' in London on 11th December 1873 applying to 'The Lords of the Committee of the Council of Education in Scotland' for a grant to build the new school, the plans of which had been drawn up by a Mr Gibb.

Meanwhile there were other important matters to be attended to, such as deciding on which Class Books to use throughout the school. After much thought and consideration, 'Nelsons' were chosen. They were to be bought direct from the publisher and stocked by the local book-seller -'Culross' where parents could purchase them for their children from the shop. The Widow Martin was employed to clean all the rooms used by the scholars for 1/6d ($7^1/2$p) per week and a decision taken regarding the coal supply for heating the various class-rooms in winter. It had been suggested that each pupil should pay a little towards the cost of the coal, but after discussion it was agreed that the School Board would meet the cost. It was also decided that the Shorter Catechism be taught to every child in school apart from the infants, unless their parents specifically objected.

> Summary of Inspectress's Report
> 26th Feb, 1908
>
> Considering the circumstances, the practical results produced by the pupils were on the whole commendable. There is practically no apparatus, however, provided for the teaching of Laundry Work, and in consequence, the instruction given, has been of a very limited nature. For the further continuance of this work, suitable tables for ironing purposes, wash tubs, wringer, and other necessary apparatus must be provided; and, in addition, a properly qualified (**) teacher should be employed.
> The inspectress further states that the present teacher of Laundry Work, Miss Dow, has no qualification to teach the subject, and in these circumstances the provisional recognition (Article 66 of the Continuation Class Code) accorded her by the Department at the beginning of the session must be withdrawn.
> G. T.

The teaching staff in 1873 was made up of the following:

Mr Logan who taught - 1st and 2nd Standards - Salary £140 plus school-house
Mr Loutet - 3rd and 4th Standards - £150 plus £20 in lieu of house
Mr Watson - would teach - Standards V & VI - £150 plus £20 in lieu of house
Miss Reid - Standard 1 & 2 and Industrial Instruction - £85

Several pupil teachers were taken on at this time who would serve a five year apprenticeship, starting with a salary of £15 with annual increments of £2 50 for males, while females were paid at the lower rate of £10 per annum.

The disparity between salaries of men and women was generally accepted in this Victorian Era, and it may be difficult for young people today to understand why this type of discrimination continued until 1970 when the 'Equal Pay Act' was introduced.

In 1874 the Board decided to reduce the teachers salaries - Mr Logan's by £40, Mr Loutet's by £50 and Miss Reid's by £20.

Until 1890 when fees were abolished and education became free to all, those pupils whose parents could afford to, paid fees for tuition - 1/6d ($7^1/2$p) for English - Writing and Arithmetic 2/6d ($12^1/2$p) - Latin and French 3/- (15p). We know from old records that French was being taught in the Parochial School as early as 1843. It was also the responsibility of the teacher of the relevant subjects to collect the fees and pay them over each month to the School Treasurer.

Mr Logan who had taught in the town for many years previous to the formation of the School Board, seems to have had his feathers well and truly ruffled by the autocratic behaviour of the Board and he, in turn, was a constant source of irritation to them. He dug his heels in at every opportunity and would not comply with many of their demands without a struggle. He complained (not without justification) of under pay and over work. He demanded that his daughter be appointed to assist him, which surprisingly the Board did, but only 'at their pleasure' and on condition she 'qualify herself', which through time she did. When directed to teach extra subjects, Mr Logan refused to do so unless he was paid extra.

From a report by Her Majesty's Inspector of Schools, we gather that Mr Logan was not much of a disciplinarian as it included the following -

"THE MASTER SHOULD KEEP BETTER ORDER AND IN THE ABSENCE OF IMPROVEMENT BY NEXT INSPECTION THEIR GRANT FOR DISCIPLINE WILL NOT BE RECOMMENDED".

Matters came to a head when he issued an ultimatum that he would retire if a pension of £70 was given him. This was turned down and in its place, an offer of £45 was made. After a rather acrimonious dispute which was eventually settled by lawyers, Mr Logan finally agreed to a pension of £60 per annum. In his Log Book the last entry dated 16th March 1877 reads..."WORK HAS GONE ON AS USUAL" From this one must conclude that when the deal regarding his pension was finalised, he immediately retired without even recording the event in the Log Book so carefully kept over the years in his beautiful hand-writing.

It is sad that after so many years teaching the children of Coupar Angus that he retired on such a sour note.

Mr Loutet, the former Master of the Free Church School, was appointed as Headmaster of the soon to be opened new Burgh School of Coupar Angus.

## EVENING CLASSES
### 1893 - 23rd October

"THE EVENING CONTINUATION SCHOOL WAS OPENED ON MONDAY EVENING AT 8-15 p.m. THE SUBJECTS TO BE TAUGHT ARE:

READING FROM 'OLIVER TWIST' AND RECITATIONS ON MONDAY FOLLOWED BY GEOGRAPHY, ARITHMETIC AND COMPOSITION.
ON TUESDAY 'LIFE AND DUTIES OF THE CITIZEN' AND ON WEDNESDAY, 'THE HISTORY OF QUEEN VICTORIA'.
PHONOGRAPHY *(SHORTHAND)* ON THURSDAY AND ON FRIDAY, SEWING.

THE TEACHERS ARE - J. S. HALLIBURTON, PRINCIPAL, J. RAFFERTY AND LIZZIE ADAM *(ASSISTANTS)*"

The above is the first entry in the Evening Class Log Book and over 140 pupils enrolled. Numbers are not given for the individual classes but not too surprisingly by 16th November the classes in 'Life and Duties of the Citizen' and 'The History of Queen Victoria' had been discontinued.

As the Evening School also relied on government grants, it was visited twice each Session by Her Majesty's Inspector to see that all was as it should be.

In 1894 only Arithmetic, Reading, Writing, Composition and Sewing were being taught.

All those attending would have worked a full day, often until quite late, hence the starting time of 8.15 p.m.

By 1900 the subjects on offer had expanded to include - Shorthand, French, Technical Drawing, Book-keeping, Arithmetic, Writing, Cookery, Laundry, Needlework and Building Construction. These classes were the responsibility of the School Board whose members visited regularly to check the all important numbers in the register upon which grants were based.

The Inspector's report of 26th June 1901 reads as follows:

THIS SCHOOL IS SKILFULLY ORGANISED AND THE GENERAL QUALITY OF THE INSTRUCTION VERY SATISFACTORY. SPECIAL MENTION MAY BE MADE OF THE TEACHING OF COOKERY, BUILDING CONSTRUCTION, SHORTHAND AND DRAWING.

---

**Coupar Angus School Board**
**CONTINUATION CLASSES.**

# CERTIFICATE

In . . . . . . . . . . . . . . . .

IN FAVOUR OF

. . . . . . . . . . . . . . . . .

---

## COUPAR ANGUS SCHOOL BOARD
## CONTINUATION CLASSES.

### SYLLABUS.
### Book-keeping and Shorthand.

**Shorthand** - Pitman's "Teacher" and Manual. Writing from Dictation. Transcribing notes.
**Book-keeping** - "Jackson's Book-keeping" Preparation of Balance-Sheet. Ledger, Cash Book, Bank, Real and Personal Accounts.
**Business Procedure** - Pitman's Commercial Copy Books and Forms. Hooper and Graham's "Business training" The mechanical operations of an office. Press and carbon copying of letters. Indexing Letter Book. Correspondence.

### Machine Construction

Practice will be given in the class in the drawing of simple parts of machines and engines, special attention being given to accuracy of measurement, proper projection, speed and neatness of work, and the knowledge of machine parts as shown in the ability to fill in missing details. Practice will also be given in the making of rough sketches of machine models. The models will be carefully measured and the sketches dimensioned, from which complete working drawings will be made. The subjects will be chosen from the following:-

Elementary - Riveted Joints, Bolts and Screws, Scales, Various Machine Parts, Engine details, Pipe work
Advanced - Boiler work and fittings. Engine details. Machine details. Strength of materials. Design of beams. Bending moments. Moment of inertia. Modulus of Section. Graphical methods. Use of Slide Rule.

Plumbing Section - Lead work on roofs, various details. Sanitation in Building Construction. Materials used. Compounds of Lead.

### Building Construction

Use of Drawing instruments. Brickwork. Masonry. Brick and Masonry foundations. Joiner work. Plumber work. Slater work. Plaster work. Glazing and Painting. Design for small cottage (to give pupils lesson in Plan Reading).

At this period the Book-keeping Class met at 9-10 p.m.

On 26th December 1901 the entry reads: "Being Christmas week and many entertainments locally, the attendance this week, especially in the early part, was rather poor. *(sgnd)* John Robertson, School Board".

In February the weather was frosty and skating apparently was too much of a temptation, and consequently attendance suffered.

The Government Grant in 1901-1902 was £49 7s 1d, the Town Council Grant - £18, and the County Council Grant - £30

By 1903 Business Procedure *(Office Practice)*, Commercial Arithmetic and Ambulance classes had been added to the subjects on offer.

These were still times of Victorian virtues and ideals and on 25th September 1903 it is recorded that:

*"Owing to the regulations of the St Andrews Ambulance Association, the Board are to attempt a separation of sexes in the ambulance class next week"* then a further entry states:

*"The ambulance class will continue to be conducted as a mixed class as the Board has been unable to secure another lecturer".*

What the 'Board' would have thought of todays society and moral values doesn't bear thinking about!

Miss Crichton of the Aberdeen School of Cookery, was appointed as teacher of Cookery and Laundry at a salary of 4/6d ($22^1/2$p) per night, from 8-15 p.m. to 9-45 p.m.

The School Board had formed a sub-committee at an early stage to attend to matters pertaining to the Night School and some children attending school part-time because they were working, were allowed exemption from day-school if they attended night-school on a regular basis.

A typewriter was purchased by the Board and used 'in connection with the book-keeping class'. There was now tuition in Machine Construction *(Steam)*

and early in the session, this class visited Blackness Foundry in Dundee. By 1907 a small library had been started which was recorded as being *"a great asset to pupils"*.

In 1908 Miss McRitchie, a day teacher in the school, was instructing evening class students in the skills of Laundry and Cookery, and although some 'new apparatus was secured for the Laundry class' *(wash-tubs, wringers, scrubbing boards)*, it was still sadly lacking enough to go round but students carried on as best they could in the circumstances.

In the Inspector's Report of this year he was pressing for improvements in lighting and equipment.

In 1911 Classes in 'Laws, Health and Citizenship' and 'Poultry Keeping', were on offer.

From time to time attendance suffered drastically because of other activities in the town. On 29th September 1910 it is recorded "Dancing Classes upsetting Shorthand" and on 8th December "Attendance affected by Political Meetings". In 1912 the reason for non-attendance was that students were "too tired for night-school due to potato lifting".

In 1913-1914 Sick-nursing and Invalid Cookery classes were introduced. It had always been difficult for pupils from the country to attend the classes on time, and permission was obtained from the School Board to take the attendance twice - once at the opening of classes then again when late arrivals had turned up. Because of the exodus of so many young men for National Service in 1914 the classes for Building Construction and Practical Maths had to be dropped. Dressmaking however was introduced and proved popular.

On 19th October 1915 the last Evening Class was held for the school had been requisitioned by the government as a billet for troops.

Classes carried on however, meeting in the Town Hall for academic subjects while cookery instruction was carried out in the Royal Hotel.

In 1916 classes returned to the school, but now new legislation made it essential that they finish by 9-15 p.m. at the latest. Classes which were always held during winter months meant students had to travel to them in the dark, which was quite an ordeal for street lighting, if it did exist, was poor. Roads too were often pot-holed and rough outwith the town, and as bicycles were expensive, most people had to use 'Shanks Pony'.

*(Top) A 1920's class with the late David Reid centre top row.*

The last entry in the Evening Class Log Book is dated 30th November 1916 and reads:

"SEVERAL GIRLS IN THE COOKERY CLASS HAVE GONE OFF TO DOMESTIC SERVICE AT THE TERM".

Although this was the end of the records of the first evening classes in Coupar Angus, it was by no means the end of Night School tuition for this continued through the decades allowing people who left school at an early age, or without qualifications, a second chance. Known now as Community Education, Coupar Angus has for many years had a varied and interesting variety of subjects on offer which include crafts and leisure pursuits.

There is one difference from early times however, for many taking part in classes at present are much more mature than in the past, and some could even be called 'elderly'!

Community Education whose activities are held in the former gymnasium block, is a separate entity now from day-school education.

## THE BURGH SCHOOL

Although not fully completed, the new school, which cost £2700 to build, was opened on 16th February 1877. All pupils, except infants, were transferred there from the temporary accommodation - the old Parish School - The Industrial School - The Free Church School and the Masonic Lodge. The infants followed on 16th March and the school, which was planned to hold 502 pupils, opened with a roll of 394. The staff was made up of 7 teachers, an attendance officer and school cleaner.

Great emphasis in this Victorian era, was placed on learning the three R's - Reading, Writing and Arithmetic - but Maths, Latin, French, German, History and Geography were also taught. As time progressed, Domestic Economy, Sewing and Military Drill were added to the syllabus.

*(Top) Mr Strain's house "Ellerslie" on the corner of School and Blairgowrie roads.*

With regard to the Military Drill, there is a very interesting reference to this in the School Log Book dated 6th February 1903 - *"Mr Stuart Honeyman (of the Tannery) has kindly given us the use of the Rifles belonging to the Boys Brigade"*. On investigation it is thought that these 'Rifles' were made of wood and carried only for effect.

The school was visited twice yearly by H.M. Inspector of Schools and from his reports we know that education and discipline, were of a very high standard. Although the pupils 'shook in their shoes' as the time for the visit of HMI approached, it would seem that it was the teachers and not the pupils who were being inspected, for it reflected badly on them if their pupils were not up to scratch in any of their subjects. In addition to the official inspector, the School Board members also paid regular visits to check the Register and to make sure that every effort was being made towards achieving full attendance, for the grants necessary to run the school were based on this. There was always at least one Minister on the School Board and he along with other members, usually on the eve of the summer vacation, visited the school to test the children's knowledge of Religious subjects.

Quite a number of children had a fair distance to come to school, and in 1896 a 'Soup Kitchen' was opened during the winter months, 'to supply children who had some distance to come, with a hot meal'. This was the fore-runner of the School, Meals Service.

By the turn of the century, the population of the town had only risen marginally from the time the school was built, and the roll had only increased by 24.
In 1900 Mr Loutet retired and Mr G. W. F. Strain, who had taught in the school as his assistant since 1894 became headmaster in his place.

## MR STRAIN'S HEADMASTERSHIP 1900-1932

The new headmaster *(whose wife was Miss Wallace of the firm Ross and Wallace, Saddletree Works)*, built a very fine house, 'Ellerslie' which stands on the corner of Blairgowrie and School Road. At this time the back garden of the house ran right down to the school, with no buildings in between.

Conditions in the school which initially were considered to be first class, were now no longer acceptable in matters of class numbers, facilities etc, for there was a shortage of space. In 1901 the Town Hall was being used by the Infant Department but this was put right in 1902 when a new Infant Block was added to the original building. It was formally opened by Mr Smith, His Majesty's Inspector of Schools who had strongly recommended in his reports, that it be built.

In 1887 as part of Queen Victoria's Jubilee celebrations, the Town or Jubilee Hall as it was known then, was built. It was to prove a very great asset, not only to townspeople, but to the school in particular. Very popular and well supported concerts, which became annual events were held there on two consecutive nights, which raised money for many extras. In 1902 the profit cleared the sum still owing on the school piano with cash to spare. The following year (1903) 91 books were bought for a 'Reading Library' from the concert profit which as time went on became a tradition in the life of the town.

In 1903 a 'Supplementary Class' was introduced whose pupils had passed the new 'Qualifying Examination'.

Absenteeism was still a problem but the following item from the Log Book shows that this was not taken lightly - *"The Board secured convictions against two defaulting parents at the Police Court today"*.

In 1906 a 'School Savings Bank' was opened with 300 children bringing along deposits of 3d and 6d which totalled nearly £5 each week. On one occasion a pupil banked £10, an enormous amount for the time, and an occurrence of such magnitude that it was recorded in the school Log Book.

By 1907 girls were being taught Dressmaking while boys had to be content with 'Cardboard Modelling'. Paper for written work was also supplied in place of slates.

This year also saw the start of senior pupil visits to various workshops and industries in the town. The first was to the Ross and Wallace Sawmills. In the Supplementary class in 1908 Household Management for girls was being taught, and Woodwork replaced the Cardboard Modelling for the boys. Miss McRitchie, who had joined the staff in 1907 took charge of the Household Management course. She was to spend her whole life in the service of the people of Coupar Angus, not only as a teacher but as a Town Councillor, a public office usually held by men at this time. Miss McRitchie was a strong minded lady who made her presence felt in school and at Council meetings, but her first priority was always the welfare of the school and its pupils. The McRitchie Memorial Prize for Household Management was donated by her relatives, and although this subject is no longer taught in the

page 68

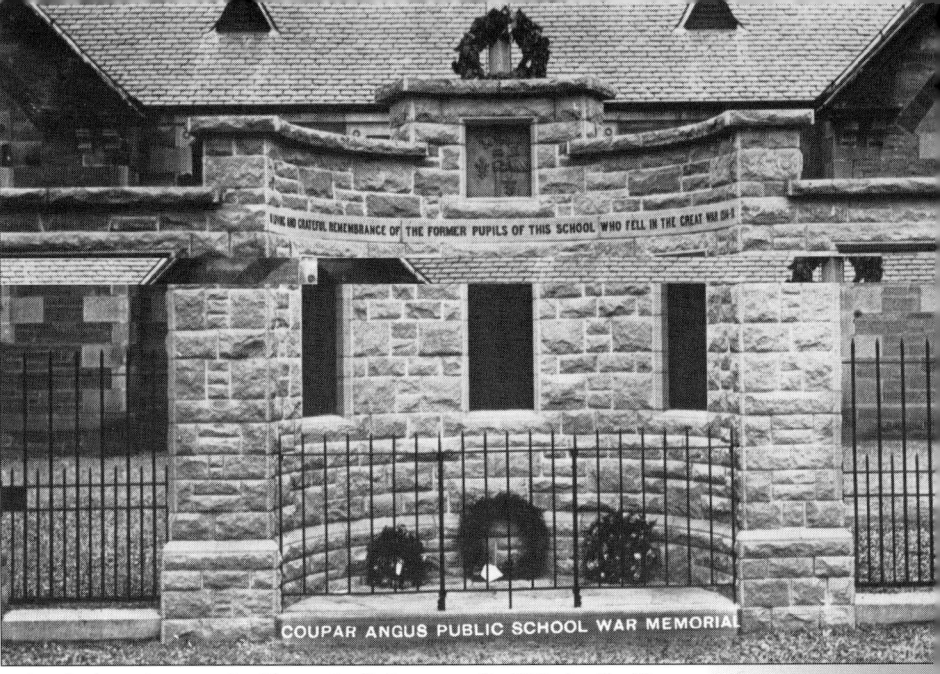

school, there is record of it on the Prize Board in the present day school assembly hall.

By 1912 a start had been made to a School Museum, and in December 1914 Mr Duncan of Denhead gifted 50 volumes to the school library.

This library, kept up to date with books purchased from some of the funds raised at school concerts, would serve the pupils until 1918 when the Rural Library Scheme was formed, and took over the responsibility for keeping it well stocked.

The War years were ones of such activity that a separate chapter is devoted to them and to those of the Second World War.

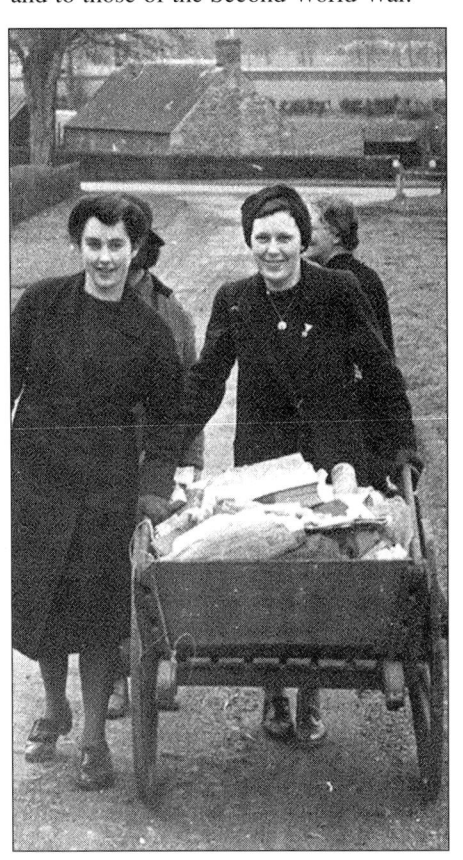

In 1919 the Staff attended a conference in Perth on 'Moral and Religious Instruction and *(surprisingly)* Sex Education'.

In 1920 the school was receiving an annual visit from the School Dentist. In 1921 an Intermediate Department was introduced and in 1923 Room 8, was fitted up as a Science class.
In 1924 a new block for Science, Drawing *(most likely Technical Drawing)* and Physical Education, was built immediately in front of the present school *(now private business premises)* for the Intermediate Section which had been introduced in 1921.

The 50th Anniversary of the School was celebrated in grand style on 18th February 1927 when all ex-pupils were invited to come along to the Infant Department, where as part of the festivities, 'tea was served and fruit and sweets distributed to the guests'.

In 1932 Mr Strain retired after 38 years service in the school as teacher and Headmaster.

*(Top) No fewer than 68 pupils lost their lives in the 1914-18 war, and on 11 September 1920 this memorial gateway was unveiled by Mr F. Norie-Miller, then Chairman of the Perthshire Education Authority.*
*(Left) Jean Murray and Jean Coogan on a waste-paper collection mission.*

## THE SCHOOL DURING TWO WORLD WARS

World War I commenced in 1914 and by March 1915, a 'Roll of Honour' had been placed in the main corridor of the school, containing the names of 140 former pupils. All over the United Kingdom young men had flocked to volunteer to serve their King and Country and the youth of the town were no exception.

The school at this time was in a frenzy of fund raising activities in order to send small parcels *"to those who had volunteered for service in the present great National crisis"*. Money was raised by schoolchildren throughout Perthshire for Motor Ambulances which would be used by the Red Cross at the 'Front', and one of these came to the school on 7th May in order that all could see the result of their labours.

Waste paper was collected and sold and the money donated to the Red Cross. Children and their parents knitted socks, scarves and mittens for the boys in the trenches on every occasion *(at fund raising concerts)* not spent on some other essential task.

In October 1915 the School was requisitioned by the Government to house troops and pupils were moved to the Town Hall. The Infants were taught in the North Free Church Hall, and Practical Subjects in the hall of the Royal Hotel. In April 1916 the troops left the school which was given a very thorough cleaning before the pupils moved back in.

### THE HEAD TEACHERS OF COUPAR ANGUS SCHOOL

MR LOGAN - MASTER OF THE PAROCHIAL SCHOOL     Retired 1877
MR LOUTET FIRST HEADMASTER OF THE PUBLIC SCHOOL .. 1877-1900
MR G. W. F. STRAIN  ... 1900-1932
MR W. B. ROBERTSON . 1932-1954
MR J. TUCKWELL ..... 1954-1964
MR A. BLACK         ..... 1964-1978
MR B. G. JOHNSTON ... 1978-1982
MRS PRATT           ..... 1982-1996
MRS ORR             ..... 1996-1997
MISS CAMERON        ..... 1997-

There was a strong feeling of 'patriotism' then and the National Anthem was sung on every possible occasion. On 'Empire Day' in May children saluted the Union Flag and Patriotic Songs were sung.

The war years saw a considerable increase in the number of pupils taking lunch in the 'Soup Kitchen' for food was scarce. With regard to food, many were to remember with distaste, the black very coarse rye bread which was all that was on offer then. At the time, it was not appreciated just how nourishing and full of protein and goodness this bread was, and which had been the staple diet of many on the European continent.

In February 1918 the School Board and Staff presented Pte Alex Macpherson with a wristlet watch on the occasion of his winning the Military Medal. The presentation took place in the Playground in the presence of pupils and a number of his friends.

In February part of the field in front of the school was 'secured' to allow some of the pupils to cultivate vegetables for use in the Soup Kitchen, and in June a further presentation took place to honour Sgt Neil Boyd winning the Military Cross.

During Red Cross Week £36 was sent to Red Cross HQ and £5 to the local branch from the sale of waste paper. In July it is recorded that Lieut Ralph S. Paterson, had won the Military Cross and that £10 10s. was sent to the Prisoner of War Association from the sale of the 7th consignment of waste paper.

The school roll in Sept 1918 was 365, when the Tank 'Julian' arrived in Coupar Angus. The visit of the tank, which was making the rounds as part of a War Savings campaign, was considered to be of such great interest and importance that the school was closed for the event. Tanks had been recently introduced to the war zone amid fervent hopes that this new and hitherto secret weapon would speedily end the fighting and secure victory.

There now was a 'School Hero Fund' and from this a wristlet watch was presented to Sgt Mitchell on his winning the Military Medal.

In January 1919 six newly returned Prisoners of War were honoured at a Presentation at which Col Clark of Princeland was the Guest of Honour. In February further presentations were made to returning heroes - Capt D. T. MacIntosh and Corp D. Irvine. When the Soup Kitchen closed at the end of the winter months it had served 8097 meals.

By 1920 fund raising activities were being held for the 'School Memorial Fund' to honour those ex-pupils who had lost their lives in the War. Many donations were received and a whist drive in March raised £65 which was added to the fund. Other fund raising activities followed and on the 11th September 1920 the Memorial Gateway was opened and used for the first time, upon which the names of the 68 'old pupils' who had died in the cause of freedom, were inscribed. The very moving unveiling ceremony was carried out by Mr F. Norie-Miller, who was then Chairman of the Perthshire Education Authority.

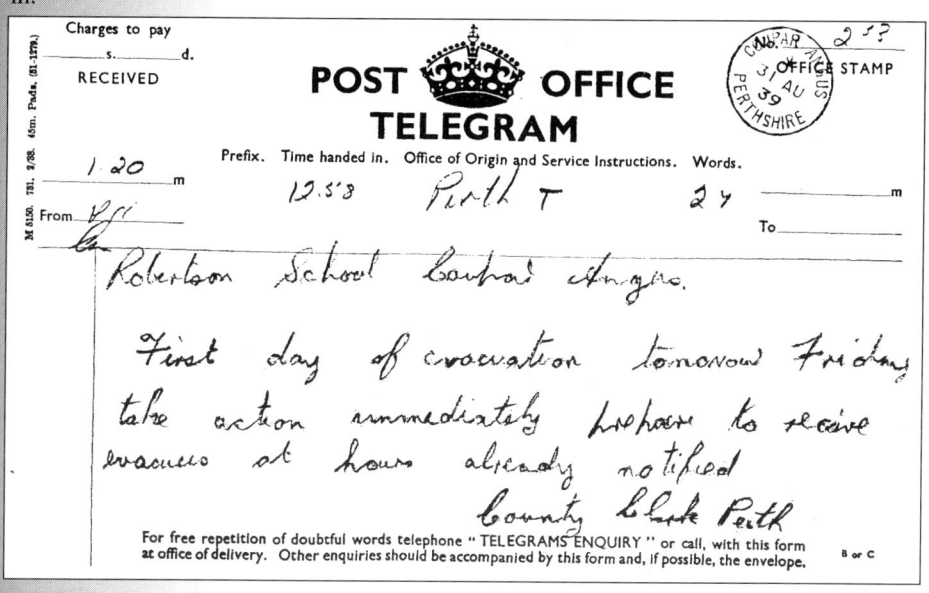

From this time on, wreaths would be laid on the 11th November 'Armistice Day' and pupils would attend a special service of Remembrance.

The years up until 1939 passed uneasily for only the very young had no sad memories of the loss of life and hardship of World War I. The International situation was so grave by the end of August that a 'State of National Emergency' was declared and the school, along with all others throughout the country, was closed for a week. This may have been a holiday for the pupils, but the Headmaster, Mr Robertson, and the teaching staff had their work cut out, for a telegram sent on the 31st August notified them that the first batch of evacuees from Dobbie's Loan School in Glasgow would be arriving the following day. The day after that more evacuees arrived this time from Anne the Saint School also in Glasgow. On 3rd September 1939 War was declared. When a genuine air raid warning sounded on 20th October the Headmaster was very pleased with the conduct of the pupils during what he described as a 'novel experience'. In November because of 'Black Out' regulations, the school was forced to close early.

The Guide Hut had to be rented to accommodate the extra numbers which were given as:

NATIVE CHILDREN.......297 *
PRIVATE EVACUEES...... 16
OFFICIAL EVACUEES..... 60
(* as described in the log book)

There were now many changes in teaching staff with some members being 'called up' for active service. Cups of cocoa were now issued to country children instead of soup and in March 1941 the first Inoculations against Diphtheria were given. This consisted of 3 'jags' at monthly intervals. The after effect of the second was unpleasant and the third could only be described as terrible.

During War Weapons Week in June 1941 the Town Council presented each child with a 6d. ($2^1/2$p) Savings Stamp in the hope that this would encourage regular saving for the War Effort from that time on.
Evacuees were still arriving in the town -

*(Top) The Common, from the back of the school showing Mr Robertson's schoolhouse third from left C1900.*
*(Centre) The Coupar Angus Home Guard pose for a picture in front of the Town Hall. Note the sandbags over some of the windows.*
*(Left) Home Guard Captain James Anderson of Balbrogie.*

page 70

24 from the Highland Academy at Greenock, as a result of the horrendous 'Clydebank Blitz', in which whole families were wiped out.

This year pupils were given 4 weeks 'tattie holidays' for labour was scarce, and it was left to the young people to bring in the harvest which was so essential to the wellbeing of the nation. Ministry of Information films were being shown from time to time in the Town Hall on subjects of National Importance. There was now a 'War Weapons Week', a 'Warship Week' and a 'Wings for Victory Week', to raise money for these which were so vital to the survival of the Nation.

On a lighter note, a new Handbell was presented to the school by ex-Provost Miss Annie Robertson who rung it for the first time on 22nd September 1942. During all this time the children of the school were taking part in concerts in the Town Hall, in order to raise money which went towards the 'War Effort'. These were very popular and very financially successful. In April 1944 a start was being made to a proper Dining Centre in the school and pies and hot drinks were supplied to country children during one of the most severe winters on record, when school meals and milk failed to 'get through' on many occasions.

The two-day holiday on 8th and 9th of May 1945 to celebrate Victory in Europe was a joyous occasion indeed in the town and nationwide, after the deprivations of War. On 5th July 1945 a Labour Government was elected to office and this would bring far reaching changes to a country still reeling from a horrendous European War. Victory over Japan was secured in August and the National Holiday on 21st and 22nd ended the conflict which had taken a dreadful toll of our manhood and added a further 23 names to the School War Memorial. The lives of every person throughout the country had been touched in some way by a war which had almost brought the Nation to its knees.

## MR ROBERTSON'S HEADMASTERSHIP
### 1932-1954

When Mr Robertson was appointed Headmaster, the Education Authorities purchased a house at the corner of Princeland and Forfar Road as a Schoolhouse, for the previous head-master *(Mr Strain)* had owned his residence.

In 1934 specialist subjects were being broadcast by Radio to pupils *(elocution was one)*. By now the original school buildings were showing the signs of age and were described as being 'very overcrowded', although the roll had not risen appreciably and had averaged 350 over the years. Times were changing however, and more and more room was required for teaching the additional subjects introduced over the years, and now considered to be an integral part of the school curriculum. Because of the shortage of space, Domestic Science *(formerly Household Management)* and Technical Subjects had to be axed. The lighting also was poor, the rooms badly ventilated and the central heating system was not working well.

The cloak-room facilities were described as 'scanty' and the school 'offices' *(toilets)* were also in need of modernisation.

In 1935 a scheme was introduced to supply school children with milk. These neat little bottles, contained 1/3rd of a pint and cost half an old pence (1/5th of 1p).

In May of this same year the Silver Jubilee of King George V and Queen Mary (1910-1936) was celebrated amid great festivity with each primary pupil receiving a 'commemorative mug' to mark the occasion. Senior pupils were

*(Top) Mr Robertson (at left) at his retiral presentation.*
*(Left) A selection of commemarative mugs dating back to the Victoria era.*

presented with a copy of John Buchan's 'The King's Grace'.

By this time, Specialist teachers travelled to Coupar Angus several times each week to teach their specific subjects. As the school holidays at Blairgowrie High School were not the same as those of Coupar Angus, the pupils here often missed out on classes due to this anomaly which surprisingly continued up to the closure of the Secondary Department in 1977.

The day to day running of the school proceeded as normal at the death of King George V and during the trying period of the 'Abdication'. The Coronation of George VI and Queen Elizabeth in 1936 came as some light relief and looked on as a joyous occasion which was celebrated in great style. There were Sports in Foxhall Park followed by tea, served to the pupils by the teachers. Souvenir boxes of chocolates and fountain pens were presented to pupils by the Rev Wylie Smith, Chairman of the School Management Committee. A week long holiday rounded off the festivities.

At this time the School Curriculum included knitting for boys. One business man - who shall remain nameless - objected so strongly to his son having to take knitting to school that he clashed with the authorities who issued an ultimatum -"Knit or Quit".

The boy was heralded as a hero by his fellow class-mates who did not particularly fancy knitting, but others enjoyed it and were justly proud of the garments they produced.

One boy suggested *"they would be better wi' fretwork"*, and Mr Robertson the Headmaster had the unenviable position of being between the Devil and the deep blue sea in the furore caused by the knitting issue.

The Education Authority released a statement to the Press:

*"The parent will be given an opportunity to fall into line with the recognised curriculum of the school. If he fails to assent, the boy will be immediately excluded from school and a prosecution will be instituted against the parent"*. A compromise was reached!

In 1938 the school was graded as a 10 teacher school. This was the year that the town's water supply was so bad that the Medical Officer of Health ordered all drinking water to be boiled and every drinking fountain in the school playground, was turned off.

It was a momentous year for 35 pupils, who along with the headmaster, travelled by train to Glasgow to visit the never to be forgotten and never to be repeated, 'Empire Exhibition'.

Term Report Cards were issued for the first time and two gas cookers were installed in Room 8 for Cookery Lessons.

The clouds of War were again looming on the horizon and on 31st August 1939 this entry appears in the Log Book -

**"Due to the gravity of the International situation a State of National Emergency has been declared and the School, along with all others, will be closed for a week".**

The War years were to be difficult for everyone, and the school had to make many changes and adjustments, but carried on despite teachers leaving for National Service. Pupil numbers rose due to the influx of Evacuees to the town.

In 1944 the school had a 'Dining Centre' in place of the old 'Soup Kitchen' started in 1896. Meals were now delivered to the school from Dundee, which was to prove to be far from ideal.

In November, the Perth to Blairgowrie 'bus was involved in an accident which injured a number of pupils travelling to school, one of whom was admitted to Dundee Royal Infirmary.

The winter of 1944/45 was to be one of the coldest on record. The country was still suffering from the deprivations of War, and the severe conditions caused even more power cuts and coal shortages. Road conditions were frequently so bad that milk and meals could not be delivered.

When in 1946 the School Leaving Age was raised to 15, very major problems of overcrowding were experienced. The Headmaster now had many additional administrative duties to attend to, and a School Secretary - Miss Jessie Reid - was appointed.

If the winter of 1944/45 was thought to be bad, that of 1946/47 was even worse. For weeks on end, roads were impassible, and teachers from outwith the town came to school by train, for road conditions were treacherous. It was a miserable time throughout the country due to the severe weather which lasted into March.

This year saw the end of French being taught in the school and the start of pupils following the A & B Courses, being transferred to Blairgowrie High School.

The country was suffering from a severe labour shortage and in October a party of 'Harvesters' from Glasgow used the school as a Hostel during their stay to help on the land. On 31st October 1947 Miss Annie Doig retired after 26 years service in the school.

## THE POST WAR ERA

Perhaps the only bright spot in 1947 was the wedding in November of HRH the Princess Elizabeth to Prince Philip, Duke of Edinburgh.

The school roll was again nearing the 400 mark due to the rise in the school leaving age and despite some pupils being transferred to Blairgowrie High School to complete their studies.

Overcrowding was eased slightly when the Guide Hut became available as extra accommodation. At the start of the potato holidays, 65 boys from St Pauls School in Glasgow arrived in town to help with the harvest and they like those of the previous year, made the school their base. This annual visit was to continue until 1953 when extra labour was no longer necessary.

A mobile film unit now made periodic visits to the school and school work was on annual display. In 1950 Hugh Watt, the Moderator of the General Assembly of the Church of Scotland, visited Coupar Angus and talked to the pupils and a H O R S A hut was erected in the grounds as a class-room for technical subjects. On 10th November part of the Science room ceiling collapsed but fortunately there were no casualties, and in January 1951 bad weather kept more than half the pupils from attending school.

In 1952 a Youth Employment Officer was visiting to advise senior pupils on career options. On 8th February the staff and pupils listened to a 'wireless' broadcast of the Proclamation of Queen Elizabeth's accession to the throne after the sudden death of her father, King George VI. The memorial service which took place in St George's Chapel, Windsor, was also broadcast to the whole school.

The pupils were now having regular talks on Road Safety and their bicycles were brought to school for inspection by Police Officers, to ensure that they were in safe condition. Cycling instruction and proficiency tests were soon to follow.

Britain was entering a new era, with a young Queen who it was hoped, would lead the nation in a time of Peace and Prosperity. To celebrate her Coronation, it was decided that all schools would have a 3 day holiday - 1st, 2nd and 3rd June 1953. Each Protestant pupil was presented with a New Testament and Roman Catholic children received Missals from the Education Committee. The local Coronation Committee gave each child a souvenir mug and a box of chocolates and there was a free show for them in the local Cinema, the 'Playhouse'.

In 1953 B C G vaccination, as a protection against T B, was introduced and on 2nd July 1954 the Headmaster, Mr W. B. Robertson retired after 22 years in Coupar Angus school.

## MR TUCKWELL'S HEADMASTERSHIP
### 1954-1964

When Mr John Tuckwell arrived from Blairgowrie High School on 10th August 1954 to take up the post of Headmaster, the Roll was 392 and the Staff numbered 19. With this number of staff, the administrative duties were considerable and the Log Book deals mostly with them. One such example of these extras is in 1955 when it became mandatory for the school to keep a 'Record of Accidents'. A sub-committee was formed to look into 'accommodation difficulties' as the roll was now 406 and the school was 'bursting at the seams'.

In September 1955 the Rose Hip collection passed the 2 ton mark bringing the total for the season to over 3 tons which benefited the school by £90.

In August 1956 the Evening Telegraph carried an article on the school with photographs of each class, and copies of the newspaper were on sale to pupils within the school.

By August, 1957 Poliomyelitis inoculations and Speech Therapy classes had been introduced and in February 1958 a bus load of pupils was taken to Blairgowrie High School to be X-rayed at the Mass Radiography Unit based there. By now more and more visits were taking place, of Advisors and Supervisors of the various subjects being taught in the school, and the staff had risen to 22.

In 1960 the school library started in 1903 and for many years located in rooms 13 and 14, was transferred to 14 Queen Street.

The much needed new Secondary Block was under construction and on 1st February the Director of Education Mr L. Young, visited the school to see that all was progressing well. The Staff now was 23 and the Chief Probation Officer for the area, was added to the list of visitors to the school.

In 1961 the Mass Radiography Unit came to Coupar Angus, which did the children out of a bus trip to Blairgowrie where it had previously been based. Two Youth Employment Officers were now advising pupils on career options.

In 1962 the Infants moved back into the renovated 'old building' from their temporary quarters in the Town Hall and Guide Hut. A Road Safety Mobile Unit paid a visit, and in June the senior pupils visited Edinburgh, while the younger ones had to be content with going to Arbroath. These visits or 'trips' were now an annual event.

Serious problems of absenteeism had been experienced for many, many years, by the school authorities at Tattie planting and Lifting times, not only in Coupar Angus but throughout all country areas. October 1962 saw the start of an 'exemption scheme' which allowed certain pupils to be absent from school to take part in this work. In this first year, 50 children applied with their parents consent and were granted leave of absence for an additional 15 days.

In November 1962 the Rt Rev Dr A. Neville Davidson of Glasgow Cathedral and Moderator of the General Assembly of the Church of Scotland, visited the school, and a parents morning was held in the Infant Dept, which would become a regular event.

By now second and third year pupils were travelling to Perth Baths for swimming lessons and pupils were competing successfully at the Perth Music Festival. All members of Staff now had to be X Rayed for T.B., and pupils were visiting Isla Bank farm to see Mr Colville's prize bulls.

*(Top) L to R - Sandy Dow, Alan Gilzean, Alan Grant and James Craig.*

page 73

When Mr Tuckwell left to go to Crieff in 1964 there was a senior girls hockey team and a cricket team taking regular part in 7-a-side events. Pupils were venturing further afield and 37 pupils, under the charge of Mr Sturrock, paid a two day visit to London.

## MR A BLACK'S HEADMASTERSHIP
## 1964-1978

A long-to-be remembered event took place on 19th June 1964 when every pupil in the school assembled in the hall to do honour to MR ALAN GILZEAN, the Dundee and Scottish International Footballer who was a former pupil. Mr Gilzean was presented with a trophy cabinet, and in return he presented the school with one of his Scotland jerseys complete with SFA crest.

The school trip for the younger pupils this year was to St Andrews, while the seniors went by train from Coupar Angus to Edinburgh, where they visited the Castle, the Scottish National War Memorial, the Zoo, Princess Street Gardens and the then unique, Floral Clock. On their return journey they apparently had a spectacular view of the Forth Road Bridge which was in the last stages of completion.

During the summer vacation, 80 children and 20 Supervisors from the Motherwell and Wishaw area, used the school as hostel accommodation. It is recorded that they *"proved to be a thoroughly well organised and well supervised body and left an excellent impression on all concerned"*.

Pupils were now travelling to Coupar Angus from other schools, to compete in games - football for boys and rounders for girls. Skiing instruction was available for those who wished it and a memorable skiing weekend was spent at Lawers Hostel by a party of the boys.

The new block consisting of a Gymnasium, Dressing-rooms, Showers, a Rural Science room and a Music room, was ready for occupation in 1965. Staff, parents and pupils alike, thought that all their problems were over and that they could look forward to a long period of progressive education in congenial surroundings.

The School Log Books from 1964 to 1977 unfortunately are missing. I contacted Mr Kiddie who taught for many years in the school, and he felt that nothing momentous had happened during this period.

## SESSION
## 1977-1978

Is a date that never should be forgotten for the Secondary Department closed finally at the end of June bringing an end to the type of schooling which had been available to children of school-age in Coupar Angus, since 1877. Now on leaving the Primary department, they had no option but to travel to Blairgowrie High School, to complete their education. A few parents at this time and in the future, would opt to send their children to other schools in Perth or Dundee, but Blairgowrie High School was the official school and almost

```
✺✺✺✺✺✺✺✺✺✺✺✺✺✺
ALL THE NEWEST AND ALL
THE BEST NOVELS
ARE TO BE HAD AT THE
Strathmore Library.
AN UNRIVALLED COLLECTION,
AND ALWAYS BEING ADDED TO.
─────────────
THE BEST QUARTERLY AND MONTLY
MAGAZINES.
SUPPLIED TO READERS.
─────────────
Special reduced terms to Subscribers, who
may enter at any time
─────────────
Wm. CULROSS & SON,
THE CROSS
Coupar Angus
✺✺✺✺✺✺✺✺✺✺✺✺✺✺
```

all pupils travelled there each day during the school session. The roll dropped to 237 and classes 1 to 4 were settled in to the 'Old' block, and classes 5 to 7 occupied the spacious, former Secondary Block.

The Gym Block would be used by classes until October 1978 when it became the 'Community Centre' for 'Community Education' which replaced 'Further Education', 'Evening Classes' and the old 'Night School' of long ago and was no longer under the jurisdiction of the school but an entirely separate body.

Fire Drill was now part of the school routine and Fire Officers regularly visited and inspected the premises to see that all was well. Regarding games which had always played an important part in school life, pupils travelled to Alyth, Meigle and Blairgowrie, to play cricket, football and rounders in conjunction with the East Perthshire Primary League.

Successful school concerts were still an annual event and in December 1977 an audience of three hundred attended both performance held in the Assembly Hall, on two consecutive nights.

Educational visits, greatly enjoyed by the participants, continued and in January 1978, 35 pupils travelled to the Scottish Fisheries Museum in Anstruther, Fife. During Mr Black's time as Headmaster, the policy was introduced to allow tenants to buy their Schoolhouses which Mr Black did.

Over the years the aquatic skills of the Coupar Angus children had progressed by leaps and bounds, which greatly pleased the retiring Headmaster who was especially proud of the swimming achievement of a Spina Bifida pupil.

At the retiral ceremony in the school, the children presented Mr Black with a car radio and the youngest pupil handed over a bouquet of beautiful flowers to Mrs Black. A huge card, which was signed by every child in the school, was also given to Mr Black.

## MR JOHNSTON'S HEADMASTERSHIP
## 1978-1982

On 21st March 1978, Mr B. G. Johnston was appointed Headmaster.

At this time a number of pupils were being coached by Mrs Hanslip in Roller Skating. They reached a very high standard and had great success in many competitions.

Among the places visited by pupils this session were:-

*DUNDEE MUSEUM
CAMPERDOWN PARK
KINGUSSIE WILD LIFE PARK
CARNOUSTIE
PERTH MUSEUM
KINNOUL NATURE TRAIL
CHESTER*

There was a School Tuck Shop now, the profit, which amounted to £285.32p, was added to school funds.

The Session of 1978/79 opened with a roll of 257 and the staff consisted of 9 full time teachers, 5 visiting teachers of specialist subjects, and the headmaster. This Session, visits from Heads of the various Departments of Blairgowrie High School were first made, in an exercise designed to help ease the transition of pupils from a small Primary to the very much larger Secondary School.

In January 1979 Mr Hugh Fraser became the new Janitor and to the delight of the boys, took on the extra curricular task of coaching the football team and proved to be a coach of considerable ability.

In May 1979 the sum of £720 was raised from concerts, despite a power cut which 'blacked out the proceedings' at one of the performances, but which continued with the curtains opened to what daylight was left. The power cut was a result of a thunder storm earlier in the evening. On another evening the entire performance was filmed by Police fromTulliallan keeping a promise they had made to Primary 7 pupils on a visit to the Police Training College.

The class 7 trip to London this year, costing £59, was joined by their contemporaries from Meigle. After 28 years teaching in the school Mr Tweedie retired and he and Mrs Tweedie presented a cheque to the school to fund an annual prize which would be known as 'The Tweedie Prize'.

Educational Television broadcasts were now a regular feature, and among those visiting the school during the Session were representatives from the SAVINGS BANK, DR BARNARDO'S, POLICE HQ, TULLIALLAN, the SCHOOL DENTIST, the SCHOOL DOCTOR, the NURSE, the RSPCA, a THEATRE COMPANY, a BOOK REPRESENT-ATIVE, and the BLAIRGOWRIE PLAYERS. The Infant Mistress, Mrs Dorie Jackson retired at the end of this year after 16 years in the school and in January 1980 the following statement was recorded in the Log Book:

*"DUE TO CUTBACKS IN PUBLIC EXPENDITURE THE SCHOOL HAS LOST 2 TEACHERS - MRS BARBOUR, MUSIC AND MRS KING, NEEDLEWORK"*.

The twice yearly visits of HMIS were long gone but this year a 3-day inspection of the school took place.

In 1978/79 a Chess Club was formed; the school was broken into for the first time, and the girls won the Strathmore League Rounders championship.

Those pupils who did not go to London this Session went to Glasgow instead, and additional visits were made to Edinburgh, Dunfermline, and Camperdown Park, Dundee.

Mr Kiddie the last member of staff of the former Junior Secondary School, retired after 33 years as Technical Teacher and organiser of the Evening Classes.

The Session of 1980/81 saw the start of visits by a teacher of Remedial Education. This was to be a time of great sadness for both Staff and Pupils due to the illness then death, of the School Chaplain, the Rev William Cochrane, who was highly respected and greatly liked. He was described by Mr Johnston as *"a pillar of strength within this community and will be greatly missed by many especially the staff and pupils of this school"*. These words were to prove prophetic!

The highly organised routine of the school ran smoothly with additional visits and fund raising events added to those which had become traditional. The coffee evening raised £615 and a party of pupils participated in a tree planting operation at Grampian View as part of an environmental project. On several occasions, groups of pupils entertained members of the Toc H. The Alyth Operatic Production, the Blairgowrie Players Pantomime and the Caithness Glass Factory in Perth were added to the list of places visited.

Mr Rattray, the very popular Lollipop man, retired after 7 years and Mrs Walker too, after 16 years. The children enjoyed a new experience by sailing down the Tay in the 'Tay Queen'.

Staff numbers had crept up again and were now - 10 full time teachers, 6 visiting teachers, plus 1 Remedial teacher.

## MRS PRATT AS HEADMISTRESS
## 1982-1996

When Mrs Pratt arrived as the first Headmistress of Coupar Angus School, the list of visits to and by the school was indeed impressive. Among them were representatives of - Health Education, the Milk Marketing Board; Help the Aged; Child Hearing; Road Safety; The Red Cross and Dr Barnardo's. The pupils went on all kinds of visits from Farms to Fire Stations and a local shop *(Davidson Chemists)*. The Police Stations were also on their list and further afield, parties travelled to London, Camperdown Park,

*(Top) The road to the school, off the Blair road.*

Stirling Castle, the Field of Bannockburn and Lochore Meadows Country Park. Football, rounders, cricket and chess were still being played and the coffee evening this session raised £800.

In November 1982 the school hosted the 'Scot Quiz' which was organised by Perth Chamber of Commerce. Along with pupils from Collace, Burrelton and Kettins a concert was held at which £450 was raised for the charity 'Action for the Crippled Child'. At the Aberfeldy Mod, the Recorder Group came first in their class and several pupils took part in a cross country race at Scone Palace. The Staff was now 9 full time teachers, five part time teachers plus 1 Remedial teacher.

On 7th September 1983 when word reached the School that Diana, Princess of Wales was to pass through Coupar Angus on her way from Balmoral to Keillers Works in Dundee, pupils and staff lined Blairgowrie Road to welcome her. Sadly, this was to prove to be the only occasion townspeople would have to see her pass through Coupar Angus. The severe winter of 1984 caused a great deal of disruption to the school itinerary and the school was closed, as well as most roads, for a time. 2000 skiers were trapped in Glenshee and were only rescued after a massive operation to open the road long enough to get them out. Large helicopters were ferrying food and medicines from the Cricket ground in Coupar Angus Road, Blairgowrie to the stranded skiers. After almost two days, the skiers were brought down to Blairgowrie in convoy.

The Session of 1984/85 was marred by Industrial Action when Unions called Strikes, and ordered their members to 'Work to Rule' which meant that several classes had 'unofficial holidays' from time to time.

The music room was moved then to the main building to 'facilitate movement and class organisation'. Now the era of the Computer had arrived and staff were having to attend 'In Service Training' in Computer Studies. Cavity wall insulation was installed on the direction of the Regional Council in an exercise to cut heating costs, and pupils took part in the Blairgowrie High School production of 'The Magic Box'. Those who had participated in the Perth Music Festival, the results of which were excellent, entertained the 'Thursday Club'.

In April a Nursery Nurse started work in the Infant Department and in May Mrs Kathleen Kench, on behalf of former pupils of the school, presented the 'Hossack Cup' as a Music Prize. The part time Staff rose to 7 teachers for now Gaelic was being taught. During the summer vacation of 1985/86 the former Technical Room was converted to a Primary Classroom, and in November another 'break-in' occurred.

By now the Headmistress had more and more administrative duties to attend to. The industrial action by some teaching staff had caused difficulties but amazingly the school continued to visit and be visited. Perth Theatre, the Scottish Opera and Perth College were among places visited and the residents of Belmont Eventide Home were added to the list of groups entertained by pupils.

## THE SCHOOL SAVINGS BANK

In October 1985 the School Savings Bank which had been opened in 1906 closed due to lack of support. Perhaps saving for the proverbial 'rainy day' was a thing of the past, but giving to charity was not, for in 1985 the pupils raised over £243 for Dr Barnardo's.

Industrial action was still causing administrative problems, but on the whole, the work of the school carried on. There were still talks on various subjects of interest, and book companies visited regularly with attractive reading material, which could be purchased by pupils. Mr Frazer the Janitor attended a course on the fascinating and mind-boggling subject of 'Floor Care' and the Mills Observatory in Dundee was visited.

In 1986 two teams from the school took part in a swimming gala, and Primary 7, along with pupils from Meigle and Burrelton, went to London on an educational visit. Inchcolme Island in the river Forth and Pitlochry Theatre were also visited in the summer term.

The pupils of Primary 7 were bitterly disappointed when the two day visit to introduce them to the much bigger Blairgowrie High School was cancelled due to what was considered to be, unwarranted Industrial Action on the part of the Blairgowrie High School Staff. At the start of Session 1986/87 the staff consisted of nine teachers plus the Headmistress and eight visiting teachers - two Physical Education and one each for Needlework, Music, Music Adviser, Strings, Art and Gaelic. A teacher of Remedial Education also visited on a regular basis when required.

In September the school and the town were very shocked when Mrs Betty Robertson collapsed and died in her class-room. Highly respected and much liked by colleagues and pupils her loss was deeply felt.

In step with the times, staff in-service included instruction in computer technology. In March 1987 the Staff/Parents and Pupils annual coffee evening raised a staggering £1064. As usual, Primary 7 pupils went to London while Edinburgh Zoo, the Mills Observatory and RRS Discovery (Royal Research Ship), Dundee were visited by other classes.

The roll was now 245, but the school buildings were suffering from the ravages of time, and dry-rot in the Infant Department had to be eradicated, and in the Hall boards which had become

*(Top) The Coupar Angus School football team with Eddie Sturrock at right, and Mr Dawson, Janitor at left.*

wood-worm infested, were replaced.

By 1990 the roll had dropped to 213 and because of rising costs, the Primary 7 pupils visited York instead of London. Other educational visits continued with Blackwater Dam and Duthie Park being added to the impressive list of places visited over the years.

On 17th August 1994 former Headmaster Mr Andrew Black died, which saddened both school and town. In the Session of 1995/96 the highly respected and popular Mrs Pratt retired and Mrs Orr, who had formerly held posts at Glenprosen (1984-1989) and Edzell (1989-l995) took her place.

The new Headmistress introduced a school Newsletter as a means of keeping parents informed of the school's many activities. The roll was now 202 and the Lintrathen Water Treatment Works, Pitlochry Hydro Dam, Athole Bakery, the Abbey Church and fragment of the Cistercian Abbey ruin, were added to the list of places visited by pupils.

A nursery garden was constructed at the rear of the Infant Block by pupils working under the supervision of the Countryside Ranger while others took part in bulb planting in Larghan Park and other areas of the town, as part of an environmental exercise.

In January 1996 'Friends of Coupar Angus School' held a Quiz Night which raised £500 for school funds. On 20th August 1996 the following appears in the School Log Book:-

*"After consulting with other Head teachers, discovered Logs are not really kept any more. No one has asked to read this one in over a year. Decided to stop".*

The reason for this decision possibly stems from the fact that the great amount of paper-work in school now renders a Log Book unnecessary, So many records have to be kept of every possible aspect of school life, that they may no longer be so essential. Certainly over the years the entries have become quite commonplace and deal mostly with the hum-drum everyday life of the school, whereas the early Log Books contained a wealth of information on many aspects of life in both school and town.

We have come a long way from the days of the 'School Board' whose members made regular visits to inspect the Register and to make sure all was in order.

Mrs Orr's stay in Coupar Angus was rather short for she decided to take early retirement. Her replacement was Miss Margaret Cameron whose teaching career had started in 1978 at Hayshead School in Arbroath.

Her first promoted post was at Carlogie School, Carnoustie. She was lecturer in Environmental Studies at Northern College for seven years before coming to Coupar Angus in January 1998. Miss Cameron felt Coupar Angus Primary School had a lot to be proud of, with a dedicated teaching and support staff lovely classrooms and halls, up-to-date resources, and a supportive community.

## EDWIN STURROCK

No history of Coupar Angus Public School would be complete without a few words about Edwin Sturrock, who came to Coupar Angus School as Form Master of Form 1 on 25th August 1936 two years after qualifying. He was full of enthusiasm and fresh ideas, and although his official remit was to teach English, History and Geography, was keen to use his other talents to enrich the school curriculum. One of these was Sport - cricket and rugby - and he had gained Full Rugby Blues in 1934 while playing for Edinburgh University. Before long the senior boys were undergoing regular football training, despite the fact their Coach was frequently suffering from injuries inflicted at his weekend rugby sessions. Although an academic of the highest order, Mr Sturrock was anxious to see practical subjects introduced, and due to his insistence a School Garden Club was introduced for those boys who did not study French. This was followed by the appointment of a teacher for Technical Subjects which greatly pleased him, for his prime concern throughout his entire teaching career was for the welfare of his pupils, and how best to prepare them for life beyond the school gates.

Although Mr Sturrock's own school report had described his singing ability as "Fair", it did not deter him from taking classes for music. Until this time these lessons had been quite formal, and bordering on the classical, but Mr Sturrock changed this and soon had them singing at the top of their voices, the popular songs of the day.

In 1940 he was called up for army service and spent the war years as an Instructor in the Army Physical Training Corps. He returned to Coupar Angus School in 1946 and before many years had elapsed became Principal teacher of English, History and Geography. The next obvious career move would be that of Headmaster but to achieve this would have meant leaving the town. He was often heard to say *"what is the point of ascending the career ladder if you leave happiness behind?"* He took his own advice and stayed in Coupar Angus where he eventually became Deputy Headmaster, a post he acquitted well, but was always happiest in the classroom.

In the days when it was generally considered that pupils of a Junior Secondary School, as Coupar Angus was then, had limited career aspirations, Mr Sturrock was never happier than when his pupils went on to achieve success in life. He was genuinely proud of his pupils and his support and encouragement, spurred them on to achieve qualifications far greater than might have been expected. He was quick to spot potential and had no patience with those who tended to "write off" a pupil.

Mr Sturrock was a life long member of the Boys Brigade, initially in his home town of Perth, then when he came to Coupar Angus he led their Drill Class and took their Sunday Bible Class until he retired.

Gardening figured largely in his personal interests, and for many years he was involved in the local Gardens and Allotments Society, and served as it's Chairman for a time.

His daughter Mrs Lynda McGregor who furnished this information, has fond memories of him at his happiest on holiday at their rented cottage at Lunan Bay, hoeing the weeds in the large garden, dressed in the scruffiest of garden clothes, with a radio propped up in a clump of lupins and tuned to the cricket commentary.

# THE SCHOOL I REMEMBER
## 1942-1945

*by Mrs Betsy Parsons, Ohio USA*

I must have started school at Coupar Angus in 1942 because my first teacher was Miss Robertson, then Miss Reid, Miss Lindsey, and I was in Miss McRitchie's class when I left in 1945. One can't remember everything that happened 55 years ago, but I do have lots of good memories of my time there.

I really didn't want my mother to leave me that first day of school: I cried when she left. That was probably the last time that I minded though. Let me just tell some of my memories.

Miss Robertson, a pretty, young teacher with a lovely highland voice, had lots of interesting things for us to do in that first class. Shapes to fit into spaces; lacing, buttoning; tying frames; designs to make with coloured tiles; songs to sing; games to play. My daughter now has the first primers I used then.

I enjoyed Miss Reid's class too and must have learned a lot. I never was very quick at arithmetic though, and this was a disadvantage in one activity she occasionally used. At dismissal time, we gathered around her as she posed questions about things we had been learning. If you got your hand up quickly and she called upon you and you had the right answer, you could leave. My best friend, Violet Wood, usually had to wait for me to walk home!

Walking to and from school was a good part of the day, too. I lived in Hillgardens so didn't have far to go. Violet lived at Bogside, so we enjoyed walking together. I still have pictures my mother took of Violet, Margaret and me on our way to school with a bunch of flowers clutched in my hand. We liked to take flowers to the teacher. The vase was a jar that had been painted on the inside, but Miss Reid always used our flowers. Sometimes Violet had to go on to school without me if I were late.

At first the wall around the school grounds was surmounted by an iron fence. This meant running all the way to the gate to get in. World War II did help me out there. The scrap metal drive caused all the iron fences to be cut down. I could then climb over the wall at the corner and save time.

World War II was a major influence on our lives as children, but we were lucky in Coupar Angus. Some of our schoolmates were refugees from Glasgow and were lucky to be in a safer place, but it must have been hard for them to be away from their families. I was away from my father, but lived with my grandfather, had my mother, and was near other relatives. The war was the reason I attended Coupar Angus School, too. Mother returned to visit her family in 1939 and brought me. When the war broke out, civilians had a difficult time returning to the United States and so we stayed in Scotland until early 1945 when war brides and other civilians began to be sent back.

The war meant that children as well as adults did their patriotic duty. For children that meant collecting scrap paper, knitting squares to be sewed together for blankets for sailors (I often wondered if they really used some of them !), and having money-making projects to benefit the Red Cross. Miss Lindsey always had ideas for us to make good use of our spare time. We made book marks and calendars from pictures and wallpaper scraps. We used up our mother's left-over bits of wool to make pompoms that were made into baby toys. We probably spent more time on those projects than we should have, but they were fun and we learned to do something to help others.

School became more serious when we moved into Miss McRitchie's class. The room even looked more serious with its tiers of desks that truly allowed some to be at the head of the class and some at the bottom! Periodic examinations determined who did sit in the desks at the head of the class. Sometimes misbehaviour could move a pupil very quickly to the bottom. Misbehaviour in any class could result in having the leather strap applied to the palm of the hand. Serious misbehaviour meant being sent to the headmaster, Mr. Robertson.

During my time in Coupar Angus, the gymnasium was in the building across the road. I think a science laboratory was in that building also. We smaller children did not do very much in the gym, but I'm sure the older ones made good use of the ropes and ladders and other equipment there.

That was also the scene of Scottish dancing classes led by Mr Abercromby, and I remember that we beginners were in the back row so we could watch the more advanced pupils. How exciting it was when we had the dressed-up "recital". My father sent me taffeta dresses from America for those. We also dressed up for our children's parties. Children now wouldn't believe their grandmothers could have fun at a party dressed like that. I wonder if today's children still enjoy plum pudding as a treat at their parties!

By 1945 the end of the war was in sight. We all collected bits of the netting that was being removed from the windows at school. We no longer were required to carry those horrible gas masks with us at all times or to practice putting them on. One evening the policeman came to the house with a message for mother. She and I were to leave in a very short time to return to America. Mother had known this would happen and was prepared. All the trunks were packed. We just had to say our good-byes and pack our personal things. I think I realized that I'd never see my grandfather again, but probably couldn't have known it would be 50 years before I would return to Coupar Angus in 1995. Two years later, in 1997, I was able to visit again and this time go back to Coupar Angus School.

When I left Scotland and arrived in the United States, I found the school to be different, although my Scottish education probably had me a bit ahead. When I returned, I felt perfectly at home as the school, activities, and teachers were so similar to the ones I had been a part of before I retired as a teacher in Ohio, USA.

Another war time memory. Paper was scarce, so the old school slates that may have dated to my mother's time were found stored somewhere and brought out for us to use. We didn't use them very much!

The history of Banking in Scotland goes back to the year 1695 when the Bank of Scotland was founded in Edinburgh. The Royal Bank was founded thirty two years later in 1727. Both banks then were supported by powerful political figures - the Bank of Scotland was Tory and leaned towards Jacobitism while the Royal Bank was Whig and Hanoverian.

# BANKS - the Coupar Angus money market

Initially, the business dealings of these banks was confined mostly to Edinburgh and the surrounding district.

Wealthy merchants in other parts of the country found themselves at a disadvantage, which resulted in small private banks being set up with money borrowed from the two giants. These Banks were run by agents who tended not to have fixed premises and it was only in the 1770's and 80's that Banks began to develop what is looked on now as a branch structure, and that developed very slowly.

Most of the provincial Scottish Banks were partnerships, and few had more than a dozen shareholders. Most were under capitalised which limited the business they could do and they did not survive the 1830's and 40's in the face of the large scale joint stock Banks which could fund railway development etc. At this time no shareholder had limited liability, so if a bank went bankrupt he was liable for the appropriate portion of the total debt involved.

### EARLY BANKS

| | founded |
|---|---|
| BANK OF SCOTLAND | 1695 |
| ROYAL BANK OF SCOTLAND | 1727 |
| BRITISH LINEN COMPANY BANK | 1774 |
| became BRITISH LINEN BANK | 1906 |
| NORTH OF SCOTLAND BANK | 1836 |
| CLYDESDALE BANK | 1838 |
| UNION BANK OF SCOTLAND | 1843 |

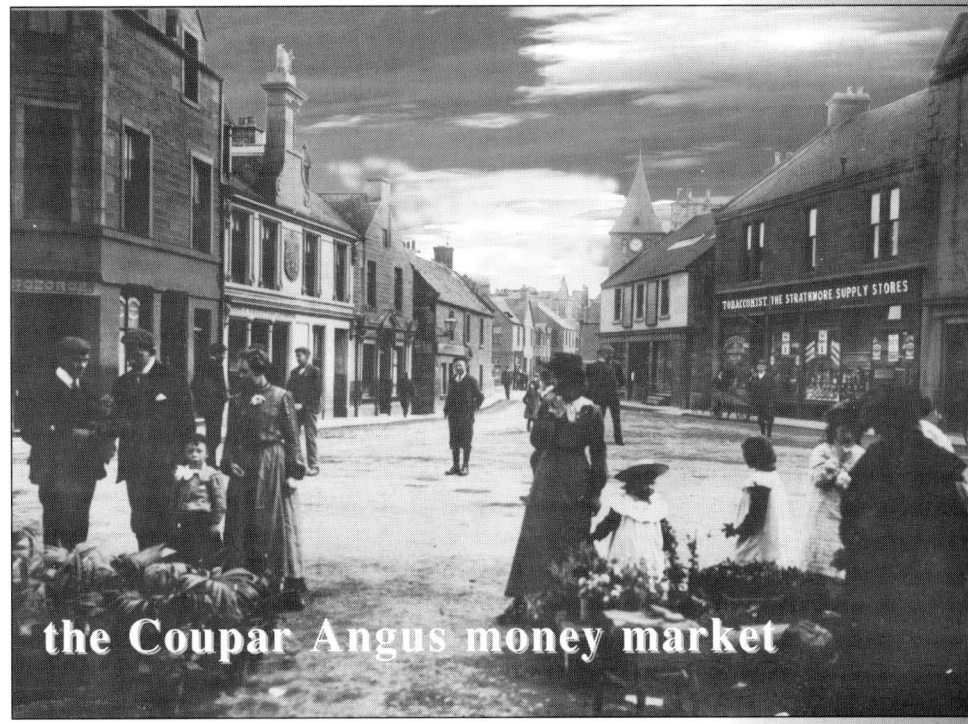

Eventually the bigger banks quashed all their rivals, and the only one which survived was the Dundee Banking Company.

In an attempt to develop the linen trade further, the British Linen Company which was founded in 1746, founded a Bank in 1774 which was the first to introduce branch banking throughout Scotland.

Although at the time Coupar Angus was a weaving town, there was no branch of the British Linen Company Bank here, but the reason for this may be that as weavers earned little more than a starvation wage, they had no need of one, and the proprietors of the large estates in the area, would possibly have banked in the cities - Perth or Edinburgh. In 1906 it became the British Linen Bank.

The British Linen Bank survived until 1971 when it was taken over by the Bank of Scotland.

The first Savings Bank was founded in 1810 in Dumfriesshire and from there spread to other parts of the country. It was an entirely different system of banking from the other banks in that it did not then lend money and did not issue bank-notes. Savings Banks have been given the credit for contributing greatly to the widely held belief of 'Scottish Thrift'. An off-shoot of this bank was the 'Penny Savings Bank' which brought banking to the less well-off members of Scottish society.

Even with this new banking facility by 1860 less than 10% of the adult population in Scotland had accounts. One hundred years later the figure had risen to 33%. This figure had dramatically risen by the start of the 21st century.

The various Scottish Banks had their own bank notes and in 1826 the government tried to outlaw all their notes under the value of £5. This caused a furore throughout Scotland and very strong opposition against it was led by Sir Walter Scott. The campaign met with such success that the plans to abolish the notes were abandoned. The Bank of Scotland £1 note still carries a portrait of Sir Walter Scott as commemoration of this event.

The Scottish Banking system was exported all over the world in the 18th and 19th centuries. Many Scottish bankers spent their entire professional lives in parts of the British Empire now the Commonwealth of Nations.

The Institute of Scottish Bankers was formed on 6th June 1875 and is the oldest professional body in the world for practising bankers.

*(Top) The Cross in the old days - the rendezvous for many business transactions.*

# BANKS IN COUPAR ANGUS FROM THE EARLIEST DAYS

In 1793 the Perth Banking Company, founded in 1787, opened a branch in Gray Street, Coupar Angus in the building now named 'Mercat Cross'. On a downstairs door within the building, although somewhat faded, is the sign 'BANK OFFICE'. The Perth Banking Company proved itself to be very forward looking for it financed the construction of the Coupar Angus and Newtyle Railway and profited handsomely from the transaction. It was a very prosperous bank which ran into trouble when it invested heavily in the United States of America, and the investments turned sour.

In 1857 it was taken over by one of Perth's oldest banks - the Union Bank of Scotland (1843-1955)

## THE UNION BANK OF SCOTLAND 1843 to 1955

This bank, was a Glasgow based joint-stock Bank created in 1843 as a result of the amalgamation of the Ship Bank, the Thistle Bank, the Glasgow Union Banking Company, and Hunters & Co of Ayr. In 1849 the Banking Company of Aberdeen was added and the Perth Bank followed in 1857. In this same year (1857) there was a bank in Calton Street - which is still known to the present day, as the Union Bank Buildings. After taking over the Perth Banking Company in 1857, trade was possibly carried on in the Gray Street premises of the former bank until the new building was built and ready for business transactions.

Over the years there were several unsuccessful attempts by the Bank of Scotland to take over the Union Bank. However in the summer of 1952 negotiations began once again which ended in an amicable agreement. In 1954 the Union Bank was assimilated with the Bank of Scotland and the full amalgamation of the bank systems was fully complete by 1st March 1955.

The former Union Bank is a 'B' listed building now occupied by a local law firm.

## THE NATIONAL BANK OF SCOTLAND 1825 to 1969
## THE ROYAL BANK OF SCOTLAND 1727 -

The National Bank of Scotland opened a branch at 7 Gray Street, Coupar Angus - the corner of Gray Street and Causewayend now a private dwelling - in 1847. As the town developed and Union Street became the main thoroughfare, it moved to there in 1873. Over the years the property was altered and refurbished and in 1958 extensive renovations to the exterior of the building were carried out. In 1959 the National Bank of Scotland and the Commercial Bank of Scotland merged to become the National Commercial Bank of Scotland with over four hundred branches.

In 1969 the National Commercial Bank and the Royal Bank of Scotland amalgamated and became known as the Royal Bank of Scotland Ltd. Soon after this, much of the bank building was sold off, part of the ground floor being retained as the branch office. Alterations and upgrading have been carried out over the years and in 1994 in keeping with the times, a cashline machine was installed outside the bank where cash and services are available on a 24 hour-a-day basis.

*(Top) Former premises of the Union Bank of Scotland, now Watson and Lyall Bowie, Solicitors.*
*(Left) Present day Royal Bank of Scotland, formerly The National Bank of Scotland.*

> **1991**
> Mr Snip (J. L. B. Apedaile) the local Councillor, cut the ribbon at the opening ceremony of the Bank of Scotland's Autoteller.

## THE BANK OF SCOTLAND
## 1695 -

The Bank of Scotland opened a branch in Coupar Angus in 1868 in purpose built premises which are still used to the present day, although over the years extensive refurbishment has taken place. In the mid 1990's the very fine bank house was sold and is now a private dwelling.

Over the centuries the Bank of Scotland has merged and amalgamated with many smaller banks. After several previously failed attempts, negotiations for merger, with the Union Bank of Scotland started once again during the summer of 1952.

This time they met with success and the full and amicable amalgamation of bank systems was completed by 1st March 1955. Throughout the country certain staffing difficulties were experienced as a result of the merger but as time passed solutions were found to those.

In 1990 a very fine 'Silver Bowl' was gifted by the bank to the Community Council for 'Citizen of the Year' award. The recipient is chosen by means of nominations from groups/clubs/societies and individuals of the local community. In 1991 a 24 hour cash machine was installed outside the bank as an additional customer facility.

## THE SAVINGS BANK

In 1839 a Branch of the Savings Bank opened in the town Post Office which at that time was situated in the building occupied by the Co-Op before its move further down George Street. Then it was known locally as the Post Office Building, and the Printer and Postmaster Mr Culross, acted as bank agent. As business grew the bank moved to roughly where the Co-op butchery was until 1999. For many years it was purely a savings bank accepting both large and very small amounts of money on which interest was paid. Then, it did not lend money and it has never had its own bank-notes.

On 20th April 1906, the Parish School, in conjunction with the Coupar Angus Branch, introduced a savings bank for pupils. Out of the 483 children on the roll then, three hundred joined the scheme and made regular deposits which averaged £5 per week. Most individual deposits would have been 3d or 6d *(old pence)*.

In October 1985 the School Savings Bank closed due to lack of support.

In 1937 the bank moved to premises at the other side of the building, in George Square where it has remained to the present day.

In 1975 in keeping with the times, many changes to the Savings Banking system were introduced, and new business activities soon followed, which enabled the bank to become more competitive with the ever expanding commercial banks.

In 1986 the Savings Bank was privatised, and after further restructuring, Scotland was left with only one - the TSB Scotland, plc.

On 28th June 1999 Lloyds and TSB joined forces as Lloyds TSB giving investors access to their money from the UK's largest network of branches and Cashpoint machines.

*I wish to acknowledge the help of Mr Alan Cameron, Archivist, Bank of Scotland, Edinburgh.*

*(Top) Present day TSB in George Square.*
*(Left) The present-day Bank of Scotland in Union Street.*

Nowadays we take for granted the important work provided by the Police and Fire Services - but this was not always the case.

# COMMUNITY WORK - our essential services

### THE FIRE SERVICE.

In the 19th century in large towns and cities, Insurance Companies used their influence to have Fire Brigades formed for they had first hand knowledge of the devastation caused by fire raging out of control in narrow and congested streets.

> **Messrs Durie and Miller, Station Works, has been destroyed by fire. Damage is estimated at £15,000.**

In Coupar Angus however, although there were serious fires from time to time over the years, and as early as 1861 the Press was agitating for a fire engine to be purchased. It appears that it was not until the early 20th century that the town had a fire engine with Captain D. Adams as Fire Officer.

The Jute Factories in town had their own appliances for fire was a very real risk, as the air was laden with inflammable dust caused by the spinning and weaving process. In 1907 when the fire engine at the Strathmore Linen Works broke down, the factory had to be closed for a few days until it was repaired.

Also in 1907 an exhibition of the Minimax Fire Extinguisher took place on the Common which no doubt had been arranged by the Town Council in an effort to encourage homes, shops and business premises to be more fire conscious.

The first fire station in Coupar Angus was Provost Davidson's garage in Union Street, where a Water Tender, a car and a trailer-pump were kept. With the outbreak of the Second World War a larger fire fighting force was formed at Smedley's Factory yard. Fire practice was held regularly there and the Austin Auxiliary Towing Vehicle or A. T. was stationed there for easy access should the need arise.

After the war 'The Pend' beside the Royal Hotel housed a Commer Water Tender and an ex-army gun tractor which had been converted for firefighting purposes. These were in service until 1962 when an up-to-date purpose-built Fire Station was erected in Blairgowrie Road.

Almost immediately the Brigade was put to the test when it was called out to attend to a very serious fire at the Marshall Chicken Processing Plant, now Grampian Country Foods.

There is a highly trained group of volunteer Firemen/women in Coupar Angus who meet for regular practice in modern fire fighting techniques.

Not only do they deal quickly with outbreaks of fire in the town and landward area, they are often called out to assist fight serious fires further afield. Their training now includes the techniques of dealing with serious road accidents which often involves cutting through the bodywork of vehicles in order to remove the injured.

### POLICE

The first regular police force was introduced to the United Kingdom in 1829. London alone had a force of 3,000 men who were known as 'Peelers' or 'Bobbies' after their founder Sir Robert Peel.

> **The Fire Brigade has left their base at Smedleys' for the Royal Hotel Garage in Todds Pend.**

*(Top) Coupar Angus Fire Station.*
*(Right) The former Police Station in Hill Street, now flats.*

> A travelling woman who stole ten shillings (50p) from a shop in town and picked two shillings (10p) from a lady's pocket, was caught, fined and given a jail sentence.

The first Police Station in Coupar Angus was recorded in the Valuation Roll as being in Calton Street although no clue to its location was given.

By 1860 changes were taking place in the penal system, and Reform Schools were set up in an attempt to teach young offenders the error of their ways, and to train them for worthwhile work when they were released back into the community. There is no record of a Reform School in Coupar Angus although records show that most large towns and cities had them. Many of the boys sent to them had been convicted of theft, which most often was of food. Some of them had no father, due to death or desertion, and one ten year old who stole some glass bottles, was sentenced to five years detention while a fifteen year old who had stolen bread, was given a sentence of three years. Both were first offences.

> Two local Pearl Fishers were fined twenty shillings (£1) or seven days for stealing four young Poplar Trees from the Island Wood, the property of Lord Lansdowne.

Industrial Schools too were set up, and in many towns children were rounded up and taken there in an attempt to train them for worthwhile work, and keep them off the streets. There was an Industrial School, which was also called the Episcopal School, for Girls in Reids Close. It is thought that the pupils here were not waifs and strays, but girls whose parents wished them taught useful skills for perhaps 'big house service'.

Alyth also had an Industrial School which trained both boys and girls in useful skills to equip them for the job market.

In 1871 the address at the Police Station changed from Calton Street to Hay Street, but recently evidence has come to hand through title deeds, which suggests that the Calton Street and Hay Street stations were one and the same, and was housed in part of what we know now as the Victoria Inn in Gray Street. An explantian for the confusion and mix up may be that the details for the Valuation Roll were recorded then by people who had no connection with the town and that street name signs were few and far between.

In 1890 a purpose built Police Station was erected in Hill Street which consisted of an office, cells and a police house.

It was to this Station that a group of the town's youngsters were taken when a game they were greatly enjoying went wrong. Among the boys were the Police Officer's son and the late Mr David Reid of Hay Street, who told me this tale just days before he died. The friends had gathered on the bridge which spanned the Blairgowrie railway line. Each had a little pile of stones and when a train passed below, they tried to drop the stones down the chimney of the engine.

Unknown to the boys, some of the stones had landed on the Guard who, on reaching the Rosemount Crossing, reported the matter back to Coupar Angus. Quite oblivious of this, they were still standing there with their stones waiting for another train to pass, when the local Policeman arrived, rounded them all up and marched them to the Police Station in Hill Street, where he locked them in the cells. By this time humiliation and fear had got the better of them, and all were not merely crying but howling. After being left in the cells for a time they were finally given a lecture then allowed to go home. The very chastened boys never played that game again.

The Police Station in Hill Street served the community of Coupar Angus for seventy years, then in 1960 an up to date Police Station and two Police Houses were built in Blairgowrie Road.

> A Census of Vagrants was taken in the town with the following results: - Males 12; Females 6; Total 18 of whom two were natives of Perthshire, 15 of other parts of Scotland and one was Irish.

The former one in Hill Street was converted to flats which became private residences. In 1997 the Blairgowrie Road Police Station was closed down and the property sold. Policing the town is done now from Blairgowrie and a daily patrol by police car is carried out at intervals. Although response to a police call out is rapid, the people of the town regret very much the loss of their Bobbies.

Before the Boundary change of 1891 the lower part of the Steeple was used as a Prison for the miscreants in the Angus side of the town.

---

# SHAVE, SIR?

"How's the Razor going, Sir?"

"Weel, if it's skinnin' it's easy; but if it's shavin' it's michty coorse!"

And the barber's hand slipped again.

*NOT A BAD STORY EH?*

The Jokes we tell are always good and fresh, but the above never occurs at

## ..THE CENTRAL..
## HAIRDRESSING SALOON,

The Cross, COUPAR ANGUS.

On 5th July 1695 the Scottish Parliament established a General Post Office and mail was taken between large towns by men on horseback, then boys on foot delivered it locally. As can be easily imagined, the system was exceedingly slow.

# COMMUNICATIONS

*Coupar Angus Post Office*

When the turnpike roads were completed, mail was carried by coaches which at this time then travelled all over the country. In 1843 Rowland Hill introduced the 'Penny Post' which meant that a letter, no matter how far it had to travel, cost one penny for every half ounce it weighed.

There is no record of when Coupar Angus first became a 'mail town' but by 1843 letters were being delivered daily, and many of them would have arrived in the town, via the Defiant Coach which passed through daily on its way from Edinburgh to Aberdeen.

By 1897 however, the town did have a fine Crown Post Office, situated in the building now occupied by the Co-operative Society and known then as the Post Office Building. It was open for general business from 7.30 a.m. until 8.00 p.m. and for money orders, from 9.00 a.m. to 6.00 p.m. The first Savings Bank in town was also based here with the Postmaster William Culross acting as bank agent.

In 1960 the Post Office was moved from there to premises in Causewayend. In 1964 however, it lost its Crown Post Office status and became a Sub-Post Office.

On 31st January 2000 the Sub Post Office moved to the Co-Operative shop in the former Post Office building where it had been prior to 1960.

*(Top) The original Post Office was next to the Co-op on the corner of George/Athole Streets.*
*(Inset) Albert Crll, the last of the Telegram Boys.*
page 84

## TELEPHONES

It was a Scotsman living in America, Alexander Graham Bell, who invented the telephone in 1876. This new invention was not immediately popular for it was an expensive service, and by 1900 there were still only 10,000 in use nationwide. The telephone company was eventually taken over by the Post Office.

The first small manual telephone exchange in Coupar Angus was opened on 1st February 1906 in George Square, above where the Savings Bank is now, but which then was a China Shop. It later moved from George Square to larger premises in George Street opposite the cottage of the District Nurse.

The system was run by telephone operators who worked on shifts, and a night operator who handled calls from 8.00 p.m. until 8.00 a.m., when the day shift came on duty. The operators, who were mostly women, were known as 'Hello Girls'. In 1962 the system became automatic and the George Street exchange became redundant. The present day automatic exchange is situated off Campbell Street on land which had been the Burgh Gas Works.

Now, hardly a home is without a telephone connection. With the modern technology of our age, we now have telephone answering machines and recall numbers which tell us who called when we were out. Telephones can also be linked up to computers and FAX Machines.

## TELEGRAMS

The telegraph system was invented by an Englishman named Wheatstone, but it was an American named Morse - founder of the Morse code - who carried out the improvements which made it so efficient.

By 1838 the railway network was spreading throughout the country and at the same time, telegraph poles were erected along the path of the railway lines to enable messages to be passed along the wires to the specially constructed telegraph offices. The Post Office introduced a public telegraph service which proved to be a great boon, for now news could be sent quickly and cheaply from one place to another, no matter the distance. When a message arrived at the telegraph office, it was dispatched immediately to the addressee by a Telegram Boy, dressed in a distinctive uniform and who rode a red bicycle.

From the 1970's onwards, telephones became very popular with practically every household being connnected to the system which rendered the telegraph service surplus to requirements.

According to some experts, present day Scotland has one of the poorest health records of a so-called advanced country due to - Chest Diseases, Lung Cancer, Coronary Thrombosis, Mental Illness and Alcoholism - although a better than average standard of health care is available.

# IN SICKNESS - and in health

From "Strathmore Past & Present" published in 1885 comes the following: *"The Parish has always been noted for longevity and sometime before 1790 it is recorded that a woman lived to be 116 years of age"*.

In the First Statistical Account of around 1790 Mr John Ritchie a student of Divinity wrote: *"The situation in the parish is healthy, there being no marshy ground or stagnant water nor anything to obstruct a free circulation of air. There are no diseases peculiar to the place. Nervous and hysterical disorders are said to be much more common now than formerly, owing, without doubt, to the way of living, particularly to the more frequent use of spiritous liquors and tea"*.

**1900 Vital Statistics for the past quarter were - 17 Births; 3 Marriages; 12 Deaths. Of parties deceased one was 90 - three were over 80 and 4 were between the ages of 60 and 80.**

So there you have it - drinking spirits and tea is bad for you - or so it was thought in the 18th century. I feel sure that Mr Ritchie's conclusions would be hotly disputed now, but in his defence, I think that the 45 Public Houses in the town at that time may have somewhat influenced his judgment. It is interesting to learn however, that inoculation was available here at this early date.

It is unlikely that Coupar Angus would have been left unscathed by the killer diseases which swept the countryside over the centuries. Bubonic Plague, Typhoid, Smallpox and Cholera took a heavy toll on life, and nationwide thousands died in the first half of the 19th century. About this time Bubonic Plague struck the then small village of Balbrogie, and no one was left to remove the dead. On hearing of the tragedy, a party of men from Coupar Angus went there, removed the bodies, and arranged for their burial. Although no official records exist of numbers, we do know that around 1850 Cholera struck in Coupar Angus with such force that the undertakers were quite unable to cope. The Rev Dr Stevenson of the Parish Church worked ceaselessly, tending to the sick, comforting the dying, and helping to coffin and bury the dead, not only of his own congregation but from every denomination in the town.

Sanitary conditions improved when the town became a Police Burgh, with Commissioners running day to day affairs. A few years later this was replaced by a Town Council, and improvements continued to be carried out. In 1875 a water supply carried by a 5" pipe from Pitcur, was brought to the town at a cost of £4000. In 1887 a drainage system was installed at a cost of £4500 which greatly improved matters and put an end to Cholera outbreaks.

In the early 1900's the water pipe was enlarged to 8", and in the 1940's the sewage works was updated at Buttery Bank. In the 1950's the town was experiencing a water shortage and D.B. Marshall sank a bore-hole to keep the factory in production. A further water supply was brought in via Blairgowrie and then from Lintrathen which solved the problem. The Buttery Bank sewage works was completely modernised in the 1980's.

It is difficult to estimate the number of dead in the epidemics which struck over the years, as it was seen as shameful either to suffer or to die from the disease, and therefore few details have been recorded. Sometimes there was no family member left to erect a memorial stone. Often Cholera victims were buried in mass graves, perhaps in the corner of the kirkyard or in unhallowed ground such as a field, which would be left undisturbed for many years lest the dreaded plague escape.

From the 14th to 18th centuries, Bubonic Plague spread in phases over much of Scotland. It was called the Black Death and the victims of this were most often buried in mass graves, often without coffins, for the authorities made rules preventing their use in order that more bodies could be buried. At Brechin Cathedral a plaque was erected many years after the plague of 1647 to the 400 people who were buried in the cathedral yard.

**Coupar Angus Town Council is to defy the Department of Health's ruling and build a Public Convenience in the town despite the ban.**

Typhoid raged between 1640 and 1694 then again in 1707.

In Scotland in 1873 Diphtheria wiped out whole families of children within days of each other, and in many cases the parents were too poor to do more than bury their youngsters.

*(Top) Coupar Angus Health Centre (see page 88)*

If, as was thought in the early days, Coupar Angus was healthier than other areas, it could be attributed to the legacy from the monks. They had advocated - yea insisted - that their tenants go off in isolation should they suffer some infectious disease. Again the monks had been great herb growers, which not only flavoured their food, but were made into healing potions and ointments. The working classes in early times lived on very plain fare - brose, porridge and home brewed ale, but again the monks stepped in and insisted that all their tenants and workers alike had to plant a kail yard, a tradition which survived in country areas until well into the 20th century. The vitamins and minerals from this vegetable would have greatly enhanced their diet and general health.

Meat was a rare luxury for many, and when available would have been rabbit or some sort of fowl. Medical care for all but the wealthy classes was practically non-existent, and even they had little choice but to resort to courses of preventive medicine such as drinking goats whey or "Taking the Waters" at spas.

> **At the end of the 18th century a hen cost one shilling 5p (no chickens were eaten then); a mason was paid 7´p per day and a tailor 4p per day.**

In earlier centuries superstition was rife, and people wore amulets and charms to ward off evil, and visited holy wells in the hope of preventing illness or to cure it.

Many wells were dedicated to saints, and folk were convinced that the water had healing powers.

Many herbs were grown and used to great effect. Houseleek at one time grew abundantly on stone roofs and was boiled up and used as a poultice for inflammatory swellings and for the relief of headaches. For bruising, the root of Solomon Seal was grated and mixed with bread and applied to the affected area. The stems of Myrrh and Sweet Cicely were made into tea which gave relief to those suffering from bronchial colds and chest troubles. A little sprig of peppermint or apple-ringey was often carried to church inside a bible, to stop the bearer falling asleep during the long sermon of those times. A cure for jaundice however was somewhat drastic, for apparently "slaters" were collected from under a piece of wood, then toasted and ground down and mixed with hot treacle, before being given to the victim to consume. The saying was then that *"It takes a scunner to cure a scunner"*!

For any reader who does not know what a 'scunner' is, the best explanation I can give, which is totally inadequate, is that it is a very great dislike or revulsion to something, which results in one feeling extremely ill!

> **While painting the water column at the Railway Station yesterday, George Clark of Perth, was struck by a passing engine and received "rather serious injuries about the head".**

At present there is renewed interest in growing herbs and in herbal remedies, but fortunately the general public are more enlightened now, and see nothing sinister in this form of 'alternative medicine'. The use of herbal remedies in the 17th century however, may have contributed to many poor women being accused of, and tried for, witchcraft.

Witches over the centuries were either consulted or persecuted according to the prevailing attitude of the time. King James VI of Scotland and I of England, believed in witchcraft and wrote a book on the subject. It was a no-win situation to be taken into custody and tried for witchcraft, for the accused was tied to a stool and ducked in a pond. If she died she was innocent, but if she came up alive, was found guilty, wired to a stake, and burned alive.

During this century a form of hysteria had swept over the land, and misfortune or disaster of any kind, was thought to have been caused by something or

*(Top left) The Sewage Works was constructed close to Buttery Bank - to left of the photograph.*
*(Above) Some of the original stone coffins are by the Abbey ruins beside the Abbey Churchyard.*

someone. Usually an unattractive woman who was perhaps slightly odd or a bit of a recluse, who grew herbs and dabbled in herbal cures, was targeted. Although no documentary evidence has come to hand regarding these activities in this area, the fact that there was a 'Witch Knowe' at Cronan, is a sad reminder that witch hunting almost certainly did take place here.

In 1662 the last witch was burned in Forfar, and in the Meffan Institute there is an excellent exhibition of these early days and later.

From the School Log Books we learn that frequent epidemics among the pupils almost emptied the school over the decades. Measles, Whooping Cough, Chickenpox, Ringworm, 'Flu' and Scarlet Fever were common. In April 1907 the school had to be disinfected and closed for a week when sadly a pupil died from Cerebro Spinal Fever *(Meningitis)*.

Our present day Centenarian, Miss Johan Brodie born in 1896 remembers that a cure for Whooping Cough was to take the afflicted child to the Tannery to breathe in the odours, which without doubt would have been powerful. Before this, it was thought that a cure could be found by taking a cup of water from a running stream against the current, drinking a little then throwing what was left back in to be carried away with the current.

In 1908 an Old Age Pension was introduced but by no means was it available to all the elderly, and a 'Means' test was undertaken to see how needy the applicant was.

As early as 1912 the school was being visited by Col. Moffat, the Medical Officer of Health for East Perthshire, and by 1920 a school dentist was visiting annually.

In May 1921 the animals in a Menagerie which had just left Coupar Angus, were struck down with Anthrax. A leopard, a lion, a puma, a tiger and others less noteworthy, died as a result.

On 14th January 1935 a milk scheme was introduced to schools when little bottles which held one third of a pint, and which cost one old half-pence, (one fifth of to-day's one pence) were distributed to the children before the morning interval, and drunk in class, by means of a straw.
In March 1941 Diphtheria inoculation was being carried out in schools which saw the start of a comprehensive programme of immunisation against diseases such as Polio, Tuberculosis and Measles. The result of this has been that very few children now suffer any severe effects from those illnesses.

Despite the epidemics that swept through the school in the early days, some children seemed to have had immunity to them, for on 11th Jul, 1924 one pupil was presented with a wristlet watch "for having an unbroken record of attendance since entering school 10 years and 3 months ago".

In 1927 a case of Encephalitis Lethargica *(Sleeping Sickness)* was reported to the Medical Officer of Health. This I had thought was a most unusual disease to occur in Scotland, although many townspeople travelled to India for periods of work in the Jute Mills of Calcutta. It was believed however that the pupil concerned had no direct contact with anyone who had recently been there.

The late Dr Frank Milne, a retired and highly respected Coupar Angus General Practitioner told me however, that in 1927 an epidemic of Sleeping Sickness had raged throughout the United Kingdom, so the town was fortunate to have had only one case.

In 1938 the water supply was considered unfit to drink, and the Medical Officer of Health ordered that all the school drinking fountains be turned off and that drinking water should be boiled.

The post-war Welfare State, which initially promised to see to every need from 'the cradle to the grave', has certainly contributed greatly to the health and well-being of the nation. Although charges are levied in certain sectors, the Health Service has expanded and progressed over the years, and now complicated organ transplants and heart surgery are fairly commonplace.
So what of the health of the inhabitants of present day Coupar Angus? Certainly we no longer have plagues sweeping over us at intervals which is due to several factors - immunisation, an excellent water supply and sewage system *(upgraded in 1987)* and the fact that every home now has modern facilities. Food and personal hygiene standards have improved, and diet has changed immensely in the post-war period with very few people now being undernourished. In fact quite the opposite is the case with many adults being seriously over-weight. Early this century 'Slimming Clubs' and 'Diets' had never been heard of, whereas now they are big business.

Yes, most certainly we have come a long way from the daily meal of porridge and greens, but the town can still boast of

*(Top) Coupar Angus Centenarian Johan Brodie, born 1896, photographed close to her 100th birthday, died July 22nd, 2001.
(Above) The much loved and highly respected Dr Frank Milne.*

longevity, for there is one centenarian and quite a number of nonagenarians and octogenarians in the Burgh.

## COUPAR ANGUS HEALTH CENTRE

A Health Centre for Coupar Angus was first considered in April 1973 when three doctors - Dr Alex McPherson, Dr Gilbert Hope and Doctor Frank Milne, put the wheels in motion of what would prove to be a long and laborious task. In 1974 the doctors were informed that the first hurdle had been surmounted when they were notified that Tayside Health Board had become statutorily responsible for the proposed centre.

In 1976 various sites were looked at carefully before the decision was taken to build in Trades Lane.

Construction commenced in April 1981 with an estimated completion date of autumn 1982. Despite the very severe winter which caused many delays, the building was completed by the second week of October thanks to the dedicated work force.

Transfer of the surgeries took place the weekend of 11/12th December and with help from the Sector Administrators all went smoothly. Mr John Angus the Primary Care Administrator, who had worked tirelessly over the years in the planning and building of the Centre, formally opened it.

The Opening Ceremony and Lunch, was held in the Health Centre with catering by the Enverdale Hotel, which at that time belonged to the Bannerman family.

Dr Frank Milne, it must be told, worked tirelessly from the inception of the Health Centre for Coupar Angus, until its completion.

Dr Milne, in his speech of welcome to the assembled guests at the Health Centre, opened with these words:

**Coupar Angus Council is accused of dragging its feet over a scheme for providing a new sewage works.**

### GUESTS AT THE HEALTH CENTRE OPENING CEREMONY

| | |
|---|---|
| Dr F.M. Addly, | Community Medicine Specialist |
| Mr & Mrs John Angus, | Administrator, Primary Care |
| Miss J.M. Bell, | Nursing Officer, Community Service |
| Mrs Betty Bryce, | Practice Secretary |
| Mr & Mrs I. G. Crum, | District Finance Officer |
| Mr Ken Drysdale, | Asst. Secretary (Capital Building Programme) |
| Miss A. Dunbar, | Nursing Officer for District; |
| Miss S. Gentle, | Matron, Blairgowrie Cottage Hospital |
| Dr & Mrs George Greig | (Partner) |
| Mr & Mrs Ian Higgins | |
| Mr & Mrs George Howkins, | Clerk or Works, Tayside Health Board |
| Dr & Mrs Hamish Jack (Partner) | |
| Mrs Irene Lawson, | Cleaner |
| Mr & Mrs H. Leaver, | Practice Secretary |
| Nurse & Mr Lyall, | District Nurse |
| Dr & Mrs J.D. Macgregor, | District Medical Officer |
| Mr & Mrs Jack McNaughton, | Practice Secretary |
| Miss Helen McNicol, | Finance Officer, Primary Care |
| Dr & Mrs Frank Milne (Partner) | |
| Mrs Nicoll, | Cleaner |
| Mrs Lydia Porteous, | Dr William's Secretary |
| Miss E. W. Redpath | Area Nursing Officer |
| Miss Maura Redpath | (daughter) |
| Nurse J. Robertson, | District Nurse based in Guildtown |
| Nurse Stephen, | Local District Nurse |
| Miss R. Swayne, | Supervisor Cleaning Staff for District. |
| Dr & Mrs John Williams, | (other Practice) |
| Mr & Mrs W. O. Wilson, | Sector Administrator and Secretary to the Health Centre Committee |
| Mr & Mrs John Winter, | Gardener and Odd Job Man at Health Centre |

*"On behalf of the doctors of Coupar Angus, may I welcome you all to this magnificent building which we now have in Coupar Angus - the product of a great deal of time and effort on the part of all who have been involved in its planning and construction over the years".*
He ended his speech: *"Birth took place during the week-end of 11th-12th December 1982 when transfer from our surgeries took place. Thanks to the generous assistance and help from the Sector Administrators, this painless delivery took place without complication. So here we are - very satisfied doctors, staff and patients as a result of all your efforts"*

Much of the effort was expended by Dr Milne himself, whose brainchild the Health Centre was. Years on, the Health Centre is still a 'magnificent' building serving the people or Coupar Angus with the highest possible quality health care.

Time marches on and a new Health Centre was opened in 2000 in Candlehouse Lane with facilities to cater for all aspects of modern health care.

## THE RED CROSS

The Red Cross Movement was the brain-child of Henri Dunant from Geneva, Switzerland who, while travelling through northern Italy in 1859 saw at first hand the terrible suffering of wounded Soldiers after the Battle of Solferino during the Franco-Prussian War, a war which most of us know little or nothing about.

So strongly did Dunant feel that he wrote a book putting forward his ideas for the formation of societies which would care for the wounded of war, and also train volunteers to be ready to give assistance when the need arose.

A young lawyer from Geneva, Gustave Moynier, decided to put Dunant's ideas

**The new Sewage Plant was opened on 31st January, 1986. The first plant which dates from 1875 was known as the 'Water Works'.**

had gained their certificates in First Aid and 40 women in Home Nursing. Invalid cookery classes were also available, by courtesy of the School Board, which means that they almost certainly would have been held in the Burgh School. From time to time over the years the branch has had male members.

When World War I commenced in 1914 the ladies of the Red Cross joined forces with those of the Burgh Work Party to produce 'comforts', as they were then known, for local lads serving in the forces. The Town Council of the time, gave them the use of the upper hall of the Town Hall free of rent, and Jumble Sales, Concerts, and door-to-door collections were carried out.

into practice and he formed a committee of five. From this small beginning in 1863 an international meeting in Geneva was called which resulted in the first international societies being formed. The international committee of the Red Cross consists of 25 members all of whom must be Swiss for it is believed that as Switzerland is a neutral country which never takes part in war, its nationals will be totally unbiased in decision making. The emblem, or badge, of the Red Cross is the design of the Swiss flag with the colours reversed - a red cross on a white background and is recognized and respected throughout the world.

The aim of the Red Cross is to train volunteers in First Aid, Auxiliary Nursing and Welfare and its activities are not now restricted to the casualties of war. Where an emergency arises anywhere in the world be it through civil war, famine or flood, the Red Cross volunteers are quickly on the scene to alleviate the suffering of those caught up in the situation.

Nearer to home, the sick, the disabled, the aged and infirm all benefit from the work of the Red Cross.

The Coupar Angus branch of the Red Cross dates from 10th November 1912 and was officially registered as 'Perth No 44'.

From the very beginning, and over the decades, members have been actively involved in carrying out the work for which it was formed.

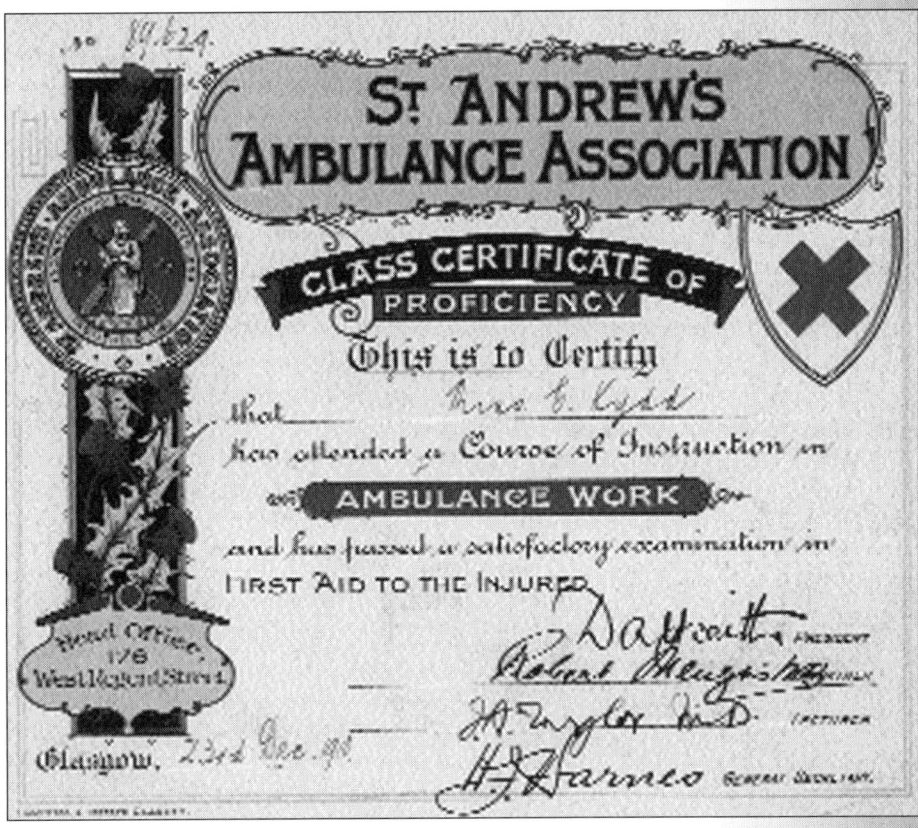

The very first classes in First Aid in the town were attended by both men and women and cost one shilling (5p) for the men and six pence (2.5p) for the ladies. The lecturer was local Dr Davidson. By November 1913, 42 women and 13 men

*(Top) Mrs Jameson, Commissioner on left of Mrs Hunter (in civvies) - a life long supporter. C 1980.*

In 1916 a Garden Fete was held at Keithick to raise money for the much needed materials. The work-party was a registered war charity during the war producing 1360 garments for the troops.

**Mention must be made of a local, totally blind lady, Miss Mustard, who knitted 800 pairs of socks.**

In 1915 four of the local detachment were nursing the wounded in the old Perth Infirmary. They were Miss Carmichael; Miss Dick; Miss Ferguson

The Red Cross bought the former Drill Hall in 1959/60 but again it is believed that they met there long before this date, so it may be that they previously rented the hall from the Territorial Army.

In the years between the wars the number of members dwindled and in 1929, 20 gained Certificates in First Aid and 16 in Home Nursing. A Voluntary Aid Detachment (VAD) was formed around this time, one of whose members served for a month during 1930 at a camp in Montrose *(no mention is made of what kind of camp)*, while 2 others spent a fortnight each at Perth Royal Infirmary. By 1935 Child Welfare classes were on offer and while on duty at the Jubilee celebrations it is recorded that "volunteers had to deal with a broken arm and several less serious injuries".

The interval between the wars was much too short but on the outbreak of World War 11, work parties were again formed and many fund raising events were organised to ensure that a constant flow of parcels left Coupar Angus for local Service men and Prisoners of War. It is a matter of record that quite a number of POW's lives were saved by these parcels. Although fortunately the flow of wounded was less than in World War I, the local group was always ready to meet any challenge or emergency, which arose.

**In 1947 the local membership was 36. The Flag Day that year raised £18 17 6d.**

As time passed, membership dwindled and by 1976 was down to 17. Despite this, 5 ladies volunteered for duty at the Commonwealth Games, which were held in Edinburgh, where they joined other Red Cross members from all over Scotland.

Needs were changing, but the Red Cross adapted to meet these needs and members now found themselves attending Football Matches, Blood Transfusion Centres, Sponsored Walks and all manner of Sporting Events and Fetes. Compassionate Driving had also been added to the services offered, and for a number of years, members accompanied handicapped people from Perth on their annual holiday to Stockport.

Although the Gulf War was of short duration, parcels went from Coupar Angus to the boys serving in the conflict in the Gulf, and when it ended surplus parcels were redirected to the troops in Northern Ireland.

In 1989 several local groups amalgamated and became known as 'The Burrelton, Coupar Angus and Woodside Centre'. Two committees were formed, one consisting of First Aiders and the other with 12 members purely for fund raising purposes. Each year over one thousand pounds is raised locally for the work of the Red Cross by organising the old favourites - the Coffee Morning *(originally introduced by Mrs Carmichael of Arthurstone)*, after-noon teas, Flag Day collection and a Good-as-New Sale, which has superseded the former Jumble Sale.

**The Red Cross have acquired the former Drill Hall in Causewayend.**

The local First Aid Group still attend local gatherings but as their number is small they often have to be supplemented by volunteers from other areas. All work well together no matter the occasion for all are members of the International Red Cross Society.

*Without the help of local members, past and present, this article could not have been as comprehensive. Special thanks must go to Mrs Walker of Perth HQ.*

---

66    The Stormont and Strathmore Annual for 1906.

## Scientific Dress-Cutting
### NO FITTING REQUIRED
### AT
### MRS L. McFARLANE'S,
**THE CORNER, CAUSEWAYEND, COUPAR ANGUS.**

*General Drapery and Millinery.*
**DRESSMAKING a Specialty—Newest Materials.**
*Style and Perfect Fit guaranteed.*

AGENT FOR J. PULLAR & SONS, DYE WORKS, PERTH.

---

**Watchmaker, Jeweller and Optician.**

**David Marshall**
ATHOLE BUILDINGS,
COUPAR ANGUS.

Reliable Goods at Reasonable Prices.
Repairs a Speciality.

---

**JOHN M. MONCUR**
.. Grocer ..
Wine & Spirit Merchant,
**5 CAUSEWAYEND,**
Coupar Angus.

J. M. M. begs to assure the Public that should they favour him with a share of their orders, he will try and merit it by supplying a good article at good value.

---

and Miss Robertson. Miss Carmichael went on from Perth to Le Touquet where she served as a nurse until the end of the war. At home, the local volunteers had plans to turn the Town Hall into a Hospital at short notice, should it be needed. A canteen, reading and writing room was also set up by the Red Cross for a company of Royal Engineers who were based in the town. A weekly collection of fresh eggs was made to help the recovery of the wounded soldiers, as food was not too plentiful.

During this time it is unclear where the local group held their meetings. It is remembered that at one time they met in rooms above the Savings Bank (Lloyd's TSB), which has been in George Square since 1937.

**One hundred of the poor were given coal courtesy of - E. Collins Wood of Keithick; Mr Geekie, Baldowrie; Mr Playfair, Wester Bendochy and others**

page 90

> In our fine motor car, we can go near and far
> The sights of the coutry admiring
> And we carry behind, 'neath the motor confined,
> The beauties we think most inspiring.

The first roads in Scotland that we know anything about were the DROVE ROADS of the early 17th century. These led from the Highlands - Caithness, Kintyre, Skye and Aberdeenshire, to the main TRYST which at that time was held in Crieff. Often they converged at certain points such as mountain passes and river fords. Other than these there would have been merely tracks or footpaths between farms, villages and towns. In the 17th century there was a route which led to Causewayend called 'the Stripe' but it is not known whether or not this was the Causewayend in Coupar Angus, for Keithick village too was known as Causewayend in abbey times. It is recorded that along the 'Stripe' in town were houses, a barn, a malthouse and a kiln.

# ROADS - drove roads to relief road in Coupar Angus

One route or track was from Coupar Angus to the north which led from Buttery Bank across the Isla at Boatlands, formerly called the 'Boat', and over the haugh land which belongs to Keithick Estate, to the Public Kirk ford at Bendochy Church. The track passed close to Bendochy Church and continued over the hill, skirting Monkmyre Loch and on to Rattray and the Glens. Although overgrown in part, the route from Bendochy Church to Monkmyre Loch is still visible.

In 1937 there was a famous Court Case in Perth between a Coupar Angus lady and the owner of Keithick Estate regarding whether a Right of Way existed at Boatlands allowing the public access to the riverbank there. In his judgement the Sheriff found that "The line of the common high road to Bendochy Public Kirk ford had not been proved and that the right of the public to use either the common high road or Bendochy Public Kirk ford had been lost by disuse". The hefty legal costs incurred had to be met by the Coupar Angus citizen but in the spirit of the times, the townspeople rallied to her aid by organising fund raising events to cover the costs.

There were a number of fords and ferries on the Isla and Ericht which were in use until early in the 20th century. In medieval times a boatman was constantly on duty at Buttery Bank *(Boatlands)* to ferry travellers over the river. The Coupar Grange mill at Ryehill was where grain was ground for many of the farms in the neighbourhood. There was a ford at this point with various tracks converging here. There was also a ford at Easter Bendochy and before Kitty Swanson's bridge was built early in the 20th century, as well as the ferry there was a crossing point at Milhorn. When the river is low during long dry spells, these crossing places are quite visible.

As the 20th century progressed, most of the old routes became overgrown through lack of use and many were ploughed up. A few which survived have been registered as Rights of Way and are shown on O.S. maps.

*(Left) Monkmyre Loch*

In 1740 Major Caulfield who had been Wade's inspector of roads, succeeded Wade but large scale road building went on. By 1763 the road was nearing completion between Coupar Angus and Fort George by way of Glenshee, Braemar and the Lecht. The bridge over the Isla at Couttie was built in 1766 so no doubt until then the river had to be crossed at the ford there. Then there was a 'Riding' stone and depending on the height of the water on it, one knew whether or not it was safe to cross on horseback. There was also a 'Wading' Stone which showed how safe it was to cross on foot.

The road system underwent dramatic change when in 1724 Lord Lovat alerted King George I (1714-27) to the danger of further unrest in the Highlands. There had been previous trouble there in 1689 and again in 1715 and the King viewed the matter so serious that he appointed Major General George Wade to travel to the areas of possible unrest and investigate. The General lost no time in assessing the situation and reported back that there were 12,000 Highlanders ready and willing to take up arms and that government troops would be at a severe disadvantage due to the lack of roads and bridges by which troops could be moved quickly to the areas of unrest.

Reaction to this report was swift and on 24th December 1724 Wade was made General Officer Commander-in-Chief North Britain. Almost immediately road making began linking Killichuimen (later Fort Augustus) with Inverness where access to the sea could be got, and Fort William, Stirling and Perth.

The Couttie bridge bears testimony to the excellence of design and construction techniques of this period for it is still in daily use carrying a steady flow of traffic to and from Blairgowrie and points north and south. The oldest road to Perth from Coupar Angus was possibly via Caddam and Keithick villages, entering the town

*(Top) The road bridge at Couttie with the Farina Mill chimney stack in the background.*
*(Centre) Cumberland's Barracks as it was, and in 2000 showing the ravages of time.*
*(Bottom) Union Street C1900 was first called New Road. It was almost as wide again as the former main thoroughfare.*

at the top of Buttery Bank Road. The present day road to Perth, which was formerly called Barlatch Street, came much later although there may have been a track between the town and the Woodside area. The little village of Woodside only developed after the arrival of the railway.

The Military Roads followed the route of some of the former Drove Roads which caused problems for the cattle whose soft hooves wore down on the harder surfaces. Cattle shoeing was introduced and it doesn't take much imagination to realise that this would have been a difficult and dangerous job. Quite a number of blacksmiths throughout the country however became very skilled in this new trade.

General Wade died in 1748 and was buried in Westminster Abbey in recognition of his service to King and Country.

After the 1745 uprising an army of occupation in the Highlands numbered 15,000. At intervals along the route of the Military roads 'Kingshouses' were set up. These took the form of Inns and were usually on the site of the former road construction camps. The name 'Kingshouse' came from the newly constructed 'Kings Highway'. What is known now as Cumberland's Barracks may have been built for the road workers then later became a Kingshouse. It is the oldest building in Coupar Angus and is thought to date from the early 18th century, pre-dating the 1745 uprising.

The title 'Cumberland's Barracks' seems to have emerged in comparatively recent history and although troops would have had short stops in Coupar, it is unlikely that a permanent force would have been stationed in this lowland town.

Troops were later stationed here however to patrol the roads in an attempt to control whisky smuggling which was rife at the close of the century.

William Caulfield died in 1767 but road building did not stop and a further 100 miles were constructed after his death. The very last stretch of road to be built was between Perth and Perth Prison which had been built in 1840/41 to accommodate French Prisoners of War who incidentally were put to work making this road.

The Military Road system led to an upsurge of interest in upgrading other former routes and tracks and a great number of Turnpike Acts were passed which allowed road construction throughout the country to be carried out by private companies and individuals.

Many landowners got in on the act by allowing roads to pass through their

(Top) The Toll House in Forfar Road, now a small car park.
(Centre) The Toll House (right of centre) at Buttery Bank beside the river Isla.
(Left) George Street, looking towards Perth - the Toll House was at the far end on the left.

page 93

property and in return they became shareholders in the company. The outlay for surfacing, repair and upkeep was clawed back by levying charges on road users. In 1844 the charge for a Coach or Gig drawn by one horse was 3d. two horses 6d, three horses 1/-, four horses 1/3d, and six horses 2/-, while a cart drawn by six horses was 2/6d. A horse, mule or ass, laden or unladen was 1d, while calves, hogs, sheep and lambs, 10 and under were one farthing each. If over 10 in number, the charge was 2d. per score. Although these charges may seem paltry now they were then thought to be expensive i.e. 8 X 2/6d = £1.00 which was a considerable sum of money.

As the need for a presence in the Highland lessened, military roads gradually became privately owned Turnpike Roads and were kept in good repair by the owners. Bars or gates were placed across them to make certain nothing or no one escaped paying the tolls.

Coupar Angus had four Toll-houses then - the one on the road to Forfar stood where the small car-park at the Common is now. The second, for those travelling between Coupar Angus and the south, was demolished in 1996 to make way for the slip road to the town centre from the Relief Road. It sold refreshments to travellers but it was not the original toll house which still stands and is named the 'Gate House'. When the branch railway line to Blairgowrie was constructed, it was felt that this toll house was too close to it for safety so the railway company built another further down the road out of harms way.

The toll house for the East and Dundee routes was at the corner of Precinct and Queen Street. The one which served traffic to Blairgowrie and the North, is at Buttery Bank and although it has been a family home for many years can still be clearly recognised as a toll house by its distinctive windows.

In 1836 the 'Defiance' coach was calling daily at Coupar Angus on its way to Aberdeen. A 'chaise' pulled by two horses and called the 'Fly' was journeying between Perth and Edinburgh and vice versa. Each journey took fourteen hours for before the Turnpike Roads maintenance was carried out by farm workers and as you can imagine the quality of work on certain stretches of road varied according to the attitude to it of the landowner. In some farm leases at the present time, one of the conditions is that the tenant must keep all the farm roads in good order.

Queen Victoria drove through the town on several occasions on her way to Balmoral - 11.9.1844, - 1.10.1844 and 31.8.1850. It was believed that at this time the name of the road by which the Queen entered the town was changed to Queen Street. Formerly it had been a part of Precinct Street but research has shown that the change of name came after Victoria's Jubilee in 1887.

Until the railway arrived in Coupar Angus those who owned haulage businesses were quite wealthy. It took a

> **LIST OF PUBLIC RIGHTS OF WAY**
>
> Asserted by Perth & Kinross Council and Coupar Angus Community Council
>
> THORN ALLEY PEDESTRIAN
>
> BURNSIDE WALK
>
> PRINCES CROFT TO GEORGE STREET
>
> HIGH STREET TO GEORGE STREET (ROYAL HOTEL PATH)
>
> FISHERMAN'S PATH

(Top) The Toll House, on the corner of Precinct Street.
(Centre) The Toll House on the Common.
(Left) A braw new road, now Union Street.
- all C1900.

week for a horse and cart to travel between Perth and Edinburgh and longer if conditions were bad. The town had quite a few carters then and some of the horses were stabled in a building at the corner of George Square *(formerly the Timber Market)*. In the 1990's this stable block was converted to an office and private dwelling with an outside stair where part of the former ramp had been. It is a most attractive building now which compliments this historic part of the town.

The horses stabled here were taken down the Wynd *(now Trades Lane)* across Barlatch Street, *(now George Street)* to Cuddies Wynd and the burn where they could drink their fill. After the railway arrived the need for horse-drawn carts dwindled but there was still a use for a few horse drawn vans for local deliveries - milk - coal - bakery goods. After World War II motor vehicles replaced the horse and cart.

With the introduction of the Turnpike Roads engineers like Metcalf, Telford and Macadam became household names because of the great improvements in road surfacing introduced by them which made journeys much more comfortable and speedy for every type of traveller.

There is some evidence that when the Turnpike Roads were constructed, some of the former tracks were closed possibly to ensure that no one slipped through the net and avoided paying tolls. From the School Log Book of 1888 - Mr Loutet's Headmastership - comes the following:

20th January
**OWING TO THE STOPPAGE OF ONE OF THE PUBLIC TRACKS A GOOD MANY NAMES HAVE BEEN WITHDRAWN FROM THE ROLL.**

Present day Scotland has an excellent road system with dual carriage/part motorway from Aberdeen to London. Road maintenance is the responsibility of the local authority concerned while the Scottish Office has the responsibility for funding the construction and improvement schemes of major roads.

*(Top) The road to Dundee C1930.*
*(Centre) Damhead with the old Coupar Angus to Perth railway bridge C1900.*
*(Left) Causewayend with gates to Coach Road on the right C1900.*

With regard to bridges which have been built in more recent years - Forth - Tay - and Skye road bridges, Tolls have to be paid.

As the Skye bridge was built by private enterprise the tolls for its use are high as a means of investors getting a worthwhile return on their considerable investment. These have proved to be extremely unpopular, especially with local residents who find the charges an additional burden to the already high costs of living in a remote community.

Before the railway was constructed the main route through the town to Meigle and Forfar was via Gray Street and Calton Street. During the second half of the 19th century due to the railway network and the ease with which goods of all kinds could be transported, the town became prosperous and started to expand.

Close to the railway businesses sprang up. A cattle market, malt barns and several yards serving the different aspects of business life - coal - timber etc., in the town and district. Fine house building commenced, firstly in Union Street, which was initially called New Road, and continued along the Meigle or Forfar Road and the newly constructed Blairgowrie Road.

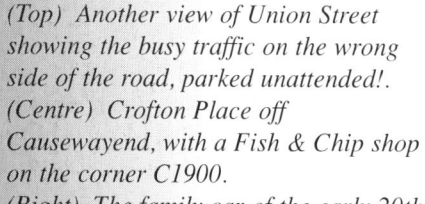

*(Top) Another view of Union Street showing the busy traffic on the wrong side of the road, parked unattended!.*
*(Centre) Crofton Place off Causewayend, with a Fish & Chip shop on the corner C1900.*
*(Right) The family car of the early 20th century ready for a run in the country.*

# STREET NAMES OLD AND NEW

**ATHOLE STREET** was named after the Dukes of Atholl who donated land to the Abbey

**BARLATCH STREET** is now GEORGE STREET

**BOGSIDE ROAD** so named as formerly the land was bog.

**BRODIE'S YARD** named after the original owner of the sawmill which was situated there.

**BUTTERY BANK** was formerly called BUTTRESS BANK and was on the old Military Road.

**CALTON STREET** - the first jail in the Perthshire part of the town, was recorded as being in Calton Street but this is thought to be incorrect. The street may have been called after the Calton Jail in Edinburgh but this is speculation for there is no documentary evidence of this.

**CAMPBELL STREET** was named after the last Abbot of the Abbey - Donald Campbell

**CANDLEHOUSE LANE** takes its name from the candle factory which was located here.

**CAUSEWAYEND** must not be confused with the village of Keithick which too was called Causewayend. It may mean 'cobbled'.

**COACH ROAD** was once the approach road or driveway to Gartlochbank and Middlehills House *(now demolished)*. Until World War II there were gates at the entrance to it which was off Causewayend and within living memory anyone wishing to cross over the Coach Road had to pay a fee.

**COMMERCIAL STREET** was once a very busy commercial area

**THE CROSS** In Abbey times and after the Market Cross stood in this area.

**CHURCH PLACE** The Congregational Church stood here and when demolished the road became Church Place but was formerly part of Campbell Street

**CUDDY'S WYND** was the road the horses were led along to the burn

**DALRYMPLE'S CLOSE** was named after the one time owner

**DAVIDSON CRESCENT** was named after Provost Davidson who held office twice.

**GRAY STREET** was named after a local Councillor T.B. Gray

**HAY STREET** was named after the Hays of Errol

**HILL GARDENS** was named after the Hill Family whose house was named 'Hill Garden'

**JAPP SQUARE** was named after the initial owners.

**PLEASANCE ROAD** is the road which leads to Pleasance Farm

**PRECINCT STREET** was so named because it lies within what were the Abbey precincts

**QUEEN STREET** was formerly a part of Precinct Street. The name was changed to Queen Street after Victoria's Jubilee in 1887 and not, as is commonly believed, after she travelled through the town on her way to Balmoral.

**ST CATHERINE'S LANE** was named after St Catherine's Croft which in turn is named after the Saint

**TIMBER MARKET** is now - GEORGE SQUARE

**TRADES LANE** was formerly 'the Wynd'. Many skilled artisans lived and worked here

**UNION PLACE** was off Causewayend, but now demolished.

**UNION STREET** is possibly named after the many roads which lead here but may refer to the parliamentary union of 1707

**THE WYND** is now - TRADES LANE

**NOTE:**
BEFORE THE BOUNDARIES WERE CHANGED IN 1891, THE GROUND FLOOR OF THE TOLL BOOTH OR STEEPLE, WAS USED AS THE JAIL FOR THE ANGUS SIDE OF THE TOWN.

*(Above) The only right-of-way in nearby Bendochy Parish.*

In 1575 the General Assembly of the Church of Scotland urged that all 'Holy Days' except the Sabbath, be abolished. A decree was issued that any person be punished *"who should persist in keeping Yule and other festivals by ceremonies, banqueting, playing (acting of plays), feasting, and sic uther vanities"*!

# HOLIDAYS AND FESTIVALS - *from early times*

In 1581 the observation of saint's days was prohibited by an Act of Parliament and Scotland became a rather sombre place devoid of all celebrations which could be linked with the Roman Catholic faith.

At this time in history every town in Scotland had an area where visiting actors put on plays, often using a cart as a stage. From early Monastic times plays, with a moral or religious bias, had been used as a form of education *(perhaps propaganda would be a better description)* the moral of which it was hoped would be apparent even to the most illiterate audience.
There is no record of where the 'play area' was in Coupar but it may have been the Common.

The lassies here are like the Pipes
They like a squeeze or two
But should you chance to "blow them
They'd skirl like bagpipes too

It is on record that the play-field in Perth was situated at the end of the High Street beside the old amphitheatre of St Johnston, while Dundee's was just outside the West Port. Aberdeen's original play-field was on the Windmillhill, but moved in 1559 to the west of Woolmanhill. These towns, especially Perth, have a long tradition of theatre going which is thought to date from these early times.

Pageants and processions were also banned by the Kirk and Scotland became a rather dreary place totally devoid of all the festivities which had been celebrated in Roman Catholic times and still carried on in England.

*(Above) A popular postcard for visitors to the town.*

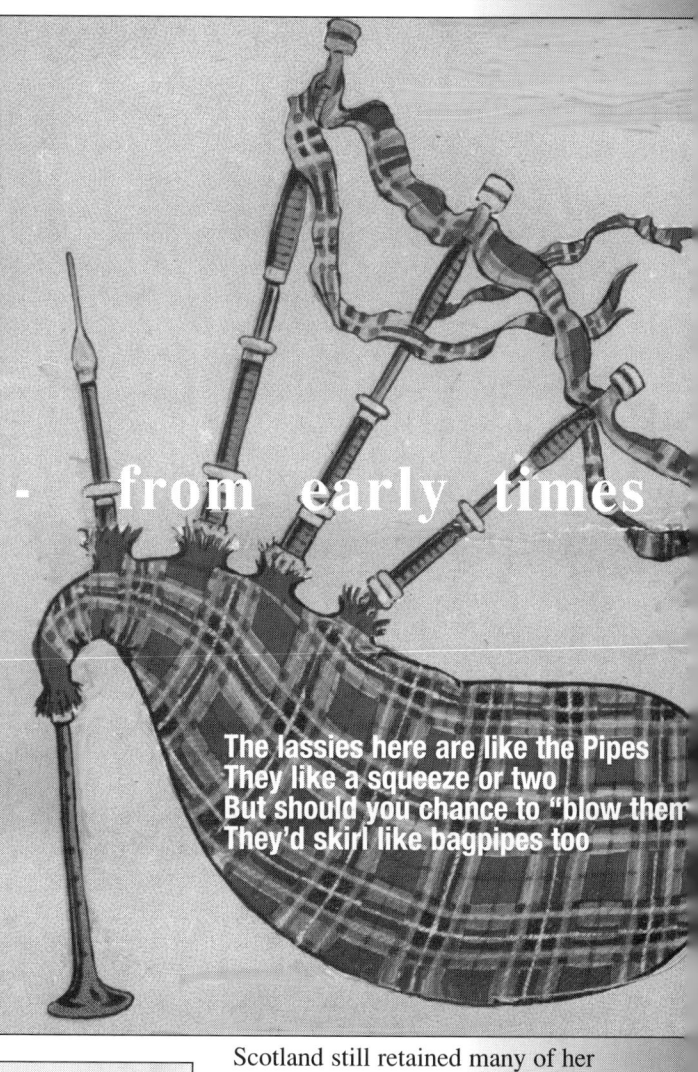

Scotland still retained many of her traditions however and Quarter Days took the place of some of the old anniversaries

1st Quarter Day  2nd February -  Candlemas
2nd    "       "   15th May -      Whitsunday
3rd    "       "   1st August -    Lammas
4th    "       "   11th November - St.Martin's Day

The old rhyme for Candlemas still survives......

"IF CANDLEMAS DAY BE DRY AND FAIR
THE HALF O' WINTER'S TO COME AND MAIR.
IF CANDLEMAS DAY BE WET AND FOUL,
THE HALF O' WINTER'S GONE AT YULE".

Formerly this had been the Feast day of the purification of the Virgin Mary, the day on which Church candles are blessed.

From the end of the 16th to the beginning of the 20th century, the only holiday for recreation and merrymaking farm workers and servant lassies had was 'Handsel Monday' - the first Monday of the New Year. Ne'erday *(lst January)* had always been a very important time for the Scots and was celebrated by certain traditional rituals such as keeping in last year's fire, first footing, making 'het' pints, drawing the first water from the well, playing shinty and other ball games. The 5th January or 12th night was previously Auld Yule, Christmas old style.

It was still a rather dreary and sombre Coupar Angus in the 19th century when education became mandatory for all 5 to 13 year olds. The tradition of schools being used as Polling Stations is a long one and dates from when they were newly built in the late 19th century. It was not until 1918 that all men over twenty-one had the right to vote, for the lower working classes had been excluded from doing so until then. Women had to wait until 1928 before they could vote. At election time there were no complaints from the pupils when they were given the day off.

On the third Thursday of March, the famous 'Horse Market' took place in the town. This must have been quite an occasion for in the early years of the school's history (1874-1890) the pupils had two days away from lessons to join in the fun. Mr Logan the Schoolmaster of the Parish School which stood close to where the Red House Hotel is now, described them as 'Playdays' which may mean that the traditional travelling players had re-emerged on occasions such as this.

By the 1890's sadly the Horse Market was petering out and no longer a school holiday. Many of the pupils however took the time off anyway much to the annoyance of the School Board. All we have as a reminder of this once splendid occasion, are the gingerbread horses still produced by the local bakery firm in the town.

In Victorian times the Queen's birthday was marked with a day off school. At first called 'Victoria Day' it became known after her death as 'Empire Day' but after World II, when the Empire was fast diminishing, it was done away with.

On 30th June 1887 the school closed early for the official opening of the Jubilee Building or Town Hall which was built to mark Victoria's 50 years as Queen. The following day was proclaimed a holiday to mark the historic event.

On the death of the Monarch, the school always closed as a mark of respect and on a happier note at Coronations, holidays were given as a gesture of patriotism and to celebrate the start of the new reign. Pageants took place then with children sporting garments *(often made of crepe paper)* in red, white and blue. A small boy and girl would have little crowns placed upon their heads and then driven through town in a horse-drawn carriage, followed by their flag-waving school companions, to an area where sports would then be held. A splendid picnic, with the eats in individual bags, would round off the day.

Sometimes trees were planted to mark the occasion and new pennies, mugs, small boxes of chocolates, books, Bibles, Missals *(for the Roman Catholic children)*.

> **FOOTNOTE**
>
> The Coates Family produced thread and latterly fine materials i.e. Clydella and Vyella. The huge factory in Paisley like so many others now, is no longer in operation. The Coates family had several country houses most of which were gifted to local authorities in the 1950's when they became too unwieldy to run in private ownership. Fornethy House near Lintrathen was one which for many years was a holiday retreat for deprived children from the West of Scotland.

*(Top) Forfar road looking towards the town - the common on the right.*
*(Left) Ally Pearson at a Rattray ploughing match with Clydesdales Donnie (left) and Davy.*

page 99

and pencils were distributed as souvenirs, at such events over the decades.

1911 was a memorable year for the children of Coupar Angus when on 10th November, every pupil in the town and indeed throughout the country, was given a school bag by 'James Coates' Esq of Paisley. Schoolteachers were not forgotten for they were given leather attache cases of such excellent quality that many survived until well after the Second World War.

There was a very special holiday in June 1914, the 600th anniversary of the Battle of Bannockburn. Right up until the Second World War Scottish History was widely taught in Primary Schools and pupils were drilled until they knew all the important dates off by heart.

## THE COUPAR FAIR

The Coupar Angus Fair was held each year in the middle of July and the school was closed for it. Children and adults alike made the most of what was then a really wonderful occasion.

At the end of July the school closed for the summer holidays which lasted until the middle of September. Most children would spend the time at the 'berries', for vacations then were unheard of.

### SCOTTISH FESTIVALS AND HOLIDAYS
#### PAST & PRESENT

|  |  |
|---|---|
| 2nd February | Fast Day |
| 3rd Thursday in March | Horse Market |
| 22nd May | Empire Day (formerly Victoria Day) |
| 17th July | Coupar Angus Fair |
| 31st July | Fast Day |
| 29th September | Michaelmas (in the Highlands the day of the struan) |
| 31st October | All Saints Eve or Hallowe'en |
| 11th November | St Martin's Day |
| 30th November | St Andrew's Day (Patron Saint of Scotland) |
| 24th December | Christmas Eve or Yule E'en (beginning of the Daft Days) |
| 25th December | Christmas Day - Yule |
| 26th December | Sweetie Scone Day |
| 31st December | Hogmany |

On their return to school after the summer break, there were no official holidays until Christmas Day. For many years until after the First World War, the pupils were given a slice of dumpling on leaving school on Christmas Eve. These were made in the school and were a real treat for the children then who had few, if any, luxuries in their lives. One day off at Christmas then it was back to classes until New Year's Eve when they had a week's break.

During spells of extremely cold weather however, when the ice was thick enough, the children were given a 'skating holiday'. The younger ones restricted their activities to the smaller ponds in the town and the Curling pond if the Curlers weren't around, but most of them made their way to Loch Bog (better known now as Stormont Loch). Skating was not restricted to the young for many of the adults too were fine skaters in pre-World War II Coupar Angus.

Coupar Angus lying as it does in the heart of Strathmore, had a long history of townsfolk abandoning their day job, for field work when extra labour was in demand, especially at the times of sowing and reaping grain and planting and lifting tatties.

In this, the school pupils were no different from their elders and great problems were created in the early days, when the pupils absented themselves from their studies and went to the tatties.

### 1871
A public dinner for the poor was held in the Royal Hotel courtesy of Stewart the Flesher. Those who were unable to attend were given Bridies from Scott the Baker.

The School Board not surprisingly, was very concerned about this for the all important matter of funding for the running of the school, was linked to attendance.

They had tremendous powers and could, and did, take parents to Court for the irregular attendance of their offspring.

On 17th October 1874 practically every school pupil was absent and at the 'tatties'. The members of the School Board, who took their responsibilities very seriously indeed, found the task of taking so many parents to court, a bit too much even for them.

*(Left) Curlers at Stormont Loch break for lunch. Seated clockwise, from left: Pat Morris, Bob Hally, Dave Pithie, Jock Davidson, ?, Archie Blyth, Bob Dewar, Jimmy Robertson, Peter Cameron, Peter Gibb C1950.*

During Mr Strain's headmastership a solution to this problem was found and the following comes from the Inspector's Report:

### 29th MARCH 1901

"MY LORDS WOULD SUGGEST THAT A REMEDY MAY BE FOUND IN A RE-ADJUSTMENT OF THE DATES OF THE ORDINARY SCHOOL HOLIDAYS TO SUIT AGRICULTURAL CONDITIONS".

('My Lords' were the members of the Scottish Education Board)

This year (1901) saw the first of what we know now as Easter Holidays which lasted from 5th to 15th April.

For many years, the date of these holidays was only decided when the school was so devoid of pupils that the Board could safely conclude the 'Potato Season' had begun. Depending on weather conditions, the autumn break had sometimes to be extended by a further week to "accommodate the harvest". Tattie lifting by pupils in schools throughout the country, continued until the 1960's when an "Exemption Scheme" was introduced which meant that the permission of both school and parent had to be given before a pupil was legally off school.

With modern potato harvesting machines, so few hands are needed that school pupils are not required now. The autumn break continues however and is still called by many - the Tattie Holidays!

---

## James Chalmers,
### The Cross, Coupar Angus,

DIRECTS special attention to the character of DRAPERY GOODS in Stock. They are selected exclusively for a Good Family Trade, and replete with the latest novelties.

*Dressmaking*, under experienced management. Ladies' Costumes a specialty,

*Tailoring* in all its branches... Gentlemen's Suits. Overcoats. Breeches. Liveries.

J. C. with the skill and experienced workmanship at his command, can guarantee the utmost care in the build and manipulation of every garment made, thereby ensuring excellence in Style and Fit.

### James Chalmers,
*Dressmaker & Merchant Tailor,*
The Cross, Coupar Angus.

---

Nowadays, in schools throughout Scotland, there are a set number of holidays - or perhaps it would be more correct to say - a set number of attendances. The number does not vary throughout the country, but the dates and duration may do so from District to District, Region to Region.

### A GARDENERS SOCIETY
flourished in the town even earlier than 1843. It was more than a Club for enthusiastic horticulturalists however, for it acted as an Insurance Company where members paid a little each week and in times of hardship were paid regular sums of money to see them through the difficult times. The Society was considerably prosperous and invested its funds well. It owned various properties in the town which it rented out. The introduction of the Welfare State in 1946 rendered it and others like it, redundant.

*(Top)* There was no excuse for not being well dressed on holiday.
*(Above)* A reminder of the annual competition for the best garden in the town.

Before we became a society of 'Telly Addicts', the people of Coupar Angus were a lively lot, actively engaged in activities which ranged from the physically taxing to the mentally stimulating.

# ENTERTAINMENT - over the years

Until the Town Hall was built in 1887 the Strathmore Hall *(now the function room of the Royal Hotel)* was the venue for events which ranged from lectures to members of the 'Mechanics Institute', to concerts. The town had been visited for centuries by strolling players and entertainers who travelled the countryside attending the Fairs and Markets which were held regularly.

In 1861 a concert in the Strathmore Hall was given by the Precentor of the Established Church, while a Mr George Henderson of whom unfortunately we know nothing, held his 36th annual concert there, which takes us back to the year 1825. The 1861 concert however, included a selection by the Instrumental Band of the Volunteer Rifle Brigade.

Without doubt, any form of local entertainment was well supported and seems to have taken precedence over everything else. From the early Log Books of the School Evening Classes, we learn that attendance was practically non-existant when 'a local entertainment' was held.

After the school was built in 1877 the children took part in annual concerts in the Town Hall which were so popular that they were held on several nights. The profit from these bought extras for the school which ranged from library books to a piano. School concerts are still an annual event but are no longer held in the Town Hall. Since the 1960s when the school extension was built, incorporating a spacious hall, they have taken place there.

Over the years there were regular theatrical and amateur shows, visits from repertory companies, Burns concerts and dances arranged by the many clubs in the town. Although the bulk of these were primarily fund-raisers, the young and not so young members of the community looked forward to them and supported them well.

## MUSIC MUSIC MUSIC

Before the days of steam radio, music was provided as entertainment by whoever had the talent to play an instrument. One group of Coupar Angus lads - including William T. Dunbar with fiddle - played Scottish Country Dance Music in various parts of the county. Later, in the 1920s a George, William and James Dunbar, playing piano, violin and trumpet respectively, formed a Dance Band called the Windsors with a Mr Turpie on trombone, and a drummer who's name is now forgotten

The Farmers Dance was a great occasion, the catering for which was done by Dunbar the Baker, whose son John *(Jack)* now in South Africa remembers trundling the firm's two-wheeled cart back and forth between the shop and the Town Hall laden with cases of glasses, cutlery, table cloths etc. At the dance two bands might have played - Dod Michie and Ian Powrie, and it was nothing out of the ordinary for the band to be pounding out a Quadrilles or Eightsome Reel at half past three in the morning.

*(Top) Props being delivered to the Town Hall by barrow for a function - venue for many shows and dances C1900.*
*(Left) Teenage happy snap before the outbreak of the 1939-45 war.*

For every dance, the hall would be decorated with streamers, balloons etc which gave it a festive appearance. On very special occasions the decorations would be even more elaborate, particularly when the Polish army were in residence in the town. Then, big jumbo-size photogaphs of Polish landmarks might be found all round the walls of the main hall. These were reproduced from an extensive library of 35mm negatives which the army photographer had brought with him when escaping from Poland.

---

"The Rendevous of the Services"

## THE PLAYHOUSE

### Queen Street : Coupar Angus

Monday to Friday each evening at 7.15.
Saturdays - 6 and 8.30.
recently equipped with the most
Modern Sound Reproducing System
NOW and always Presenting
PROGRAMMES OF
UNEXAMPLED EXCELLENCE
Open very Sunday at 7.15

---

*(Top left) At the Town Hall, Provost John Davidson with officers of the Polish Army unveiling a plaque they presented to the town. It reads, in both languages: "In remembrance of our sojourn - the soldiers of 1 Med. Reg. A - 1941"*
*(Top right) Dod Michie in session.*
*(Inset) Provost W. T. Dunbar.*

When the 'Picture Playhouse' was built in Hay Street around 1920 it was an additional pleasure for the townspeople and did not detract from the 'live' entertainment in the town. The old wooden Playhouse is no longer there, and houses have been built on the site, but memories linger on among many of the older residents.

These silent films, were shown on a solid, painted, concrete screen while a pianist played to convey the mood - anger - sorrow - joy - love etc. The front rows consisted of wooden forms, without backs, which cost four old pence, while further back, the more expensive seats had back rests. In 1921 Norma Talmadge was starring in "The Forbidden City", Charles Chaplin in "Musical Tramps" and Harold Lloyd in "Soldiers of Misfortune".

The old Playhouse was replaced in 1929 when the United Presbyterian, or South Free Church in Queen Street, which had been lying empty for two years, was converted to a Cinema. Mr W. T. Dunbar, the Baker, was Provost at that time, and he, along with council members and son John, attended a trial run there. Mr Prain of Blairgowrie, the owner of the Hay Street Picture House, arrived with a big clumsy 35 mm sound projector, which he set up at the back of the kirk and projected some film on the wall for the members of the Town Council who were also present, and whose approval was necessary.

They agreed unanimously that it was a good thing and a great improvement on the old Picture House and the conversion from church to cinema went ahead. Up in the balcony there were some rows of "chummy" seats i.e. seats for two with no arm rest between. John Dunbar remembers that as teenagers, they all had their own special chummy seats, if they were available.

## THE WAR YEARS

The outbreak of World War II saw an increase in entertainment in the town, but now the fund raising aspect took on a much more important roll in raising money for the various projects which became known as the 'War Effort'.

Dod Michie and his band played regularly at the Saturday night hops, entrance to which cost two old shillings. From the late 1930's the band consisted of a piano played by John *(Jack)* Dunbar, Ali Baxter on drums and Dod himself on trumpet.

The Michie band played all round the area, including Burrelton, Meikleour, Caputh, Alyth etc and also Murthly Asylum.

When the Polish Army arrived in Coupar Angus, two fantastic saxophone players joined the band. Dod's little Morris could often be seen chugging along to different events,

## Coupar Angus Spitfire Concert Artistes

*(Cutting from the PA) In aid of the local Spitfire Fund at Coupar Angus, what was called "The Mulberry Bush" concert was held last night and will be repeated this evening.*

DYBBC were always willing to entertain or to lend a hand in any way.

Their talents were not restricted to merely cheering up and entertaining a war weary town, for it was they who inaugurated the 'Coupar Angus Spitfire Fund', by holding an all night dance in the Victoria Hall in September, 1940. From the P.A. of that time comes the following:-

*"The dance hall was brilliantly decorated with flags. foliage, decorations and fairy lights while the tables in the buffet hall looked very attractive with their pink dahlias and pale green menu cards".*

The official slogan for the Spitfire Fund was:-

**"A SPITFIRE A DAY KEEPS THE NAZIS AWAY"**

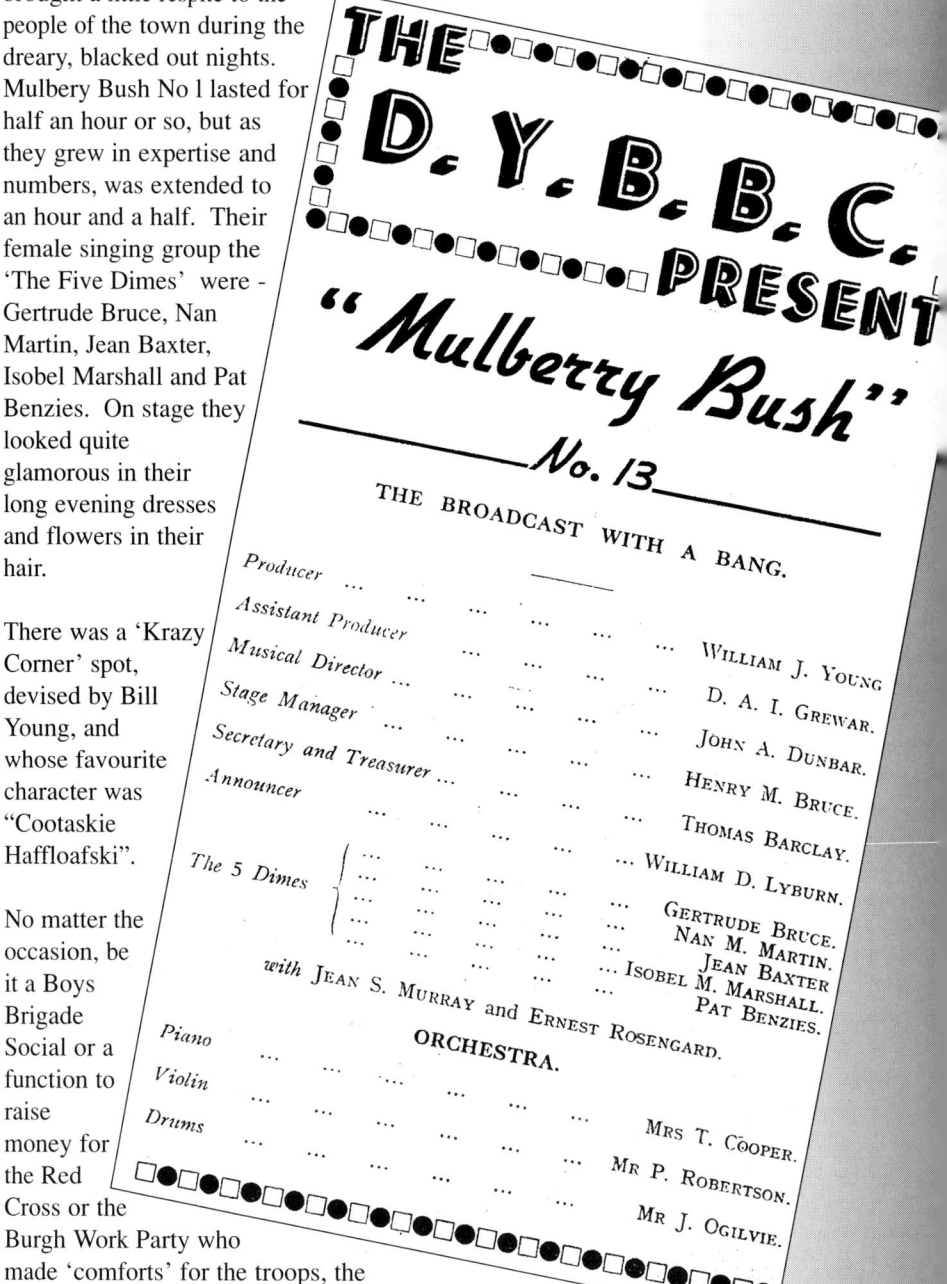

with the drums tied on the back, and all five members of the band inside.

Despite an exodus of young men during World War II entertainment carried on in Coupar Angus, but now the fund raising aspect had a much more serious side to it. In the early days of the war several young people formed an entertainment group and called themselves 'the DUNBAR-YOUNG-BARCLAY-BROADCASTING-COMPANY or 'DYBBC' *(see programme right)* The boys did not really 'broadcast' over the air, but copied the format of the day from such popular radio shows as ITMA.

Their programme of light hearted and varied entertainment was called 'The Mulberry Bush' - firstly Number l and then so on for sub-sequent shows. This brought a little respite to the people of the town during the dreary, blacked out nights. Mulbery Bush No l lasted for half an hour or so, but as they grew in expertise and numbers, was extended to an hour and a half. Their female singing group the 'The Five Dimes' were - Gertrude Bruce, Nan Martin, Jean Baxter, Isobel Marshall and Pat Benzies. On stage they looked quite glamorous in their long evening dresses and flowers in their hair.

There was a 'Krazy Corner' spot, devised by Bill Young, and whose favourite character was "Cootaskie Haffloafski".

No matter the occasion, be it a Boys Brigade Social or a function to raise money for the Red Cross or the Burgh Work Party who made 'comforts' for the troops, the

*(Top) PA cutting showing the team.*
*(Above) Professor Halfloafski.*
*(Right One of the DYBBC programmes.*
page 104

**THE D.Y.B.B.C. PRESENT**
**"Mulberry Bush"**
**No. 13**

THE BROADCAST WITH A BANG.

| | |
|---|---|
| Producer ... | WILLIAM J. YOUNG |
| Assistant Producer ... | D. A. I. GREWAR. |
| Musical Director ... | JOHN A. DUNBAR. |
| Stage Manager ... | HENRY M. BRUCE. |
| Secretary and Treasurer ... | THOMAS BARCLAY. |
| Announcer ... | WILLIAM D. LYBURN. |
| The 5 Dimes { | GERTRUDE BRUCE. |
| | NAN M. MARTIN. |
| | JEAN BAXTER |
| | ISOBEL M. MARSHALL. |
| | PAT BENZIES. |

with JEAN S. MURRAY and ERNEST ROSENGARD.

ORCHESTRA.

| | |
|---|---|
| Piano ... | MRS T. COOPER. |
| Violin ... | MR P. ROBERTSON. |
| Drums ... | MR J. OGILVIE. |

while the DYBBC slogan was:

THE DYBBC ARE HERE
TO HELP THE BOYS ON HIGH;
SO BRING YOUR SPARE CASH
ROUND TO US
AND A SPITFIRE WE WILL BUY

These were the days when Coupar Angus housewives sacrificed their old aluminium pots and pans for scrap to help build aeroplanes, and any home with iron railings lost them for scrap to build bombs. There are still some stumps left where the railings were chopped down by municipality workers.

## THE POST WAR YEARS

For some years after World War II dances and other entertainments, carried on, then gradually a change took place and dancing to live music was replaced by the 'Disco' with its ampliified sound, and on occasions, behavioural problems.

Dancing to live music is now almost exclusively restricted to weddings and dinner dances, and even on these occasions, bands seem to feel that amplification is essential which renders social chit-chat impossible.

In the late 1940's in Coupar Angus, a Dramatic Society emerged which for a number of years brought great pleasure to the play-going public of the town. The Toc H Social Service Fund was one of the societies to benefit from their productions. Initially the Club met and produced their plays in the Town Hall then after 1951 they changed to the smaller, newly converted Abbey Church Hall.

*(Top) One of the many posters produced by Culross to help the DYBBC. Note the sugar restraint!*
*(Above) (L & R) Bill Young was lost without trace on a bombing raid, and Harry Bruce died while training as a fighter pilot in South Africa.*

## D.Y.B.B.C. DANCE IN AID OF SPITFIRE FUND

in Victoria Hall on Friday 30th August 8.30 p.m. to 2 a.m.

ADMISSION
2/- [per couple 3/6] H.M. FORCES 1/-
EXCLUDING BUFFET

BRING YOUR OWN SUGAR

Mr George Petrie was the Club's Producer and R.G. Doig the Stage Manager. Among the plays presented by them over the years were the following: "The Mistress of Greenbyres" and "Our Tommy" by Joe Corrie; "Orange Blossom" by Philip Johnson; "The Ghost Train" by Arnold Ridley; "Beside the Seaside" by Leslie Sands; and "The Honour of Drumlie" by James Scotland. Among the cast of these plays were: Helen Graham; Susan Wilson; Judith Benzies; Edna Bonthrone; Morag Richards; George Walker; Betty Irvine; Christine Harris; Wilson Graham; John Stewart; John Forsyth; George Robertson; Jack McLaughlan; Robert Benzies; Andrew Young; Isobel Lamond; Elma Strachan; Mrs J. McDonald; Mrs A. Lamond; Marie Kermath; Mrs M. Wilson; Joseph Casciani; Ellen Whytock; David Clark; Margaret Sutherland; George Petrie; Neville Williams; Rita Syme; and David Rioch.

## CORONATION 1953

The celebrations for the Coronation of Queen Elizabeth on 2nd June 1953 saw a splendid programme of events, which started on Sunday 31st May with a United Coronation Service in the Abbey Church.

On Monday June 1st at 6.00p.m., the senior citizens, then called the 'old folks', were taken on an outing to Blairgowrie, Alyth, Kirriemuir, Forfar and Dundee, which at that time would have been considered to be a 'real treat'. On Tuesday June 2nd from 10.00 a.m. on, the 'old folk', if they wished, could watch the Coronation Ceremony on Television *(black and white only then)* in the front hall and billiard room of the Town Hall. At 1 oclock there was a Decorated Vehicle and Fancy Dress Parade and at 1.40 p.m. a Religious Service was held in Foxhall Park. At 2.00 p.m., Childrens Sports took place, followed by other Local Sporting Events. Between 5 and 6 p.m. a Country Dancing Display was given by dancers from Alyth, Burrelton and Coupar Angus, with music by the Martin Hayes Scottish Dance Band. From 8 p.m. until 2 a.m. an admission-free Coronation Dance to the Ambassadors Augmented Dance Band, was held in the Town Hall. The proceedings were halted between 11.00 and 12.00 p.m., so that all could attend the Fireworks Display and Bonfire in Larghan Victory Park. During the afternoon and evening, the St Margaret's *(Old)* Silver Band from Dundee added to the festive atmosphere with rousing selections.

The activities carried on into Wednesday with a free Picture Show for children in the Playhouse Cinema in Queen Street. Every child born within the burgh on Coronation Day received £5.5s., and there were competions for the best decorated private houses, shops, and business premises. The Judging of the best Coronation Garden Display was postponed until August when the gardens entered would be looking their best.
At the time of the Coronation in 1953 television was still in black and white. Due to the fact that the ceremony was to be televised, TV sales rose dramatically as people who had put off until now, decided to go ahead and purchase one in order to view the proceedings in the comfort of their own homes.

There are always exceptions to the rules however for in the 1960's and early 1970's the folk of Coupar Angus were entertained in a most delightful way when a bit of a mystery man - Roy Harness arrived in town as a Partner in the Cafe at the Cross. He was a man of musical genius and he rounded up many of the young people and trained them to act and sing. He also displayed great ability as a producer and presented programmes of such excellence that people flocked to the performances. These shows which included selections from 'The King and I', 'Oliver', and even 'Madame Butterfly' have never been forgotten.

As time has passed and colour television was introduced, very few, if any, homes are without at least one set, with many children having their own TV's in their bedrooms. Now in addition to television, the dawning of the 'Computer Age' has meant that many homes have one, plus a personal computer (PC) with games which have become very popular. Television with its video recorder, is now taken for granted as an essential part of daily life. It was the death knell of the Cinema in all small towns like Coupar Angus but is now gaining popularity once more in large towns and cities with modern multi-choice cinemas. Television without doubt is a great asset, for many programmes are not only entertaining but are highly informative and educational. By televising State Occasions and Parliamentary affairs etc, a new

> **THE LADIES SOCIETY**
> This society of a purely charitable status, distributed money, coals and clothing, to elderly women who found themselves in straightened circumstances through retirement, widowhood or ill-health. This type of society has been superseded by charities like 'Help the Aged'...

*(Above) Workers at Durie & Miller celebrate the Coronation in 1936.*
*(Right) The Coupar Angus Dramatic Society in the late 1950s.*

dimension has been brought into our lives, while sad events like the funeral of Diana Princess of Wales, was watched by millions of people throughout the World.

Although entertainment, like so many other things, not only in Coupar Angus but in the country as a whole, has changed, it goes on in different forms in the town. Whist Drives and Bingo Teas take place regularly as fund raising events and the Toc H does much by having regular meetings and tea parties for the elderly, with entertainment of one kind or another.

### 1950
"Six girls were selected to represent Coupar Angus in the Miss Strathmore 1950 Competition. They are - Cathie Gallacher, Aileen Thomson, Mary McLaren, Betty Lowson, Olive Black and Jean Whyte."

There is a well supported Country and Western Club in town and each Sunday afternoon a Ceilidh takes place in the 'Red House Hotel'. In addition, line dancing, keep-fit classes, and Karate are all popular with old and young alike.

The school pupils still hold their annual concerts, which are well supported by parents and friends, and school sports days are looked forward to with eager anticipation.

Time moves on and nothing stays the same be it good times or bad, but in many ways, the town of Coupar Angus although different from former years, is still alive and kicking.

## ADAM RENNIE 1897-1960
### By Ron Stephen

A small boy watched fascinated as an old man played merrily on a fiddle at a Silver Wedding Celebration in Coupar Angus. The Year was 1906 and the boy was nine-year old Adam Rennie, who in later years gained International fame as a Violinist, Composer and Scottish Country Dance Band Leader.

Adam Rennie was born at Kemnay, Aberdeenshire in 1897 and came to Coupar Angus at the age of five years. His parents worked on Coupar Grange Estate in the nearby Parish of Bendochy and Adam went to the school there where he got his first music lessons from his teacher, Miss Elsie Birrel.

On leaving school Adam went to work on the land, and he was 'Fee'd' *(employed)* as a 'Halflin' *(Odd Job Man)* at Ryehill Farm on Coupar Grange Estate and by the age of fourteen was in charge of a pair of horse.

Further fiddle lessons were to follow from 'Dancie' Reid of Newtyle who nurtured so many of the fine fiddlers in the Angus and Perthshire district.

After the days' work was over, Adam delighted the older men in the Bothy with his music, and as his playing developed he began to be asked to play at various local parties and functions. His first public engagement was playing for the dancing at the Bendochy Sports to celebrate the Coronation of King George V. He was paid ten bob (50p) for this and said "I thought I would never be poor again".

In 1916 he joined the 5th Gordon Highlanders and did not touch a fiddle from then until he 'won' a fiddle from a shelled music shop in the deserted town of Arras in Northern France in the Spring of 1918.

The Battalion had fortyeight hours rest leave there and were billeted in two cellars when Adam arrived back with the fiddle under his greatcoat. He took it out and started to play "Take Me Back to Dear Old Blighty" and was an instant success. Every time the Battalion moved into the line the fiddle which had charmed the Gordons many times was handed over to the Padre for safe keeping. Then came the fateful day of 28th July 1918 at Soissons where at Soissons Adam suffered a severe leg wound. He lay unattended for two days before being picked up by the Germans and taken prisoner. The French Red Cross found him in 1919 and after a series of transfers across Europe he managed to write home asking for cigarettes to be sent to him. This caused a sensation for his family had thought him dead. Back in London he had to have his leg amputated and spent a year in various hospitals before returning home.

In 1920 Adam opened his Tobacconist and Newsagent Business at the Cross in Coupar Angus, with financial help from the Minister at Bendochy Church the Rev A. Wylie Smith who had known him as a pupil at Bendochy school and was only too willing to help a wounded hero. It was to prove to be an excellent investment for both, for Adam ran his business in Coupar Angus for thirty eight years.

Adam never saw the Arras fiddle again, but twelve years after the War ended memory of it was brought home to him in a very strange way when he was travelling by train from Dundee to Coupar Angus with only one other passenger in the compartment. The man put down the newspaper he was reading and asked him if he was Adam Rennie? Adam replied in the affirmative and the man went on to say that the last time he had seen him was in a cellar in Arras playing a fiddle that he had just 'pinched'!

Fact is indeed stranger than fiction! Adam was to become a member of the greatly loved 'Angus Occasionals' and in 1943 made his first ever broadcast with them.

He formed his Quartette in 1949 which made its first broadcast on the old 'Home Service' on 8th December of that year. They also broadcast on the 'General Overseas Service Country Magazine' in the 'Journey through Scotland' and he also had a solo spot in the 'Fiddlers Six' series.

*(Top) Adam with Neil Gow's fiddle.*

The famous Quartet came about in a most casual fashion. When Adam was judging a competition in Blairgowrie and like all the other Judges taking part, was behind a screen so they could not see the player, he was particularly struck by the expertise of one competitor whom he resolved to meet after the competition. The musician turned out to be sixteen year old Bobby Brown, who incidentally won the competition, and Adam invited him to come to Coupar Angus "for a tune".

### ADAM RENNIE COMPOSITIONS

**JIGS:**
Sir Torquil Munro; Elizabeth Donald; Mrs Grace Bowie (of Coupar Angus).

**REELS**
Bill Sutherland (Blair Athol); Jean Kirkpatrick's Fancy (Alyth); Pat Donald; John Donald; The Reverend Peter Fenton (Ardler); Kemnay House; Kinclaven Brig'; The Bonnie Dancers; Mrs Monair of Bruach.

**STRATHSPEY**
Innes Russel (Perth).

**POLKAS**
Janette Gibb's Polka; Silver Wings Polka; Military two Step; Up With The Lark

Adam on occasions had previously played with pianist George Robertson and on this occasion they were joined by Jock White who played Bass. From this informal and casual get-together the famous 'Quartet' was born. Later George Robertson introduced Adam to Ed Robb who took over playing the double bass for the duration of the Quartet. Over the years they had some very prestigous venues and on several occasions played at Balmoral Castle for

page 108

the Ghillies Ball - twice in l953; twice in l954 then again in l956 when her Majesty the Queen, the Duke of Edinburgh and the Queen Mother were all present. Adam Rennie's fiddle is perhaps the most famous in Scotland for it was the 'Neil Gow Fiddle' which he won at the Perth Festival in 1932 for 'Distinction' in Scottish Music. During l930/3l he won the 'Open Violin Championships For Strathspey and Reels' which was sponsored by the Forfar Burns Club.

Not surprisingly the Rennie Quartets' radio broadcasts attracted the attention of several recording companies and records were recorded with Pye *(Nixa)* and the Parlaphone Company which were released as 78's plus one small 7" extended playing disc.

The band was also in great demand South of the Border, and one thousand mile round trip in January l952 saw them journey to Chelmsford in Essex to play at the Chelmsford Farmers Batchelors Ball where dressed in their Royal Stewart tartan dinner jackets they were much admired.

On a trip to London in January 1957 they played in Porchester Hall on the Friday and at Holborn Hall on Saturday where the dance was sponsored by the Scottish Reel Club.

At the Holborn dance they took part in a Documentary Film produced by the Pathe Company to promote the Tourist Industry in Britain. The first part of the film had been made throughout the year in different parts of the country and culminated with scenes of the Scottish Reel Clubs ending with the playing of "Auld Lang Syne".

Adam Rennie eventually retired to Muirton House,* Blairgowrie where he died.

At Christmas l986 the original recordings of the 1950's were re-released and tapes and records produced. The profits from the sales of these benefitted the Toc H in Coupar Angus, who had their meeting place in Trades Lane refurbished and an efficient heating system installed.

## THE PIPE BAND

Pipe Bands in general date from the early 19th century when Highland Regiments were formed.

Bagpipes have been played in many parts of the world from the earliest times but the 'Pipe Band' as we know it, is entirely of Scottish origin. Although many are found throughout the world most are modelled on the Scottish version and those from the former Colonies - Australia, Canada and New Zealand - have reached a very high standard. If a pipe band is to reach world class, a very high degree of technical skill is required for piper and drummer to play in complete unanimity.

We know for certain that there was a Pipe Band in Coupar Angus from early last century, which, along with the Municipal Brass Band took week about in playing round the town each Saturday, ending up at Dunbar the Bakers, where they refreshed themselves with the famous bridies and mutton pies. The band's expenses were amply met from donations, collected by loyal supporters, as they made their way through town.

The Boys Brigade had been founded in Coupar Angus in the late 19th century by the Parish Church Minister, Finlay Robert MacDonald during his ministry (1881 -1901), and they had a Pipe Band which was very popular with the lads some of whom played not only in it, but

*\* Muirton House has since been a Country House Hotel and is now a much extended Private Nursing Home*

*(Top) Adam Rennie's corner shop on the Cross.*

in the town band too. When the boys were considered to have reached adulthood they joined the town band which meant that the Boys Brigade Band acted effectively as the 'feeder' for the town band. It is not surprising therefore, to learn that the town Pipe Band was of a very high standard. They made quite a visual impact in their kilts of Gordon Tartan with matching tunics of green.

Over the years they were sought after to play at Fetes and other open air gatherings but what was considered to be the highlight of the season, was to be asked to play at a Football Match at Muirton Park in Perth, the home of the St Johnston Football Club. In those days the club gave the band permission to take up a collection, and a large sheet was carried around the arena into which spectators tossed their pennies.

> A group calling themselves the "Illuminators" has been formed and will manage all aspects of the Christmas Lights and Decorations in the town.

Nowadays, the Club gives bands a fee for playing! In the 1920's and 30's the band met for practice in a wooden building in Candlehouse Lane, behind the White House Hotel which was owned at that time by Mr Frank Ross, who was a staunch supporter. Full band practices took place on the area of land now occupied by Johnson Ventilation. In the later 1930's they moved to the school and practices were held where the additional school buildings now stand. Between the Wars, all the Youth Organisations in the town, along with the Ex-Servicemens Associations, assembled in George Square on Armistice Sunday, and marched behind the band to the Abbey Church.

For the duration of World War II, the band was disbanded and the uniforms were stored at Balbrogie which at that time was owned by its President, Mr James Anderson.

The first Pipe Major we have record of was Mr William Mason, who lived in Precinct Street, and was married to a local dairyman's daughter. When he and his wife moved to Grey Park, Burrelton as Caretakers, Pipe Major McDonald took over for a short time then Mr Robert Pitkeathly of Stormont Crossing, assumed control. Mr Pitkeathly's time with the band saw them rise to new heights of perfection, for he was a member of a very distinguished family in the world at piping, and a Pipe Major second to none. Andrew his son, went on to become the personal piper to Her Majesty - Queen Elizabeth II. Under Mr Pitkeathly's leadership, the band went from strength to strength, but when in the 1950's he left Coupar Angus to assume control of the Blairgowrie Pipe Band, sadly, he could not be replaced and the band folded. The uniforms were eventually sent to the British Legion in Perth.

Apart from a short period in the 1970's when T. L. B. Apedaile formed a very successful Scout Pipe Band, there has been no Pipe Band revival in Coupar Angus since then, but Blairgowrie's has survived over the years and has several lady members.

*August 2000 saw a revival of interest in forming a Pipe Band when Pipe Major Kevin Douglas started recruiting nmbers*

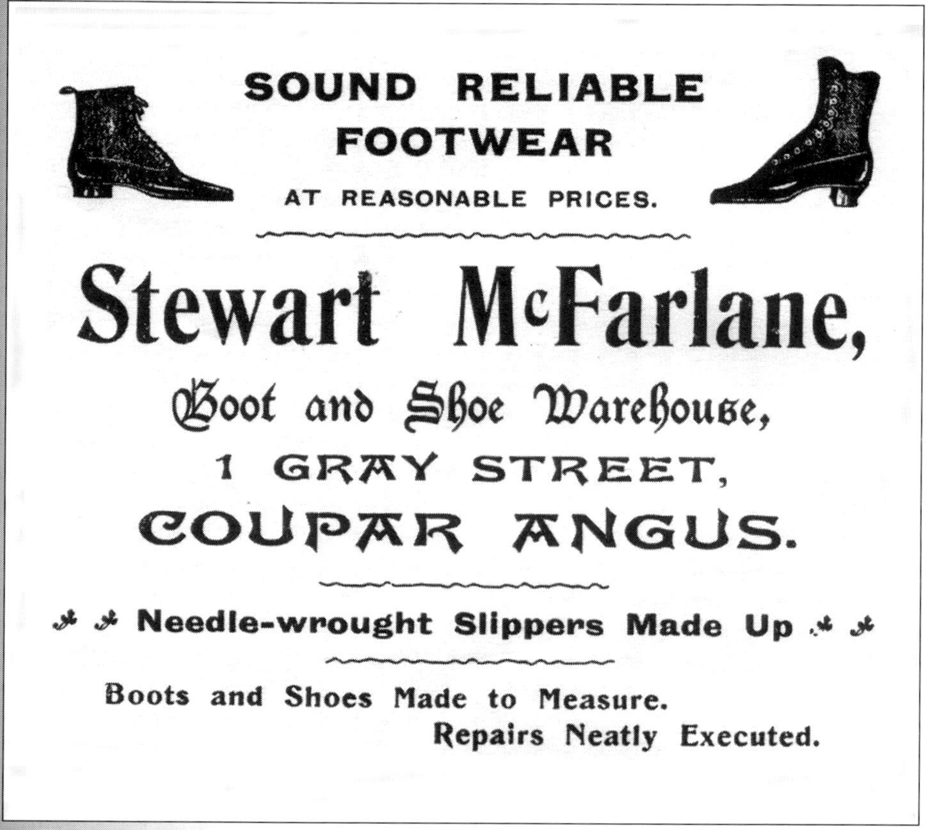

*(Top) The pipe Band pose for a photograph in George Square along with the ex-servicemen of the British Legion.*

---

**SOUND RELIABLE FOOTWEAR**
AT REASONABLE PRICES.

# Stewart McFarlane,

Boot and Shoe Warehouse,

**1 GRAY STREET,
COUPAR ANGUS.**

Needle-wrought Slippers Made Up

Boots and Shoes Made to Measure.
Repairs Neatly Executed.

## THE INSTRUMENTAL OR BRASS BAND

The 7th Perthshire Rifle Volunteers, or the 'Rifles' as they were better known, had their Drill Hall in Causewayend *(now the Red Cross Hall)*. As a result of the Jacobite Uprising, groups of 'Militia' were formed in 1797 to support the army at that time, in order to counter any threat to the Nation should it arise.

We do not know when the Coupar Angus contingent was formed but by 1861 they were drilling regularly and had an Instrumental Band, which not only played while they were marching or assembling for weekend drill at the Cross, but took part in concerts which in the days before the Town Hall was built, were held in the Strathmore Hall, now the function room of the Royal Hotel.

Quite a number of concerts were held there over the years to raise money for various activities in the town, and in 1861 they took part in one to raise money for the 'Soup Kitchen' which at that time was feeding over one hundred Coupar Angus folk each day, due to the crash of the hand loom weaving industry. The Captain of the 7th Perthshire Volunteer Rifles in those days was Murray of Lintrose, and in his honour the men wore bands of silk Murray tartan ribbon round their caps. In 1861 they numbered 72, and were described in the 'Advertiser' of March of that year as "gallant defenders of their country".
In 1881 reorganisation took place and new regiments were formed for each area of the country. The Royal Perthshire Rifles were affiliated to the 3rd Battalion Black Watch, and during the Boer War 1899-1901 many of the local group volunteered for service in South Africa. In 1908 changes again were introduced and the Territorial Army was formed. There is little recorded information of when the Volunteer Rifles Instrumental Band fizzled out and the Municipal Brass Band was formed, but Mrs Flora Whyte, who was born in Coupar Angus and now lives in Luton, has supplied valuable information for, according to family legend, it was her Grandfather, James Slidders, who started up the brass band around the turn of the century.

It appears to have been disbanded, as so many other activities were, at the start of World War I but was reformed in 1920 when Mr John Lamb became its Conductor.

Mr Shepherd of Hill Gardens, well remembers the uniforms were known to have been those of a previous band, and were poorly tailored and ill fitting. One band member who worked with a tailor tried to alter them and make them look a bit smarter, but unfortunately his efforts proved to be futile for they still looked terrible.

The post-war Municipal Brass Band, met for practice in the Town Hall where the instruments were kept underneath the stage. It had between 20 and 26 members who played various instruments including - Cornet - Bass - Double Bass - Euphonium - Horn and Trombone. Despite the ill-fitting uniforms, the band was popular locally and carried out many engagements in the town and district. Unfortunately, despite its success, the decision to disband it was taken in the mid 1930's.

*Grateful thanks are extended to Mr Jim Dawson, whose father Robert was treasurer of the Pipe Band during Robert Pitkeathly's time as Pipe Major, and to Mr Shepherd, Hill Gardens for information on the Instrumental Band. We are indebted also to Mrs Whyte, Luton for valuable information and for a copy of what has proved to be a rare photograph of the Municipal Brass Band.*

---

**THE CROW CLUB**
The members of this musical society supped together at the Railway Hotel on Wednesday evening. Mr Irving occupied the Chair and Mr D. E. Forbes was Croupier.
The Croupier at this time sat at the very end of the table and acted as assistant Master of Ceremonies.

---

*(Top) The Coupar Angus Municipal Band with its Conductor James Ogilvie ACV.*

Coupar Angus has a long tradition of sporting activities. Some have long gone but some have survived well despite difficult times.

# SPORTS ACTIVITIES - the competitive spirit.

## CURLING

It is generally accepted throughout the world that Scotland is the home of curling.

Evidence from old pictures of the 16th century show however, that it was played then in Holland with frozen clods for stones. A similar ancient game with wooden 'stones' was played throughout parts of Europe - Holland, Germany and Switzerland and in Iceland.

The Scots however took the game very much to their hearts and made it what it is today. The present day world wide rules were first devised by the Duddingston Curling Club of Edinburgh and recorded in their minute book of 1804. The Duddingston Club is by no means among the oldest in Scotland for it was founded in 1795. The Coupar Angus Club is some forty six years older and was formed in 1749 in the aftermath of the Jacobite Uprising and is the seventh oldest in affiliation to the Royal Club.

| | |
|---|---|
| KINROSS | 1668 |
| KILSYTH | 1716 |
| DOUNE STRATHALLAN | 1732 |
| MEATH MOSS | 1736 |
| DUNFERMLINE | 1738 |
| MUTHILL | 1739 |
| COUPAR ANGUS | 1749 |

The club rules in the early days were extremely strict. When a new curler became a member he had to provide himself with two good stones. These would not have resembled much the beautifully polished 'Ailsa Craig' ones that are played with today but if within a year he had failed to bring the stones along, he was fined ten shillings - 50p in today's money but worth about fifty times more. If another year passed and he still had no stones a further ten shillings had to be paid and if after the third year there were still no stones, he was asked to leave and his name deleted from the roll.

Yet another rule stated that should a member leave the district, his stones became the property of the club. A further rule was that when a member moved to another district he could never play against the Club.

There were rules governing the conduct of members and from Provost John Davidson's "Rules and Reminiscences" comes the following:

"There was the famous incident concerning John Crocket, who had been reported to the Society for swearing and who had also lost sixpence on the ice. The delinquent was asked several times to appear before the society, but having ignored these summons, a party of members was detailed to fetch him. John Crocket presented a gun at them and threatened to shoot the first one to lay hands on him and struck one of the party on the breast.

For this unseemly conduct, Mr Crockett was dismissed from the Club and all members debarred from curling with him - "UNTIL HE SHALL, IN THE FULL MEETING, ACKNOWLEDGE HIS FAULTS AND MAKE SUCH COMPENSATION TO THE SOCIETY AS THEY THINK THE NATURE OF THESE CRIMES REQUIRES"

*(Top) Curling on the frozen river Isla with the Farina Mill chimney stack in the background.*
*(Left) L to R Alex Gatt, Pat Henderson and J. R. Anderson at Stormont Loch.*

The story ended happily for two years later, the culprit gave full and ample satisfaction and was again entitled to enjoy the privileges of a Brother Curler".

In the early days the Club had a number of stones which were described as giants:

| THE SAUT BACKET | 116 lbs |
| SUWAROFF | 84 lbs |
| COG | 80 lb |
| BLACK MEG | 66 lbs |
| CRECHE | 58 lbs |
| TOM SCOTT | 58 lbs |
| WELLINGTON | 53 lbs |

From this list we can tell that whatever else they were, the Curlers of Coupar Angus were very strong men indeed and that the ice must have been exceedingly thick before they could play. From a study of the records of the 19th century, it appears that winters were colder for matches were played from December until March on nearby Stormont Loch.

It had been believed that the stones had been left out on the pond at the top of the Common where part of the former Secondary School now stands, and that during the night there was a sudden thaw and the stones sank and were never recovered.

As a boy, Alex Gatt remembers that during a game of football, the ball went over on to the grass where a part of the pond had been, and when he went to recover it, beside the ball was the partially uncovered handle of a curling stone. At the time it was of no interest to him and as he grew older and more interested in the game of curling, he concluded that the missing stones were under the school foundations.

It came as a very big surprise therefore when Mrs Florence Smeaton, Town Hall Keeper, opened up a cupboard which had been locked for decades, and to her amazement found it to contain four strange looking stones with handles. The Community Council members were alerted to the find but none of them knew what they were.

When I heard of this, due to my research, I knew something of the ancient stones and asked Mr Alex Gatt to have a look at them, and he identified them straight away as the missing ancient curling stones. They were labelled and had the name and weight written in the beautiful handwriting of days long gone by.

| Suwaroff | 84 lbs |
| Cog | 80 lbs |
| Black Meg | 66 lbs |
| Creche | 58 lbs |

On 11th December 1882 Mr David Bett who was Chairman of the Club and the Manager of the Union Bank in Calton Street, asked that he be given 'Cog' and 'Suwaroff'. The members agreed, but on condition that they be kept and handed down through his family as heirlooms and, that they would always be available for inspection by members of the Club. Obviously they had been returned at some point to the Club, by him or his family.

The Saut Backet, Tom Scott and Wellington may well be under the foundations of the school, but these four have been locked away in the Town Hall cupboard for no one knows how long.

Before the Coupar Angus Club amalgamated with the Kettins Club in 1908 friendly rivalry existed between the two.

The Kettins Rink was at the corner of Beechwood, next to Beechwood House and it is believed that they also curled on a small loch at the top of Tullybaccart near to the turn-off to Abernyte. Due to the altitude there, the ice lasted several days longer than at Kettins.

There is a tale of an interesting incident which happened in the late 19th century at Beechwood, when Coupar Angus visitors were playing Kettins by lantern light. It was getting late and the Coupar Angus players wanted home but the Kettins Skip, described as the local 'Bigwig' kept insisting on yet another and another end. When it came to his turn to play, one really fed-up Coupar Angus curler, upped his stone, smashed the lantern and cleared off home without more ado!

**Two stones with ornate ebony and brass handles have also disappeared without trace. They were last seen in yet another cupboard in the Town Hall in February 1954 and could now perhaps be enhancing someone's rockery.**

For many years they graced the top table at the annual dinners of the Club and were on display at Curling Courts when new members were admitted to the Club. Despite this loss some of the old traditions still survive in a special

> **Thirty members of the local roller skating club took part in a marathon sponsored disco.**

Curlers handshake and password. Until the 1930's when artificial ice-rinks came into being as a direct result of the influence of films of the time, curling matches were always played out of doors. Initially this would have been on lochs and natural ponds, then later curling ponds were constructed which held just enough water to freeze easily and give a surface good enough to play on. The first pond to be used for curling that we know of, was at the top of the Common where the school extension stands now. There was a hut across the road from it where the stones and brushes were kept. It is thought that around 1908 the Club moved to Coach Road where a pond with several rinks, and a Pavillion were constructed. The Pavillion is still there but the former pond is now a grassy area which may formerly have been a bleaching green. It was at this time the Kettins and Coupar Angus clubs amalgamated.

There is some evidence that the Kettins pond at Beechwood was used by the Coupar Angus Curlers around the time of amalgamation and this may have been in the period before the Coach Road rink was constructed, Beechwood being preferable to the pond at the Common. Now-a-days the Curlers travel to Forfar, Perth, Pitlochry and on occasions to Kirkcaldy to take part in matches.

The present day membership is around thirty - women now are among the members - and each year the Club holds its General Meeting and supper in one of the local hotels. Unfortunately it no longer has any of the famous old stones to grace the table!

At the present time, during winters of very severe frost, 'Bonspiels' are held. In this area Stormont Loch is the usual venue for local clubs, although it is a number of years since the ice was thick enough for this.

When the railway line was built from Coupar Angus to Blairgowrie in the 19th century, a special 'Halt' at the loch-side, complete with platform, was constructed, solely for the use of the curling fraternity.

'Bonspiel' simply means - 'a game of curling' and is now synonymous with the outside game when curlers come together to play as they did in days gone by.

On the natural ice and in the crisp air the stones are heard to roar as they slide along the ice and this has led to the epithet 'The Roaring Game'.

*Footnote: Since the find of the ancient curling stones, Mrs Smeaton has searched every nook and cranny of the Town Hall and is satisfied there are no more mysteries awaiting discovery.*

*I wish to acknowledge the help and information supplied by Mr Alex Gatt.*

## CRICKET

The game of cricket in Scotland dates from 1715 when English Government Officers introduced it at the time of Jacobite unrest in the Highlands. The first match on record took place at Alloa in September, 1785 and the oldest Club in Scotland is thought to be Kelso which dates from 1821. Perthshire however holds the longest record for playing commencing in 1826.

The Scottish game of cricket differs from that of England, in that it is of amateur not professional status.

It is unclear just when Cricket was introduced to Coupar Angus but we do know that around the turn of the 20th Century, there were three teams here. They were rowed across the river at Boatlands and played on the flat area of land there while the spectators viewed the game from the slopes of Buttery bank. In 1910 the Club President was Mr S. Honeyman, Greenside; L.B. Mills, St Helen's Place was Captain, and D. Stewart, Calton Street was Secretary.

Sometime after this, play took place on 'Filshie's' field where the Abbey Road houses now stand. Mr George Dunn who was with the Club for 23 years, remembers that this field was always the first where skating took place in winter. Unlike football, no Coupar Angus cricketer ever 'set the heather on fire' in the cricketing world but there were several excellent players nevertheless who spent many years with the Club. Among them were K. McGregor, A. Hynd and W. Walker who also played for Perthshire. In the 1950's Mr Fred Aitken visited Coupar Angus and presented the Club with a cricket bat, used in an Australia/England Test Match, and which had the signatures of all the players inscribed on it. Fred Aitken was one of a large family born in the White House Hotel, who had left for Australia when he was still a lad.

The bat took pride of place on a wall of the Clubhouse for years until it was removed after a spate of vandalism and taken to a member's house for safe keeping. The present custodian of the bat is the Captain - Mr R. Edington.

The present club dates from 1946 when Larghan Victory Park was opened after World War II. In these days cricket enjoyed much support from the townspeople, and not just a few well known and highly respected persons were among its Sponsors. Perhaps the most supportive of these was Colonel Lindsay of Hallyburton who for many years until his death in 1981 was Vice-President and ardent supporter of the Club. In the Minutes of that period it is recorded that *"the death of generous Vice-President Col M. J. Lindsay was a great blow to the Club"*.

The Club has an impressive array of trophies:

- The BENZIES TROPHY
- The AITKEN TROPHY
- The JOHN D DONALSON TROPHY
- The BOWLING TROPHY
- The COL LINDSAY TROPHY
- The McDONALD CUNNINGHAM TROPHY
- Col. LINDSAY'S SPECIAL PRIZE BAT

As time passed the Club began to feel the pinch of financial pressures. No longer was the annual dinner dance and prize giving to be the only social occasion of the year, for fund raising events had to be organised as a matter of survival. The Patrons of the Club still gave their support and membership fees rose steadily over the years, but by the mid seventies difficulties were arising.

However in 1978 the Club Joined the Perthshire Cricket League and took part in league fixtures despite the occasional difficulty in raising a team when there was an away game with a 6.30p.m. start. Discussions at this period were on-going regarding the extension and improvement of the Club House although due to the absence of funding in the form of grants, this unfortunately was never carried out.

In 1978 David Pithie, a long time player and ardent supporter of cricket in the town, formed a Junior Team which played in the Strathmore League games.

*(Right) Col. Lindsay at Hallyburton presenting the cricket bat.*

Enquiries were undertaken at this time regarding the Deeds of Larghan Park and after much legal investigation these were found to be missing. In 1981 a further application was made to the Sports Council, the Playing Fields Association and Perth & Kinross District Council for funding for the erection of an extension to the Clubhouse which would provide a much needed kitchen, toilets and showers. The plans had to be abandoned once again as no money was forth coming. It is recorded that one gentleman seemed to be pleased with things as they were for he stated that *"the Club had one of the best Club-houses in the League"*. As mentioned earlier the Coupar Angus Cricket Club has always had many loyal members and supporters, one of these being Albert Croll who retired as Club Secretary in 1983 after serving as such for many years. 1984 was a black year financially for the Club which could no longer afford the services of a Groundsman, but here again loyal supporters stepped in to the breach in the form of Mr Pithie and Mr Robertson who took on the important and time consuming task.

In March 1986 a new artificial wicket was fitted by En-tout-cas but in the process a great amount of damage was done to the out-field. By now the Club was attracting the attention of vandals and help from the Police was sought to prevent damage being done to their new wicket. In appreciation of the many years of service to the Club, G. V. Drought, K. D. Pithie and J. J. Anton were offered Hon. Life Membership.

As the 1980's drew to a close the Club found themselves once more in serious financial difficulties and a 'Race Night' and a 'Sponsored Snooker Marathon' were two of the proposals put forward in an attempt to raise much needed funds. Due to a gradual falling off of younger players there was no Junior league side. However as the 1990's progressed all was not doom and gloom. Coupar Angus Recreation Association was formed with the intention of raising money from various sources to build a Club House at Larghan Park for the use of all the sporting bodies in the town. This has not yet been accomplished but the intention is still there and funding is being actively sought.

At the dawn of the twentyfirst century, the Coupar Angus Cricket Club is in a much healthier financial situation than it has been for many years and the chances of this historic sport surviving in the town is looking good.

## THE QUOITING CLUB

When asked if I knew about the 'Kiting Club' in Coupar Angus I immediately conjured up a picture in my mind of groups of individuals out in the open air holding the strings of kites which were swirling and swooping in the breeze. This romantic scene was soon banished when I realised that it was a different kind of kite - 'quoit' to be exact, but pronounced as kites in Coupar Angus at any rate.

There is not a lot of information available on the game of 'Quoiting' except that it was popular throughout Scotland as early as the 18th century. Whether it existed in Coupar Angus then is a matter for speculation but we do know that it was a very popular pastime here in the late 19th and early 20th centuries.

An ex-Coupar Angus lady, Mrs Flora Whyte from Luton has written to say that she has in her possession her grand-father's medal which has round the edge:

*"Won by James Johnston 1890*
*FOUR Times in Succession"*
and in the centre:
*Presidents Medal*
*Coupar-Angus Quoiting Club 1888*

The inscription is surrounded by a Laurel Leaf and on the reverse side are two men, one ready to throw a quoit and the other holding one.

We know that in 1906 the Quoits Courts were at the end of Precinct Street but the exact location is unclear. Shortly after 1906 however they moved to what was called the Railway Field at the end of Candlehouse Lane, near the bridge, close to where the Relief Road is now. The area where the Courts were is covered now in rough grass and weeds.

The four Courts in Candlehouse Lane resembled a large pit with a spike in the middle of each court. The area round the spike was covered with clay which was taken from the burn and the player had to throw the quoit and anchor it over the spike.

From the Coupar Angus Quoiting Club Log Book dated 1923 to 1939 which is in the safe custody of Perth Museum, some interesting information has been gleaned.

The Quoiting season lasted from late April until early October much the same as that of tennis and cricket. The Club held their General Meetings in the Strathmore Hotel *(White House)* and in

*(Right) The boys of the Coupar Angus Quoiting Club:*
*(Back row) Bert Donaldson; Will Burrie; ? ; Charlie Baxter;*
*(Front row) Colin Whytock; John Sutherland; Davie Gray; D. Sutherland; John Smeaton; R. Hynd;*
*(Kneeling) Mike Robb:*

1923 they had one hundred and seven members. They also had a hut beside the courts where they kept their equipment and sometimes held informal meetings there to decide certain matters such as whether competitions would be on a 'knockout' or 'points' system. The knockout system mostly won and the decision taken that the Club Championship Bowl and a Pair of Quoits would go to the Winner, and that the Runner-Up would be awarded ten shillings (50p).

The Following is the 1923 League Match Table

```
        LEAGUE MATCHES
   FAIR CITY   88    COUPAR   83
   STANLEY     69    COUPAR   98
   RATTRAY     68    COUPAR   94
   RATTRAY     62    COUPAR  100
   FAIR CITY   65    COUPAR   87
   ARDLER      50    COUPAR  100
           WON 5 LOST 1
        2 MATCHES NOT PLAYED
```

In the Handicap Competition James Davidson was First; J. Stewart was Second; Andrew Bowden and G. Johnston were third equal, and in the Doubles Competition J. Davidson and D. Hardie came First with J. Smeaton and J. Sutherland Second.

For the Rose Bowl and Pair of Quoits, First was J. Stewart and Second J. Davidson while D. McLaren and W. Hampton received Consolation Prizes of 10/6 and 5/- respectively.

The President's Cup was won by J. Stewart and D. McLaren won a Badge. J. Simpson who was third, was presented with a Razor of the cut-throat variety. There were quite a number of prizes donated by members and supporters and all were played for.

At the presentation of prizes in the Strathmore Hotel, mention was made that J. Davidson had been undefeated in all the Club Matches.

*(Right) Provost Davidson bowling the first jack of the season.*

The Office Bearers at this time were:

| | |
|---|---|
| PRESIDENT | F. W. DUBBER |
| VICE | J. DURNIN |
| CAPTAIN | G. JOHNSTON |
| VICE | A. McDOUGAL |
| SECRETARY | D. HARDIE |
| TREASURER | J. DAVIDSON |

COMMITTEE - W. Borrie; Andrew Donaldson; A. Boath; A. Young; R. Bruce; A. Bowden; D. Soutar.
LEAGUE DELEGATES - Andrew Donaldson; Andrew Bowden and D. Hardie.

There was also a Dance Committee so from that we can assume that this could have been an annual social event for no mention is made of fund raising.

The last entry in the Log Book is dated April 1939 when the office bearers were:

| | |
|---|---|
| PRESIDENT | T. M. ROSS |
| VICE | A. DOUGAL |
| CAPTAIN | J. SMEATON |
| VICE | R. HYND |
| SECRETARY | C. BAXTER |
| TREASURER | D. SHEPHERD |

The Rose Bowl and 15/- was won that year by W. Sutherland; the Unionist Cup was won by T. Duff and the Coupar Angus Club were the winners of the Dundee District League for the fourth year in succession.

Also written in the Minute is *"no money with cup for 1938-39"*.

One of the last entries states *"Bank Book handed over to D. Shepherd with £10.14.7. in it"*.

There is no mention of the Club discontinuing or being disbanded for the War years but Mr J. Smeaton's son who lives in Princes Croft was able to tell me that during the War someone broke into the Club shed and threw all the quoits into the burn. Mr Smeaton was able to recover his but others were not so fortunate. The loss of the quoits may have been one reason the Club did not reform after the War, but the game seems to have lost appeal and as far as can be determined, quoiting is no longer carried out in Scotland although in England the game has survived

Mr Smeaton has in his possession the Forfarshire Cup which was presented by Peter McRae of Ferry Road, Dundee. Apparently the Coupar Angus Club decided to enter and try their luck, on the understanding that if they did not win outright, they would not enter again. Such was their skill that they won it in 1935; 1936; 1937; 1938 and 1939.

It would seem that in quoiting circles they were indeed a force to be reckoned with. Despite their success the Club did not start up again and their hut gradually fell into such disrepair that it was burned to the ground.

At the back of the Log Book the following lines were written with no explanation.

NO MORE DO YOU SEE THESE HILLS BEHIND US
NOR THE ONES YOU LOVED DEARLY AND LEFT BEHIND
BUT MANY TIMES THEIR HEARTS ARE SIGHING
FOR HUSBAND AND FATHER WHO WAS ALWAYS SO KIND

I wonder who wrote those sad lines and why? Did one of the Quoiters lose his life in World War II? Can anyone remember?

# THE BOWLING CLUB

Although we know that bowling is a very ancient sport, the date it originated is not known. However, the oldest bowling green on record is in England, and dates from the end of the 13th century. Bowling had become very popular by the 16th century and it has been well recorded that in 1588 Sir Francis Drake refused to go out and challenge the Spanish Armada, until he had finished his game of bowls.

The 'Rules of the Game' were not drawn up however until 1849 and it was not until 1905 that the 'International Bowling Board' was founded. Sixty one years later in 1966 clubs in the United Kingdom began to take part in 'World Championships'.

The decision to form a club in Coupar Angus was taken on 18th November 1867 at a meeting in 'Smeiton's Inn', now the Athole, when Mr John Paterson of Garlochbank was appointed Chairman.

A piece of ground at Beechgrove *(now Campbell Street)* was obtained from Mr Thoms for an annual rent of £3.3/-. The cost of making a Green was £20 and on 5th July 1868 it was officially opened with a match between the Club Chairman, John Paterson and John Loutet, who was then a teacher at the Free Church School and who later became the headmaster of the newly built Burgh School. The first inter-club match on 14th July 1868 was played at Coupar Angus against Blairgowrie Bowling Club which resulted in Strathmore winning by 32 shots.

After a few seasons the Club decided to extend the Green, but unfortunately Mr Thoms had strong objections to the necessary foundation of metals and ashes being laid. As agreement could not be reached, the Club decided to look elsewhere for a site, and a piece of land measuring 50 yards x 45 yards, suitable for this purpose was bought for 2/3d per pole for a period of 99 years, from the Very Reverend Dean Torry of Foxhall. The cost of laying the new Green was £350, which was a considerable sum at that time, so the Club decided to hold a three day Bazaar to raise funds. The response to this was overwhelming and £598 10s 6d was realised. After paying all the expenses for the construction of the Green and Clubhouse, the members were left with a balance of £31 1s 1d. The new Green was opened on the first Thursday of June 1882.

In 1895 an unfortunate dispute arose regarding the payment of rates, and the Club decided they had no alternative but to take the now Proprietrix to Court. Fortunately for the Club, the Sheriff decided in their favour. The local lawyer Mr Watson, who had handled the case, gave his services free of charge.

By 1903 the Green was in such poor state that a Mr Wilson from Glasgow was called in to do a survey. The estimate to put matters right was £332 so once again a Bazaar was decided upon as the best way to raise the money. This was held in July 1905 and raised the sum of £564 11s. 2d. and after all expenses for the new green had been paid, the Club was left with a healthy balance of £116 5s. 5d.

1907 was a very special year for the Club when they won the Barclay Cup. The triumphant players were welcomed back to Coupar Angus first of all by a party on bicycles, at the foot of Tullybaccart. At Baldinnie, a party of Bowlers and the local Pipe Band were waiting to greet them and escort them into town. At Queen Street, the carriage was halted, the horses taken from their shafts and replaced by club members and then drawn by them to the Clubhouse where a celebration took place.

In 1907 the Club joined the Perth, Forfar and Fife Bowling Association and in 1908 the Scottish Bowling Association. Their first International Honour was secured in 1913 when R.K. MacIntyre was first capped for Scotland at Cardiff then again in 1919 and 1923.

The Strathmore League was formed in 1920 and up until 1975 'The League' had been won by the Coupar Angus Club a total of twelve times.

The centenary of the Club was celebrated by a match against the Scottish Bowling Association in 1967.

In 1971 a recreation room and bar were built where members could meet together for social evenings. By 1975 this venture

*(Top) An early view of the club house.*
*(Left) (L to R) Provost W. T. Dunbar, 1928-1931 and Provost D. C. Steen 1931-1934 on the green with old friends.*

had been so successful that the old Clubhouse was demolished and the bar extended to make a completely new Clubhouse with large windows overlooking the Green. There was also enough space for indoor Carpet Bowls.

In 1974 it was decided at a Special Meeting of the Club to demolish the original wooden clubhouse and build a new Locker room, a kitchen and a shed for the greenkeeper's machinery. The extension was completed the following year at a cost of £13,000. Improvements continued when a new automated sprinkler system was installed in 1976 which meant the green could be watered, as and when required, at the push of a button.

In 1984 the Club after due consideration, purchased just over two acres of adjacent land from the then Major General Wimberley and the following year a car park equipped with floodlights, was constructed at the south east end of the new ground, which gave the Club parking spaces for 40 to 50 cars and an area for buses should it be necessary.

In 1987 it was felt that further extension to the Club premises was needed, and after much discussion and several special meetings, a loan of £16,000 was arranged from Tennent Caledonian Brewers as part funding for the project. The original proposal had been to relocate the locker/games room, but after much deliberation it was decided that the new extension should provide a function room, bar and kitchen. The work was completed by the end of the 1991 season and the 1992 A.G.M. was held in the new function suite.

The Club has always prided itself on being progressive, so it came as no surprise when at a special meeting in 1997 it was decided to alter the Constitution and Rules to allow men and women to be equal members within the Club. These amendments were sent to the Clerk of Courts who also approved the changes.

The Club looks forward confidently to the twenty-first century having gone from strength to strength from its humble beginnings in 1867.

*(Right) The Tennis Club with guests from Blairgowrie - c1940.*

## TENNIS IN COUPAR ANGUS

Racket sports go back in time to 12th century France. It took another 800 years to reach Coupar Angus.

In the 16th century, Mary Queen of Scots played a form of tennis at Falkland Palace where the court still remains, and her son, King James VI of Scotland I of England, was a keen tennis player. Modern tennis in Britain however, dates from the 1860's. Rules of a game which was called 'Sphairastrike' *(sphaira is Greek for ball)*, played on an hourglass shaped court, were drawn up by Major Wingfield in 1873. Several versions of this game became popular then the 'All England Croquet Club' at Wimbledon decided to draw up their own rules, and in 1877 the first Wimbledon Championships were held with men's singles.

Until 1924 tennis was an Olympic sport then lapsed for 64 years before returning to the Games in 1988.

The Coupar Angus Tennis Club was formed in the 1920's on part of Foxhall where the Bowling Club car park is now. The playing season was from early May to mid-September and over the years the club had many distinguished players.

When World War II commenced, the courts were requisitioned by the government who planned to hold Prisoners of War. As the courts were securely fenced in and close to the railway station, it was thought to be an ideal place to process them before sending them on to the various Prisoner of War Camps.

The courts were never used for this purpose, but during the long war years had seriously deteriorated due to neglect. When the War ended compensation was paid, which was nowhere near the cost of restoration so a programme of fund-raising events was embarked upon.

After due consideration it was decided that the former 'Blaze' courts should be replaced with the all weather 'En Tout Cas' type, for despite their very high cost, it was generally accepted that they were the very best available, and would suit the needs of the club.

All seemed to be proceeding smoothly and the men arrived to carry out the work. A local resident of Coupar Angus for many years who was the father of one of the Tennis Club Committee Members took a keen interest in the work as it progressed. He noticed there was not much supervision from the Company during construction and that quite often a few of the men in the squad were "scoffing" off probably for a pint in the local pub! One local man had a very good knowledge of drainage work and dared to suggest to the squad that he thought they were not going deep enough to eradicate all the vegetation which had been free to grow on and under the courts during the war years.

Unfortunately his fears proved to be only too correct. All was well for about three seasons and members of the Club and other Clubs who came to play inter-club matches were thrilled with the new type of surface, which of course required no watering and no maintenance. Then the trouble began. Water began to show on the surface after rain. One heavy shower was enough. The drainage had failed.

An inter-club match would be arranged for 6.30 p.m. and if it rained at 5.00 p.m. *(which it often did)* players had no alternative but to get the brushes out to sweep the water off the courts or cancel the match. The matches were all part of the Strathmore League and it was important for each Club in the League to win as many matches as possible. The condition of the courts was now affecting all play. Members began to be totally disenchanted with the situation and it did not help to encourage new members.

Despite all the difficulties the male section of the Club had an excellent team and they qualified for the Midlands League and eventually were in the top Division.

We were all very proud of our boys and the following were all in the original team:

   Norrie Currie    Sandy Currie
   Douglas Hume    Donald Brown
   Fred Stewart    Willie Lyburn
           Charlie Porteous

The girls did not manage to attain the same standard but worked hard raising funds to keep the Club going. They also did quite well in the Strathmore League. The Tennis Club had always felt the membership was not as large as it could have been. The reason for this was that it was felt by many in the town, that 'tennis' was a game for 'snobs'. Despite great effort by members to show that this was not the case, the feeling prevailed. Even a splendid fund-raising Fashion Show in the Town Hall could not entice some of the townspeople to support what they called the 'snobby clubs' show.

To remain viable the Club needed an income of £100 per annum which was not always easy to achieve, one reason being some members simply 'forgot' to pay their dues. General Wimberley of Foxhall was very supportive of the efforts of the Club to keep going, and charged only a nominal £1 a year as rent. The Club survived until the late 1960's when they suffered a spate of vandalism which spelled the end for them. Until this time, this type of wanton destruction had never been a problem in the town,

*(Right) The first team to play at Foxhall Park in 1935 - R. Cathcart, W. Law, H. Coutts, R. Bell, J. Nixon, W. Doig, J. Low, R. Baird, J. Brown, J. Cromb, and B. Clark.*

but when the fine porcelain sinks of the 1920's were mindlessly smashed, the club, which had worked so hard and had given so much pleasure to many of the town's sports-persons, had no alternative but to call it a day.

The last trophy match was played in 1968 and shortly after that the club folded.

As time passes, many townspeople have come to realise just what a loss the tennis courts were to the town.

Some years ago the Coupar Angus Recreation Association was formed with the sole purpose of raising money to improve all the sporting facilities in the town. Although it often proves to be a thankless task, they hold regular fund-raising events and have made application to the various sporting bodies for grants. It is not generally recognised that filling in forms is a slow, complicated and time consuming business which demands expertise. Many deprived areas do not get lottery grants due to the fact that no one is willing to fill in the highly complex application forms. It is to be hoped that C.A.R.A.'s time and effort will eventually pay off. This public spirited body of men and women deserve the support of the public and should be highly commended for their efforts. Included in their plans are new tennis courts for Coupar Angus. Former members of Coupar Angus Tennis Club would be so happy to see Tennis Courts once again in Coupar Angus. They feel it is very sad to think that thirty years have passed since the young people in the town have had the opportunity to take part in such a healthy and enjoyable sport and they wish the hard working members of C.A.R.A. every success in their tremendous effort to carry out their plans which include new Tennis Courts.

*I wish to acknowledge the help and valuable information from Mrs Jean Coogan who now resides in Woodside.*

## FOOTBALL

Association Football or 'Fitba' as it is called in Scotland, is run by several associations of which the Scottish Football Association (S.F.A.) at Park Gardens, Glasgow *(founded in 1873)*, is the most important. Over seventy Clubs are affiliated to the S.F.A.

The Scottish Football League runs all competitions for the thirty eight Senior Teams while Junior Football for professional and amateur adults is administered by the Scottish Junior Football Association.

In 1972 a Scottish Womens Football Club was founded.

The game has its roots in Roman times. In the 15th and 16th centuries it was banned by Royal edict as it was thought to interfere too much with the all important 'archery practice'.

At the time of the Industrial Revolution when large numbers of the population settled in the cities, football became increasingly popular as a spectator entertainment.

After World War I there was an upsurge of interest and huge crowds attended matches. In some areas of the country now-a-days, football matches are not as well attended as formerly but big Clubs still attract a large following and millions now view important games on T.V.

Although there are few records regarding the early teams in Coupar Angus it is almost certain that the game was played here in the 19th century. In 1906 there were four teams:

**The Rob Roy**
President - Col Clark of Princeland.
Captain - F. Donnely, Causewayend
Secy and Treasurer - W. McKenzie, Campbell Street

**The Second Rob Roy**
Captain - David Scott, George Street
Secy and Treasurer - W. McKenzie, Campbell Street

**The Thistle**
President - G. W. Strain
Captain - John Guild, Gray Street

**The Volunteer**
President - Lieut Boyd
Captain - Sergt D. Adam
Secy and Treasurer - Drummer William Forbes, Causewayend

These four teams all played on the Common, so it must have taken a bit of organising ability to fit them all in. The Volunteers were originally known as the Volunteer Rifles which was to all intent and purpose the 'Home Guard' of the time.

Matches were played on New Year's Day and in 1921 the Strathmore Football League was won by the 'Coupar Angus Comrades'. There was also a a team called 'Mr Clark's Selects' whose President was no doubt Mr Clark of Princeland, and another was called the 'Coupar Angus Rovers'

Strange to relate in the middle of the 1920's the popularity of football in Coupar Angus waned dramatically and the town was left without even one team.

Because of this, hockey became very popular and many young men joined the hockey club which for a time was very successful.

When Foxhall Park was opened in 1935 football was once again to the fore to the detriment of hockey. The very first game played there was against St Johnstone with the score 10-1 St Johnstone Jimmy Brown (*centre front in pic on previous page*) scored the Coupar Angus goal and the rest of the team were:

**R. Cathcart, W. Law, H. Coutts, R. Bell, J. Nixon, W. Doig, J. Low, R. Baird, J. Cromb and B. Clark**

The glorious 1938/39 season saw the Coupar Angus Juniors win the Perthshire, the Currie, the P.A., and Constitutional Cups and the Angus League Shield.

In the team were - Tom Wann, Goalkeeper, from Stanley - Willie Cheape Left Back who signed for

(Back Row - L to R) *R. Gray, treasurer; D. Clark, assistant trainer; W. Cheape; T. Wann; D. Forber; G. Forbes; G. Gray;*
(Middle) *G. Bannerman; W. Gray; A. Forbes; H. Gow; J. Smeaton (trainer); R. Bell; T. Gray; E. Childs;*
(Front) *R. Clark; F. Brown; W. Hurrell; J. McWalter; Drum Forbes; K. Moncrieff; B. Clark; J. McVey and J. Baird, (secretary)*
(Trophies L to R) *Constitutional Cup; Currie Cup; Angus League Shield; Perthshire Cup; P.A. Cup*
(Inset) *J. Campbell*

Falkirk and Tommy Gray who later became well-known as a Dundee F. C. player

When Larghan Victory Park was completed around 1950, some of the teams played there. By 1965 the teams were:

Juniors - Amateurs - Juveniles - School - Smedley's

That year the 'Juniors' played Celtic at Perth in the League Cup

Coupar Angus Juniors 1961 team won four trophies when they played in the Angus Junior League

Harry Rodger was the President; Sandy Dow, Vice President; John Donaldson, Treasurer; Albert Croll, Hon Secretary; and other officials were Sandy Robertson; Jock Harrison; and Len Simpson. The team were very fortunate to have as their trainer Ian Campbell who lived in Ardler. Ian was a qualified Coach who after his spell with the Juniors, went on to coach with Dundee United at Tannadice Park.

The members of this successful Coupar Angus team were:-

**DOUGLAS COPELAND; IAN SHAW; JIMMY STEWART; ARCHIE GRANT; GORDON LAING; TOMMY SIMPSON; HARRY SCOTT; BRIAN BONTHRONE; HAMISH WATT; MALCOLM BELL; ACKIE SMITH and LEN DUDMAN**

Gordon Laing and Len Dudman were good all-round sportsmen who also played cricket for Perthshire and Scotland.

1961 was a good season for Coupar Angus with the team having a good run in the Scottish Junior Cup. When Broxburn Athletic visited Foxhall Park, there was a crowd of almost 4000 spectators. The visitors won 6 - 1 but Coupar Angus learned a lot from the experience of playing against such a prestigious team.

The Juniors were fortunate in that they were always able to get good goalkeepers. One of these, GEORGE NIVEN, joined Glasgow Rangers from Coupar Angus in 1947 and became first choice keeper for the Ibrox Club in 1952.

page 120

The friendly match between Coupar Angus and Rangers at Foxhall Park after George's transfer, not unexpectedly saw Rangers win 5 - 1 The line-ups were:-

**COUPAR ANGUS**
STEWART; EMSLIE; MURRAY; SMITH; MATTHEW; SNEDDON; FINDLAY; REGAN; MENZIES; BROWN and DOIG.

**RANGERS**
NIVEN; LINDSAY; McKENZIE; McDONALD; STANNERS; LITTLE; FRAME; DUNLOP; McINTYRE; LITTERS and CASKIE.

Another Coupar Angus Goal Keeper DOUGLAS COPELAND joined St. Johnstone while SANDY KEAY went to Hibs, and MIKE WINEBERRY left for Forfar Athletic, IAN FIDDES distinguished himself by being capped several times for Junior Scotland.

A number of other players went on to join the senior ranks. Coupar Angus produced some footballers in the early days who became well-known. Among them were the Forbes's; the Gray's and the Brown stalwarts. There was also Bill Abernethy who played for Coupar Angus and Blairgowrie before he went on to play Senior Football with Arbroath at Gayfield. Possibly Bill will be better remembered however as the Tay Pearl Fisher who was featured in several television programmes. David Gray played for Rangers while his brother Tommy played with Morton, Dundee and Arbroath. Stuart played for Coupar Angus Juniors, Alyth and Blairgowrie. He was a great centre-half who was capped several times for Junior Scotland.

Local boy Alan Gilzean became a big name in the footballing world. He started off playing for the Coupar Angus School Team in big "tackety buits" then went on to play for the Coupar Angus Juniors before moving on to Dundee Violet, where he was spotted by a Scout from Dundee Football Club. His goal scoring ability was second to none and he was a great 'header' of the ball. He was capped several times for Scotland and was signed for Tottenham Hotspur where he played alongside Jimmy Greaves and many other well known stars of the football world in the seventies. When Alan had some free time he would turn out for Coupar Angus Cricket Club Team and on one famous occasion he brought the Dundee Football Club team out to Larghan Park.

When Alan signed for Dundee, later that season the Dundee Football Club Team visited Foxhall Park for a friendly game. Not surprisingly the game was won by the Senior Team in front of a very large number of spectators. The Juniors groundsman at that time was WILL McKENZIE and everyone concerned had the highest praise for the excellence of the playing surface.

Over the years Foxhall Park was held in high esteem and most of the Perthshire Junior and Amateur Cup Finals were played at Coupar Angus. In June, 1964 Provost John D. Davidson (*Jock*) presented Alan Gilzean with an Omega gold wrist watch at a ceremony in the Town Hall which the Provost declared as *"unique in the annals of the town"*. The watch was inscribed *"Presented by the citizens of Coupar Angus 1964"*.

**The idea for the presentation had been conceived after Alan had scored the only goal in the Scotland V England International at Hampden to give Scotland a hat trick of wins over what was then described as the *"auld enemy"*. Twenty five year old Alan scored 52 goals for Dundee that season which was a record then, and 3 for Scotland - one against England and two against Germany.**

*(Top) George Niven.*

These perhaps were the glorious years of football in the town, and since then no outstanding player has emerged, but we live in hope.

In the present difficult times, two teams have survived - the Amateurs and the Juniors, and they have faced up squarely to the problem of finance and have organised many on-going fund raising activities which are very well supported.

## HOCKEY

Games with a ball and hooked stick were played in ancient times, but 'hockey' originated in 19th century England.

The Hockey Association was founded in 1886 and drew up the game's first rules. In 1900 the International Hockey Board was founded, and in 1908 hockey became an Olympic Sport for men. Women players however had to wait until 1980 before they could take part in these.

Hockey in Coupar Angus, as far as can be determined, dates from around 1910 with a Men's team known as the East Perthshire Hockey Club. They played at the top of the Common on what was then called 'Princeland Park.

During World War I the team went into abeyance due to the lack of players, but started up again in 1919 at Foxhall Park where East of Scotland Farmers is now. In the local paper of the time it was reported that *"the team was now resuscitated"*.

Around 1924/25 football met with a set-back and Coupar Angus was left without a team. Because of this hockey got a boost in popularity and attracted many new players and supporters. Mr John Shepherd of Hill Garden, remembers that at this time, practically every schoolboy had a hockey stick which they took to school, and practiced at every possible opportunity - to and from school, in the playground, on the Common - everywhere and anywhere!
Not only did these youngsters play for the school team, when the occasion arose they also played for the Seniors. The East Perthshire Hockey Club had now grown in numbers to field two teams, the First and Second Eleven. The First Eleven played Universities such as Aberdeen, Glasgow, St.Andrews and Edinburgh and other distinguished hockey teams, while the Second Eleven won every match it played in the Midlands League.

The Men's team was a force to be reckoned with, and it had many enthusiastic and highly skilled players, several of whom played at International level.

Such was the prestige of the town's Hockey Club that the Scottish Hockey trials were held regularly in Coupar Angus.

Fund raising events took the form of the occasional Dance and Whist Drive which added to the social life of the town, and were eagerly looked forward to and supported by members and non-members alike.

In 1936/37 football was re-introduced to Coupar Angus which proved to be the death knell of hockey in the town when people transferred their allegiance back to it. As a result, the East Perthshire Hockey Club gradually disintegrated, and members left to play for other Clubs in the area.

*(Top left) Groundsman Mr Prain*
*(Back row L to R) B Lowe, J Robertson, N Paterson*
*(Front L to R) Jack Paterson (Sadler), Fred Howison, Willie Bruce (Drumkilbo), John Anderson (Coal Merchant)*

### THE LEAGUE OF HORSEMEN

This was a secret society of men who worked with horses, of whom there were many until the railway rendered them surplus to requirements.
The fee for membership to the league was said to have been a bottle of whisky, but so well kept were the secrets regarding the rituals, that very few details exist, for they swore never to divulge anything that took place at meetings.
One test before membership was that a sheet of paper was placed on top of a barrel and the man seeking membership was ordered to write on it. If he did, he was struck on the hand with a chain. If he firmly refused to write, he had passed the test and was admitted as a member of the society.

For many years Coupar Angus did not have a park apart from the Common which was and still is, used for all manner of activities. Earlier in the century, moves were made to try to obtain an area of land at Butterybank from Keithick Estate for this purpose, but they came to nothing.

# LARGHAN - Victory Park

At the end of World War II, plans were afoot to purchase land on the outskirts of town for Council House building.

Provost Davidson approached the owner of the land however and suggested that a much better use would be for it to be turned into a park. It was through Jock Davidson's intervention that Mrs Charlotte A. Ferguson, gave the town the 22 acres of land which we know as Larghan Victory Park and a much needed want was filled. The beautifully laid out park is a haven for all, but especially for mothers with small children who can play in its safe environment. At holiday times and at weekends, families come from far and wide to spend the day in its pleasant surroundings.

There is a very safe and up-to-date play area for children complete with paddling pool, and the putting green has remained very popular over the years with locals and visitors.

The cricket club plays here and small Caravan Club Rallies have been held on a regular basis over the years.

The well planned park has adequate parking facilities, toilets, and a refreshment kiosk.

The stone gate pillars at the entrance were the gift of the Horse Society of Coupar Angus.

The park has a number of beautifully laid out flower beds and it is often said that Larghan Park is the 'Jewel in the Crown' of Coupar Angus. Sadly the 'Crown' at present is rather tarnished but plans are in the pipeline to polish it up.

No account of Larghan Park would be complete without a mention of the late Frank Agger who lived close by and had been its unofficial guardian for many years.

Frank was a long serving member of the Town Council and in on the planning of the park at grass roots level. It, and the town of Coupar Angus, were very dear to him and his vigilance over the years has been a very great service to the town and its residents. If young people were found in acts of vandalism, Frank carefully pointed out to them the error of their ways by explaining who bears the costs of their thoughtless behaviour and the harm they were doing to the enjoyment of many people both old and young.

The townspeople owe a great debt of thanks to Mrs Charlotte A. Ferguson for the Park, and to Frank Agger for his years of unofficial custodianship of it.

*(Above) Autumn leaves gather in the empty paddling pool again.*

These were not games of great tradition started many years ago, but flourished in the 1950s in Foxhall Park. They attracted competitors from the professional circuit who found it a useful date on the calendar to add to their earnings and keep in training for the big name games in the autumn.

Ewan Cameron from Lochearnhead was a frequent competitor as well as the Scott brothers from Inchmurrin Island on Loch Lomond. The event was born out of the organisation which ran the horse show for which Coupar Angus was famous in its day.

The Common itself would be covered with horses being prepared for the ring when Bob Hally was the Secretary and chief mover of the Coupar Angus Horse Society. When the Games were running the Common acted as a car park which was well used with big turn-outs to watch the sport. Chieftain of the Games was always Frank Benzies MBE whose house at the head of the Common gave him full knowledge of all the preparations for the big day.

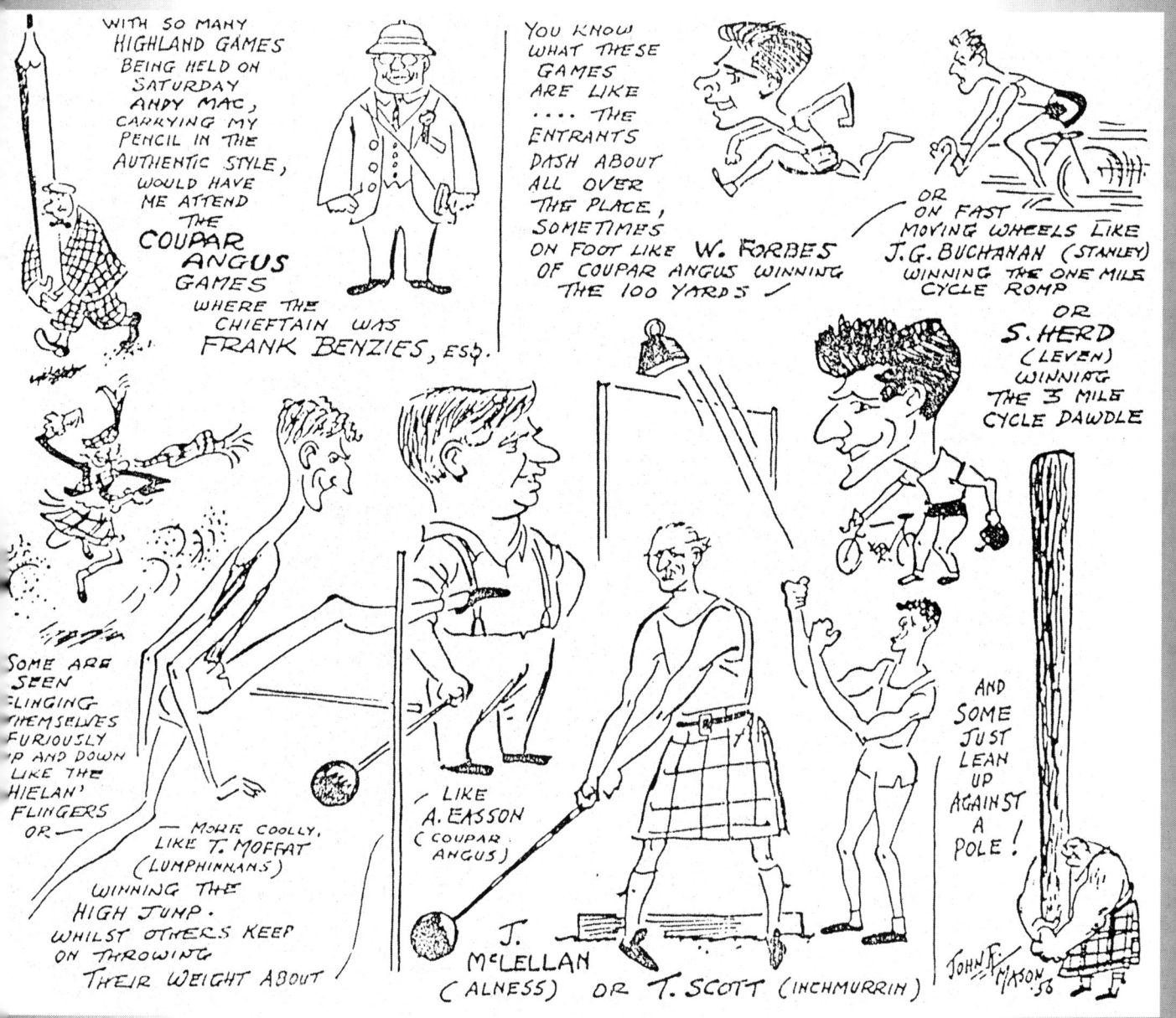

# COUPAR ANGUS - the annual highland games

The local track events were very popular and the highland dancing, heavy events and cycle racing were up to the standard of top circuit events.

*Reproduced by kind permission of P and K Museum & Art Gallery.*

The two World Wars of the 20th Century have been so well recorded that there is no need to include an account in this book.

# IN MEMORIUM - we shall remember them

It is important however that we remember the fine young men of Coupar Angus and District who died in the belief that their sacrifice would ensure that the world would be a better place for future generations. Would that the young people of today take time to reflect on this.

Coupar Angus differs from other towns and villages for there are two official War Memorials - the Memorial Gateway at the School for former pupils who died, and the other within the Parish or Abbey Church in memory of its members and adherents who also made the supreme sacrifice. Quite a number of the names on the School Memorial are also on the Abbey Church Memorial. One young man from Ardler and another from Burrelton have their names engraved on the Memorials there, as well as on the school memorial.

At the time of World War I, or the Great War as it was then known, there were five Churches in the town - the Parish Church; the South U F Church; the North U F Church (St Andrew's); the Congregational Church which stood where Church Street is now; and St Anne's Episcopal Church. At that time Roman Catholics travelled to worship in Blairgowrie.

The North and South Churches each had a Memorial to the members and adherents of these congregations who died in World War I, and both are now in the former North or St Andrew's Church which is now the Abbey Church Hall. When these Churches were closed the names were added to the Abbey Church Memorial. Although we know that several of the ex-pupils who died were Roman Catholics, there is no memorial in St Stephen's Church, Blairgowrie. St Anne's Episcopal Church has no memorial, but it is possible that no member of the congregation lost their life in the War.

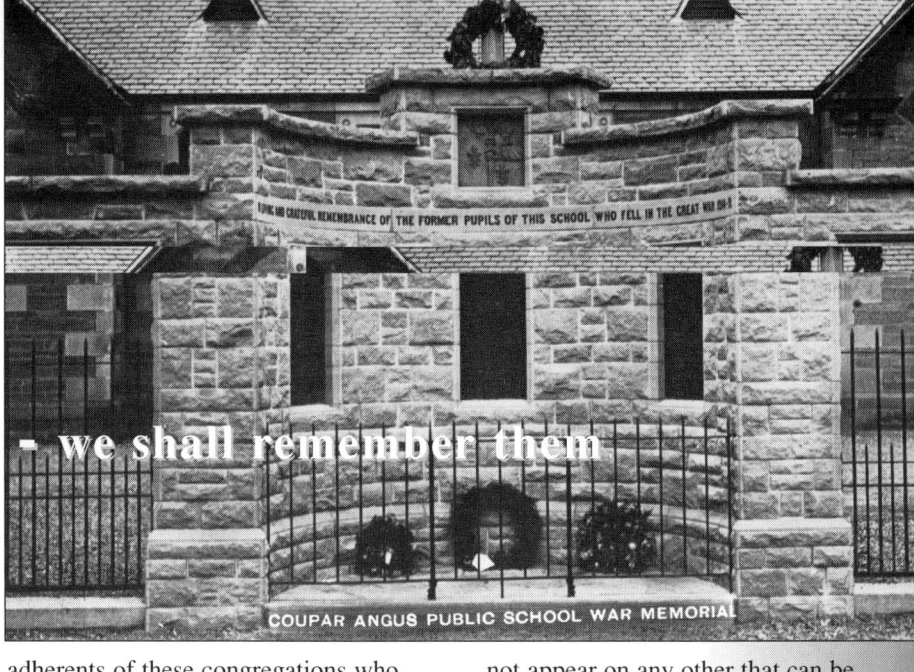

At a time when almost every home had a Church connection there are thirteen names on the School Memorial which do not appear on any other that can be traced. This poses the question - was there a Memorial in the Congregational Church and if so, where is it now?

The Congregational Church was demolished in the 1950's and no one can remember if there was a memorial, or what happened to the furnishings of the Church. Ardler Church was built by the Carmichael family of Arthurstone in Memory of their Dead Children and when it was sold by the Church of Scotland, the War Memorial was removed and became the unofficial responsibility of the then owner of the Manse. When the Manse was sold in the 1990s the Memorial was passed on. The present custodian however has arranged with the appropriate authorities to have it mounted on a plinth and erected close to the village War Memorial.

*(Top) Coupar Angus Public School War Memorial pre-World War II.*
*(Centre) Roll of Honour in the Coupar Angus Council Chambers.*

page 124

# THE SCHOOL MEMORIAL

**IN LOVING AND GRATEFUL REMEMBERANCE OF THE FORMER PUPILS OF THIS SCHOOL WHO FELL IN THE GREAT WAR**
**1914 - 1919**

*Large panel on the left of centre*     *Middle panel*     *Right hand panel*

| | | |
|---|---|---|
| AITKEN DAVID | DUNCAN JAMES YOUNG | LUNDIE KENNETH D |
| AITKEN HARRY | DUTHIE DAVID OGILVIE | MACFARLANE ROBERT |
| ALEXANDER JAMES | EDWARD JAMES | MACLAREN JAMES |
| ANDERSON SIDNEY | EWING GEORGE | MACINTYRE WILLIAM |
| BATCHELOR PETER | FERGUSON GORDON SCOTT | MACPHERSON WILLIAM |
| BAXTER CHARLES | FERGUSON JOHN ROY | MACRITCHIE JAMES |
| BAXTER JOHN | FERGUSON STEWART | PETERS CRAWFORD |
| BAXTER ROBERT | FINLAY DAVID | PETRIE JAMES |
| BLACK JOHN | FORBES JAMES | RICHARDSON ARTHUR DAVID |
| BRADLEY GEORGE F | FORSYTH ALASTAIR | ROBERTSON DOUGLAS |
| BRODIE WILLIAM | FORSYTH FRANK | RODGERS ALEXANDER |
| CLARK GEORGE | GALLOWAY ALEXANDER | ROSS EDWARD |
| CLARK JAMES | GALLOWAY WILLIAM | ROUGH JAMES |
| COCHRANE WILLIAM S | GIBB WILLIAM | SANGSTER HERBERT |
| COWNIE JOHN | GLENDAY WILLIAM | SAUNDERS CHARLES |
| CRAIG ALEXANDER | GOWRIE JOHN | SAUNDERS EDWARD |
| CRAIG WILLIAM | GOWRIE THOMAS | SIMPSON GEORGE |
| CRICHTON JAMES | GRAY GEORGE | SOUTAR WILLIAM |
| CROZIER WESLEY | HENDERSON JOHN BEATTIE | STEWART ALFRED E |
| DAIR PETER | JOHNSTON J A KIRKHAM | TAYLOR WILLIAM D |
| DONALDSON JAMES | LAING PATRICK J S | WATSON HOWARD |
| DOW ADAM | LAING ROBERT | WILLIAMSON FRED R |
| REID CHARLES | LOWSON WILLIAM H | |

**AND OF THOSE WHO FELL IN THE SECOND WORLD WAR**
**1939 - 45**

*Second panel on left of centre*     *Small panel right of centre*

| | |
|---|---|
| AUCHTERLONIE WILLIAM J | FORBES DRUMMOND |
| BAIRD WILLIAM B | HUNTER WILLIAM C |
| BISSETT DAVID | MACFARLANE LOUIS A |
| BRUCE HENRY M | MCRITCHIE FRED |
| CHRISTIE PETER | MORTALI ALFRED |
| DARGIE JOHN | SHEPHERD GEORGE |
| DICKSON ALEXANDER | STEWART CHARLES |
| DICKSON ALLEN | WHYTE JOHN |
| DONALDSON JOHN | WOOD GEORGE A S L |
| DUNCAN PETER F | |
| FORBES DOUGLAS | YOUNG JOHN H |
| | YOUNG WILLIAM J |
| | WHITE WILLIAM B |

*(Top) Two left medals relate to the Boer War, the remaining two for World War 1.*

# THE MEMORIAL AT THE ABBEY CHURCH

**1914 - 1918 WAR**

| | | |
|---|---|---|
| AITKEN | Pte HARRY | Somerset Light Infantry |
| AITKEN | Boatsn DAVID | HMS Ajana |
| ANDERSON | Dr JAMES | Royal Field Artillery |
| ANDERSON | Pty SIDNEY | Scots Guards |
| BAXTER | Sapper JOHN | Royal Engineers |
| BAXTER | L/Cl ROBERT M | Black Watch |
| BLACK | Pte JOHN | Black Watch |
| BRADLEY | Pte GEORGE F | Australian Imperial Forces |
| CRAIG | Gnr ALEXANDER | Royal Field Artillery |
| CRAIG | Pte WILLIAM | Black Watch |
| CRIGHTON | L/Cl JAMES | 11th Manchesters |
| CROZIER | L/Cl WESLEY | London M D Infantry |
| DAIR | L/Cl PETER R | Black Watch |
| DONALDSON | Pte JAMES | Black Watch |
| DUNCAN | JAMES YOUNG | Royal Engineers |
| DUTHIE | Lt DAVID C | RAF |
| FERGUSON | Tpr GORDON S | Scottish Horse |
| FINLAY | L/Cl DAVID | 1/7th Black Watch |
| FORBES | JAMES | 6th Black Watch |
| FORSYTHE | Lt ALISTER | New Zealand Infantry |
| GALLOWAY | ALEXANDER | Royal Fusiliers |
| GIBB | Sergt WILLIAM | 6th Black Watch |
| GLENDAY | Pte WILLIAM | Gordon Highlanders |
| GOWRIE | Pte JOHN | 6th Black Watch |
| GOWRIE | Pte THOMAS | Royal Scots |
| HILL | Sergt ROBERT H | London Scottish |
| JOHNSTON | L/Cl J A KIRKHAM | 4th Black Watch |
| JOHNSTON | Dr JOHN | Royal Field Artillery |
| LAWSON | Pte PATRICK DAVID | Black Watch |
| LOWSON | CL WILLIAM H | Canadian Forces |
| MacFARLANE | Pte ROBERT | Royal Scots |
| MITCHELL | Pte HUGH | Black Watch |
| MITCHELL | Pte ALEXANDER | Black Watch |
| PETRIE | Pte JAMES | Black Watch |
| SAUNDERS | Pte CHARLES | South African Scottish |
| LAING | 2/Lt PATRICK J S | Canadian Contingent |
| McKENZIE | Pte DUNCAN | Cameron Highlanders |
| McLAREN | Pte JOHN | Royal Scots |
| PATON | Pte DAVID | Black Watch |
| PURVES | CL WILLIAM JAMES | Motor M G Section |
| RICHARDSON | Pte ARTHUR D | Black Watch |
| STEWART | Pte ALFRED E | Black Watch |
| TAYLOR | Gnr WILLIAM D | Royal Garrison Artillery |
| WATSON | Lt HOWARD | RAF |
| ROBERTSON | Pte ALEXANDER | Australian Imperial Forces |
| ROBERTSON | Pte E MURRAY | Leicestershire Regt. |
| ROSS | Bombrd EDWARD J | Royal Garrison Artillery |
| ROUGH | Pte JAMES | Seaforth Highlanders |
| SANGSTER | Pte HERBERT | Royal Scots |
| SAUNDERS | Sergt EDWARD | Rifle Brigade |
| SHEPHERD | Pte ANDREW | Scottish Rifles |
| SIMPSON | Pte GEORGE | Australian Imperial Forces |
| SOUTAR | Sapper William R | Royal Engineers |
| EDWARD | Driver JAMES T | R E Artillery |

**1939 - 1945 WAR**

| | | |
|---|---|---|
| AUCHTERLONIE | Pte WILLLIAM J | 1st Cameron Highlanders |
| BAIRD | L/Cl WILLIAM B | Black Watch |
| BISSETT | Gnr DAVID | Royal Artillery |
| BRUCE | Sgt Pilot HENRY M | RAF |
| CHRISTIE | Pte PETER | Argyll & Sutherland Highlanders |
| DICKSON | Sgt A/G ALLAN | RAF |
| DICKSON | LAC ALEXANDER | RAF |
| DUNCAN | Pte PETER F | 4/5th Black Watch |
| DONALDSON | L/Cl JOHN | No 2 Troup Commandos |
| FORBES | CL DOUGLAS | Royal Armoured Corps |
| FORBES | L/Cl DRUMMOND | 2nd Gordon Highlanders |
| HUNTER | Pte WILLIAM C | RASC |
| MARNOCH | Sgt JONATHAN J G | RAF |
| McNAB | Dr JAMES | RASC |
| MacFARLANE | Lt LOUIS A | RNR |
| SHEPHERD | WO GEORGE | RAF |
| STEWART | Pte CHARLES | Black Watch |
| TAYLOR | Stoker WILLIAM | Royal Navy |
| WOOD | L/Cl GEORGE | RMP |
| YOUNG | L/Sgt JOHN H | RECCE Corps |
| YOUNG | Pte Thomas | RP Corps |
| YOUNG | P/O WILLIAM J | RAF |

> All the names of those who died in World War I and II are recorded on the Scottish War Memorial in Edinburgh Castle.
> P/O William J. Young's name is also on the memorial at Runnymead on the Thames, recording the names of RAF personnel who were lost without trace.

# THE MEMORIAL AT THE SOUTH CHURCH

TO THE GLORY OF GOD AND IN MEMORY OF THE YOUNG MEN OF THIS CHURCH
WHO GAVE THEIR LIVES IN THE GREAT WAR 1914-1918

| | | |
|---|---|---|
| SOUTER | Sapper WILLIAM R | Royal Engineers |
| EDWARD | Driver JAMES T | RFA |

**THEIR NAMES LIVETH FOREVER**

# THE MEMORIAL AT ST ANDREWS CHURCH

TO THE GLORY OF GOD AND IN HONOURED MEMORY OF THE MEMBERS AND ADHERENTS
OF THIS CONGREGATION WHO FELL IN THE GREAT WAR 1914-1918

| | | |
|---|---|---|
| BAXTER | L Cpl ROBERT McDONALD | 6th Black Watch |
| DAIR | L Cpl PETER ROBERT | 2nd Black Watch |
| DUTHIE | Lieut DAVID OGILVIE | RAF |
| FERGUSON | Trooper GORDON SCOTT | 1st Scottish Horse |
| FORSYTHE | Lieut ALISTER ELDER | New Zealand Infantry |
| LOWSON | Cpl WILLIAM HOY | Canadian Forces |
| MITCHELL | Pte HUGH | 2nd Black Watch |
| PETRIE | Pte JAMES | 6th Black Watch |
| SAUNDERS | Pte CHARLES | S A Scottish |
| STEWART | Pte ALFRED ERNEST | 9th Black Watch |
| TAYLOR | Gunner WILLIAM DALRYMPLE` | Royal Garrison Artillery |
| WATSON | Lieut HOWARD | RAF |

All these names were transferred to the memorial in the Abbey Church.

# THE ANGLO BOER WAR

## 1898 - 1901

The Boer* War which now-a-days could be described as Britain's 'Vietnam' for victory of a sort, was only achieved after much suffering and great loss of life on both sides.

The war began when a handful of Boer farmers who were impeding the spread of the British Empire in Africa, declared war on the Imperialists.

The Boers *(now called Afrikaaners)* wore no uniforms, were excellent marksmen and fought a Guerrilla type of warfare of hit-and-run tactics, mostly after taking the British troops completely by surprise. Possibly the war would have continued even longer had not General Lord Kitchener assumed command. He was looked on in Britain as a hero of the British Empire, but he was a man devoid of compassion for human suffering and he extended the war to include the civilian population when he introduced a scorched earth policy by burning farm houses to the ground, destroying crops and livestock, and taking prisoner all Boer women, children and old men. It was Lord Kitchener who devised the first ever 'Concentration Camps' and there the civilian population was kept living in tents which were quite inadequate for they gave little shelter from the extremes of the African climate - the searing heat by day and the bitter cold of night. To his, and Britain's everlasting shame, over 26,000 women and children died in these camps from starvation and disease.

Blacks also were herded up and placed in Concentration Camps lest they aid the Boers, and were given practically nothing to eat as Kitchener thought they could live off the land. Over 30,000 of them also died.

The British troops also experienced great hardship, for they arrived in Africa totally unprepared and ill equipped for the harsh Southern African continent. Their uniforms were quite unsuitable as they had been designed for the immensely different Northern European climate. Foot soldiers had to slog very long distances over difficult and alien terrain in heavy clothing. As the war progressed, certain modifications were made to the uniforms - larger brims on caps and shorter gaiters but they made slight difference. The Boers were superb horsemen, and in order to match them in skirmishes, Lord Kitchener had horses sent out from Britain. In the Southern African winter on the Highveldt it never rains, and the grass is severely burned by frost. As Kitchener had not thought about ordering feedstuff for them, many of the poor beasts died of thirst and starvation.

The very high death rate among the British troops at the battle of Magersfontein, twelve miles south of Kimberley, where the two young Coupar Angus men lost their lives, was due to several factors. Firstly the flat open terrain had prevented close reconnaissance being carried out, but despite this the Highland Brigade, who were weary and wet through having marched all night in pouring rain, were ordered to advance. As the two leading companies of the Black Watch were making their way forward, furious Boer fire opened up from an unsuspected trench at the foot of the hill. Many of the Scots who had never been in action before, tried fruitlessly to charge while others among them tried to flee. The entire Brigade was pinned down on the open veldt, and to make matters even worse, their mess tins on the back of their belts shone in the sun, and made perfect targets for the Boer marksmen.

When the British artillery did eventually come into action, the density of the Boer fire was reduced somewhat, but the damage was done and many of the Highland Brigade lay dead or severely wounded.

*Boer - Afrikaans word for 'farmer'.
(Top) Col Baden Powell at the relief of Mafeking.

> In earlier times, the Ogilvie family had strong links with Coupar Angus. On 6 November 1900 at Diamond Hill, near Pretoria, Lt. Col. David William Stanley Ogilvie, ninth earl of Airlie, was killed while in command of the 12th Lancers.
>
> At his own request, he was buried where he fell. A very fine memorial to his memory was erected by public subscription near to Alyth Square. Memorials to the fallen in the Boer War are few.

## YOUNG MEN OF COUPAR ANGUS WHO SERVED IN THE BOER WAR - 1898 - 1901

Pte G. Aitken . . . . . . . . .Gordon Highlanders
Gr J. Bannerman . . . . . .Royal Field Artillery
Tpr G. Bannerman . . . .Scottish Horse
Tpr T. Bannerman . . . . .Scottish Horse
Sh Smith A. Beattie . . . .Scottish Horse
L/Cprl. J.F. Bryson . . .Black Watch
Tpr J. Davidson . . . . . .Scottish Horse
Pte W. Erskine . . . . . . .Black Watch
Tpr F. Ferguson . . . . . .Diamond Fields Horse
Sh Smith G. Fleming . .Scottish Horse
Pte T. Geekie . . . . . . . .Scots Guards
Pte W. Gilchrist . . . . . .9th Queens Royal Lancers
Pte J. Glen . . . . . . . . . .Highland Light Infantry
Tpr D. Gow . . . . . . . . .Scottish Horse
Pte T.F. Gowrie . . . . . .Black Watch    Killed 11.12.1899 at Magersfontein
Pte A. Honeyman . . . .20th Co. Highland Horse
Sapr J. Irvine . . . . . . . .Royal Engineers Died on 18.3.1902 at Woodstock
Pte T. Lawson . . . . . . .Black Watch
Corpl W. Lowson . . . . .Royal Scots
Pte J. McIntosh . . . . . .Black Watch
Sapr J. McLagan . . . . .Royal Engineers
Pte A. McPherson . . . .Black Watch
Pte J. Morris . . . . . . . .Black Watch    Killed on 11.12.1899 at Magersfontein
Pte D. Myles . . . . . . . .Black Watch
Qmr Sgt J. Myers . . . . .Scottish Horse
Pte C.G. Playfair . . . . .Highland Horse
Corpl H.L. Playfair . . .Highland Horse
Tp. W.S. Playfair . . . . .Strathcona's Horse
L.Cpl J.M. Reid . . . . . .Scottish Horse
Pte C. Rodger . . . . . . .Black Watch
Pte J.G. Scott Highland Horse
Pte A. Smith . . . . . . . .Black Watch
Tpr D.L. Stewart . . . . .South African Constabulary
Gr D. Sutherland . . . . .R.A. Mounted Rifles

Men from the villages of Ardler, Burrelton and Woodside, which are close to Coupar Angus, and who served in the War, have been included:

**BURRELTON**
Sergt W. Baxter . . . . . .Royal Scots - Died on 5.11.1900 at Telspruit
Sapr J. McFarlane . . .Royal Engineers
Tpr W. McKay . . . . . .Scottish Horse
Pte W. Thomson . . . . .Queens Own Cameron Highlanders

**ARDLER**
Corpl A. Mitchell . . . . .Gordon Highlanders

**WOODSIDE**
Bombdr J. Amos . . . . .Royal Garrison Artillery
Sadd Corpl C. Purgavie  Royal Field Artillery

*Although not recorded, it is strongly felt that Stuart Geekie of Abbotsville was an officer in the RASC in the Boer War.*

*(Top) South African post card of the times entitled "Bad News".*
*(Above) This elegant obelisk of granite preserves the memory of three Alyth men who gave their lives in the service of their Queen and country in the Boer War. They were David, 9th Earl of Airlie, Lt-Col Lancers, killed at Diamond Hill near Pretoria, Nigel Neis Ramsay, 2nd Lt Black Watch, killed at Magersfontein, and Charles James Wedderburn Ogilvy, trooper in the 20th Company Imperial Yeomanry who died on the way to South Africa.*

# BIG TAM - A LOCAL HERO

**Major General Douglas Wimberley** moved to Foxhall, Coupar Angus in 1954 when he retired from being Principal of University College, Dundee - now Dundee University. He had no previous contact with the area, having been born in Inverness and spent his childhood there and in India, but Mrs Wimberley's father came from Achaladar, near Blairgowrie. He joined the Army in 1914 at the start of the First World War, at the age of 18, in the Queen's Own Cameron Highlanders, the regiment in which his grandfather had served in the Crimean War and the Indian Mutiny. He went to France in 1915 taking part in the battles of Loos and the Somme.

From 1916 to 1918 he was a Company Commander in the 51st Highland Division machine gun battalion which was commanded by Colonel Steven Hardie who for many years lived at Ballathie House near Meikleour. With the Highland Division he fought in the battles of Ypres and Cambrai being wounded during a big German attack in 1918 by a bullet in the leg while firing a Vickers machine gun, and being awarded the Military Cross.

After the First World War he saw active service in North Russia, Southern Ireland and the North West Frontier of India.

At the start of the Second World War in 1939 he was commanding officer of the 1st Battalion of the Cameron Highlanders, being sent to France a few days after war was declared. In 1940 he became a Brigadier and in 1941 he was promoted Major General. He became the commander of the reformed 51st Highland Division, the original Division having been captured by the Germans at St Valery after the bulk of the British Expeditionary Force had been evacuated at Dunkirk.

The reformed Highland Division was sent to North Africa in 1942 to join the 8th Army under the command of General Montgomery. They fought their first battle at El Alamein, the main Infantry fighting being carried out by the Highlanders, the Australians and the New Zealanders. Alamein was the first major battle in the war that the British defeated the Germans and St Valery was well and truly revenged. General Wimberley was blown up in his jeep during this battle, his driver and his radio operator being killed beside him. At the end of all this action he was awarded the Distinguished Service Order. For the next 6 months the 8th Army, with the Highland Division in the lead for much of the time, drove the Germans back across North Africa, with major battles at Tripoli, Mareth and Wadi Akareit, finally defeating them in Tunisia when General Wimberley was made a Commander of the Order of the Bath.

During the fighting in North Africa the Highland Division suffered 5300 men killed, wounded or missing which gives an indication of the amount of fighting they had done.

General Montgomery, with the 8th Army and the Highland Division, then invaded Sicily driving the Germans back to Italy after two months hard fighting, with the Highlanders suffering a further 1400 casualties. After Sicily the Highland Division was brought back to England to take part in the Invasion of Europe, most of them involved with the D-Day landings.

General Wimberley had then left them to become the Commandant of the Army Staff College and then the Director of Infantry. He retired from the Army soon after the end of the War to take up the University post in Dundee having earned a total of 14 medals during his 32 years service. He was Honourary Colonel of the Queen's Own Cameron Highlanders from 1951 to 1961 when the Camerons had to amalgamate with the Seaforth Highlanders to form the new regiment of the Queens Own Highlanders.

General Wimberley, who died at Foxhall in 1983 was followed into the Army, and his old Regiment, by his son and by his grandson who is at present - 2000 - serving with the 51st Highland Volunteer Battalion of the Territorial Army in Perth.

Just like the rest of the country, the people of Coupar Angus came together in groups to socialise and form little communities, all of which developed the character of the town. These are not presented in any particular order of status.

# GROUP ACTIVITIES - our upright citizens.

## FREEMASONRY AND THE COUPAR ANGUS LODGE

Freemasonry has its roots in the ancient Guilds of the working masons who built fine buildings such as castles, churches, bridges etc. In the middle of the 18th century in England, the degree of Master Mason was introduced and shortly afterwards was adopted in Scotland.

Masonry however is much older than the 18th century as the following list taken from 'The Hiram Key' by Christopher Knight and Robert Lomas, shows:

### PRE - 1710 MASONIC LODGES IN SCOTLAND WITH THE DATE OF THE FIRST RECORDED MENTION:

| | | |
|---|---|---|
| 1599 | 9 Jan. | Aitchison's Haven |
| 1599 | 31 July | Edinburgh |
| 1599 | 27 Nov. | St Andrews |
| 1599 | 28 Dec. | Kilwinning |
| 1599 | 28 Dec. | Stirling |
| 1599 | 28 Dec. | Haddington |
| 1600 | | Dunfermline |
| 1613 | 31 Dec. | Glasgow |
| 1627 | | Dundee |
| 1654 | 2 March | Linlithgow |
| 1658 | 24 Dec. | Scone |
| 1670 | | Perth |
| 1670 | | Aberdeen |
| 1674 | 28 Dec. | Melrose |
| 1677 | 20 Dec. | Cannongate Kilwinning |
| 1678 | 27 Dec. | Inverness |
| 1687 | 20 May | Dumfries |
| 1688 | 29 May | Leith and Cannongate |
| 1691 | | Kirkcudbright |
| 1695 | 25 March | Hamilton |
| 1695 | April | Dunblane |
| 1701 | 2 June | Kelso |
| 1702 | 22 Dec. | Haughfoot |
| 1703 | | Banff |

Among the early Grand Masters of Scottish Freemasonry were:
1740 - Thomas, 8th Earl of Strathmore:
1744 - James, 8th Earl of Moray.

In the 17th century wealthy and educated men started joining the various Lodges and became known as 'Free' or 'Speculative' masons to distinguish them from the 'Operative' masons who worked at the trade. The Lodges were glad to have them for they brought prestige and wealth, which was essential in times of depression, if they were to carry out their charitable work among elderly and sick Masons. The conditions of membership are quite clear and those wishing to become Scottish Free Masons must be of high moral character, respected members of the community and law abiding citizens. Religion and politics must never be discussed within the Lodge.

In Scotland there are 32 Provincial Grand Lodges but Scottish Lodges are found in many countries worldwide - Africa; the Caribbean; South America; Western Australia; India; New Zealand; Singapore; Malaysia; Hong Kong and Japan.

The present day Masonic Lodge is a 'B'

(Top) On parade - Coupar Angus Masons in full regalia.
(Photo courtesy of the P.A.)
(Above) The Masonic Lodge in Gray Street with its insignia above the door.

listed building in Gray Street, and is one of the oldest structures in the town as it dates from the early 18th century. Its origins however are unclear, for in old records it is described as the 'Gray Street Hall', and certainly over the years has not been the exclusive province of the town's Masons. Masonic Lodge No.105 as its number shows, is not among the earliest, and it started off as a 'Friendly Society'. A banner dated 1765 still survives, and was once carried in processions.

There is some evidence that in the early days the lodge met in Causewayend, most possibly in what is now the Red Cross Hall, which formerly was the Drill Hall of the Volunteer Rifles.

> **SCOTTISH LEGAL BURIAL SOCIETY**
>
> There was an active branch of this society in town, to provide fascilities for saving towards the inevitable burial costs.
> At the 1861 Annual General Meeting, which was held in the Masonic Hall, it was recorded that 60 men and some women were present.

In 1842 there were 50 Masons in the Coupar Angus Lodge and from an original photograph taken at "Laying the Foundation of the Coupar Angus New Public Buildings" *(Town Hall)* by the Most Noble The Marquis of Breadalbane Provincial Grand Master of Perthshire East" we see that there was a very strong Masonic presence. All were in full regalia, some bare-headed, others wearing silk top hats, and a few carried staffs. One can conclude from this photograph that the members included many of the affluent members of the community. In recent years the membership has dropped to around 80, but the aim of Masonry has not altered from its origins and charitable work continues to be carried out, although with the many benefits available through the Department of Social Security, the need is not so pressing as in earlier times.

## THE TOC H

The Toc H was formed first of all in England shortly after World War I. Its aim was to encourage people to meet together in Christian comradeship and to help fight the loneliness which was prevalent then, for very many people from all walks of life had lost loved ones in the 1914-18 War which was then believed to have been fought to end all Wars.

The original Head Quarters of the Society was Talbot House in Poperinge, Belgium, and the name Toc H was derived from the telegraph code for this which is now obsolete.

Since its inception in Coupar Angus, the Toc H has never lost sight of the original goal. Unfortunately it has fizzled out in many parts of the country, but not so in Coupar Angus for it goes on from strength to strength in the hands of a group of very dedicated members. Afternoon and evening meetings are held on a regular basis throughout the winter. Once a month an afternoon tea party takes place, with a variety of entertainment for the elderly of the community.

For many years, groups of local school children have regularly entertained members and guests in their meeting place in Trades Lane, which is affectionately known in Coupar Angus as 'the Loft'.

The Toc H in Coupar Angus has proved to be a welcoming place for countless numbers, for here the hand of friendship is always extended.

*(Top) A few kent faces at the Toc H*
*(Left) During World War II the Toc was a haven for the troops statione the town. They were often entertai by highland dancers.*

The world-wide Scout movement began when General Sir Robert Baden-Powell wrote a book "Aids to Scouting" which was intended as a guide for soldiers. As well as being of interest to the Army it was widely read by those who at that time, were responsible for training boys.

# SOME YOUTH ACTIVITIES

## SCOUTING IN COUPAR ANGUS

When Baden-Powell returned from serving in the Boer War he was urged by Sir William Smith the founder of the Boys Brigade, to re-write the book for boys. After giving this some thought B.P. as he would become affectionately called, decided to hold an experimental camp to test the appeal of his theories and in this, once again the Boys Brigade come into the story for they found a camp site for the experiment on Brownsea Island at Poole in Dorset. The B.B. also provided all the necessary equipment for the camp.

All this took place in 1907 and such was the success of the camp that it inspired B.P. to write the famous book "Scouting for Boys".

It had not been B.P.'s intention to form a new youth movement for he had hoped that 'scouting' would be a useful addition to the already existing youth movements, however all over Britain boys clamoured to become Scouts. It soon became very clear that they would have to be formed into a separate body for their numbers were expanding so rapidly that they could not be absorbed into the organisations which already existed - Boys Brigade and Young Mens Christian Association.

On 24th January, 1908 at a public meeting in the YMCA Hall in Birkenhead, the Boy Scout Movement was launched.

In September 1909 the first Scout Rally was held at Crystal Palace and 11,000 attended. By the end of the year the membership had risen to 100,000.

A troop of Scouts was first formed in the town in 1909 by six boys who got together to form a patrol of Scouts based on "Scouting for Boys" a publication which came out fortnightly. One of the original boys, James Crichton and his five pals held their meetings in a garden shed to the rear of a house in Causewayend, the whereabouts unknown. The boys apparently approached Sergeant-Major Toyer of the Scottish Horse, who was stationed in Coupar Angus and who lived in the house attached to the Armoury now occupied by the local detachment of the Red Cross, and asked him to become their Scout Leader, which was an understandable choice considering Toyer had served with Baden-Powell in the South African or Boer War. On 21st March 1909 the local Scouts took part in a display in honour of the visit to Perth of Lieutenant-General Sir Robert Stevenson Smyth Baden Powell, in the Roller Skating Rink, Dunkeld Road,

*(Top) Happy lads at a scout camp with a youthful Ronnie McDonald in their midst.*
*(Left) The 6th Perthshire Cub Scouts in 2001. (L to R)*
Back row: Derick McDonald (Scout Leader), Kim Smith, John Mitchell,, Stewart Sheed Snr, Andy Harrison, Martin Ellis, Brian Rodgers, Raymond Fair, James Henderson, Alan Paul, Craig Macall, Grant MacDonald.
Middle row: Lee McDonald, Andrews Stewart, Darren McDonald, Stewart Sheed Jnr, Jamie Paul, James Fleming, Shaun Smith, Lloyd Brow, Marc Macall, Andrew Henderson.
Front row: Kevin Gibbons, Paul Mchoul, Grant Stevens, Kyle Ellis, Tony Devine, Callum Hill, Callum Mitchell, Euan Mitchell, Wayne Harrison, James Powell, Jordan McDonald.

Perth. While B.P., as he was affectionately known, was inspecting the Coupar Angus Scouts, he poked Toyer in the stomach and said *"too fat Toyer, too fat"*! Toyer had obviously put on the pounds since serving with Baden Powell.

Soon after the Scouts were formed they received a blast of publicity when a boy named Alexander Macdonald aged thirteen of Hay Street, Coupar Angus, got in to a pearl fisher's boat which was moored at "Clarkie", one of the most dangerous parts then of the River Isla, and began to paddle it over the river, which was in semi-flood. At the deepest part of the river he got into difficulties and the boat capsized throwing him into the water. Local Scout, James Crichton was near at hand and rushed out into the flooded river and with great difficulty managed to pull the boy to safety with help when reaching shallower water, of local bystanders.

It was reported in the 15th June 1910 edition of the Perthshire Advertiser that "Crichton's plucky action was the subject of admiring discussion in the town all evening". But that was not the end of the matter for on 9th July 1910 James's gallantry was rewarded in a splendid ceremony on the North Inch in Perth, when he was presented with a parchment and medal by the Commissioner, Mr Herbert Pullar at a parade attended by very many local dignatories, Scouts and members of the public. A portrait was also painted of the local hero, by an un-named local artist, and it, as well as the parchment and medal are in the possession of Ron McDonald the recently retired, long serving Scout Leader. The ceremony received a considerable write-up in the Perthshire Advertiser of 13th July 1910. With such a glorious start, scouting in Coupar Angus could not fail to go from strength to strength, which it has done over the years. It has been exceptionally successful despite the fact that the boys had no official hut in which to hold their meetings until after World War II.

It was not uncommon in pre-Second World War Coupar Angus to find people who had in their lifetime never travelled further than Dundee, so when in 1921/22 several of the town's Scouts went to London with Scouter William Doig, to attend a Jamboree, it was a real red letter day. One of the early Scoutmasters was Jack Scott who has retained a life long interest in scouting and he remembers when the Scouts met in the old school gym. Later they moved to the Red Cross Hall which was known then as the Drill Hall. When this was no longer available, so keen were the youngsters that they met in the Haugh field beside the river Isla at Princeland Farm. This was not as simple a matter as it might appear to be for all the necessary equipment had to be carried there by the boys and their Scout Master of the time, Alan Blyth who sadly died in 1999. It is generally accepted that Alan Blyth with his enthusiasm and innovated ideas, made a great contribution to local scouting. Coupar Angus has been extraordinarily fortunate in its youth leaders for not only have several of them served for long periods of time, they have continued to take an interest in the movement long after their active involvement ceased.

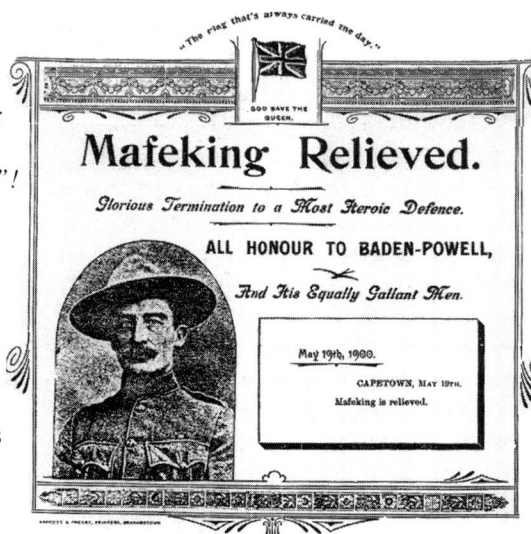

It is unclear what camps, if any, were held before 1937 when the first camp for some time took place at Lunan Bay. In 1942-43 Little Glenshee was the venue of a joint camp and Jack Scott remembers well an incident that took place there.

This was war-time and food was not too plentiful. The growing lads were feeling the pangs of hunger and pooled their resources and bought several loaves of plain bread which at that time cost around three old pence a loaf. They then approached the farmer who kindly let them help themselves freely of the cattle molasses which was stored in a large barrel. The next day all was well but the following day the boys paid the penalty of consuming too much of the treacle for there was a constant rush to the camp latrines.

In 1943 the camp site was at Kirkmichael then in 1944 it was located between Dollar and Crieff. In 1945 they went to the estate near Tannadice in Angus, of Jock Neish a famous name in the Scouting world, who dedicated his entire life to the Scout cause. To camp here was a highlight for the boys for a game of football could be followed by a dip in Jock's swimming pool, which were few and far between in these days. No one can remember if there was a camp in 1946 but in 1947 it was held at Aberfeldy. This camp was memorable for the weather was so bad the boys were completely washed out while trying to raise camp and ended up, thanks to the farmer, sleeping amongst the hay in the hay loft. Not even the rats could keep the weary boys awake for long. After a good night's sleep spirits were restored but the dampening experience would never be forgotten. It was in this year also that Ian McKay gained the ultimate award of 'King's Scout', which has never been attained before or since. *(In our present Queen's reign it would be 'Queen's Scout').*

In 1948 the camp was held at Rotmell, Dunkeld and was memorable for the antics *(which we will draw a veil over)* of one David Bruce better known to his friends as 'Brasso', at a camp-fire attended by several Dundee Guild members who were holidaying in a hut at nearby Dowally.

*(Top) Press cutting showing Col Baden Powell.*

From early days competing for the Perthshire 'County Shield' and 'Thumbstick' was a never to be forgotten event. The 'Thumbstick' consists of a weekend hike which must be well planned. A report also has to be submitted on the event. Jack Scott remembers that one eventful time when he, Ron McDonald and Alistair McKenzie set out en route to Glen Fernoch and over to Glen Tilt. Their first camp was planned for a flat sheltered area at the Falls of Tarf but before they reached there it started to snow. They were caught out on the moors in a blizzard but good training and common sense prevailed and they set up camp. The three spent the night huddled together for warmth in a small tent and in the morning when they opened the flap, the snow which completely covered the tent, fell in on them. They all agreed that good training had saved their lives on this occasion. The date by the way was June 1957. It is generally recognised that Alan Blyth was the one who changed the Scouts attitude to badge work which improved tremendously, but it has been and still is Out-Scouting in which the Coupar Angus Scouts excel.

The town has been extremely fortunate in its Scoutmasters, most of whom have stayed for long periods of time. In the Spring of 1999 Ronnie McDonald retired as Scoutmaster after a life-time in the movement for he has been keen on Scouting from a youngster. Even when he was called up and left home for his period of National Service after World War II, he still involved himself in the Scout Troop attached to the RAF base where he was stationed. On his return to Coupar Angus he became assistant Scoutmaster to Jack Scott.

In 1952 the first official Scout Hut was ready for occupancy by the boys. It was an ex-army hut which had been used during World War ll by Canadian troops at Blair Atholl. It was transported to Coupar Angus and erected on foundations built by local firm J. B. Stewart on the entrance track which had given access to the old curling pond, no longer in use. Since then additional protection of an outer brick wall has been added.

On Jack Scott's retirement in 1957 due to pressure of work, Ronnie assumed control.

During the 1960's and 1970's Scouting in the town became very popular and at one time, Ronnie was running two troops - his own and one in Blairgowrie until a Leader for it could be found. From 1971 to 1973 Ronnie held the post of District Commissioner for East Perthshire.

A very popular part of Scouting has always been the outdoor activities in which they take part, such as hiking trips which necessitate staying at Youth Hostels, and camping at home and abroad. Among the overseas destinations to which the local Scouts have travelled are - Belgium, Germany, Holland and the United States of America.

In the 1970's there was a Scout Pipe Band with Len Apedaile as their tutor. They achieved a high degree of excellence and were sought after to play at local events. For several years they piped in the New Year at the Cross but perhaps their highest achievement was when they were asked to play at a Hockey International at Muirton Park in Perth. The older boys formed a group of Venture Scouts under Len's leadership which for a time, was very popular. Unfortunately as so many youth movements catering for young adults have done, it fizzled out.

Our local Scouts play a very active part in the life of the community by always being ready and willing to assist at local events, be it a clean up of the Coupar Burn or being Jack of All Trades at locally held Game Fairs and Carriage Driving Competitions.

The parents of the local Scouts have played an important part in the welfare of the troop with their unfailing support over the years. The first Group Committee was formed on the 13th March 1949 at a meeting in the Victoria Hall to raise money for equipment and a much needed Scout hut. The Chairman was Major Wilson and members of the committee included:-

H. M. Gray (former Scouter); F. W. Doig (former Scouter); Mr MacDonald (parent); Mr Hume (parent); Mr T. S. Martin (parent); Mr A. S. Mackay (parent); Mr Robertson (Headmaster); and Mrs Coogan (Lady Cubmaster).

Among the suggested fund raising activities were - Sale of Work in Victoria Hall; Bus Tours on Saturday afternoons; Twenty Questions; and a Fancy Dress Football Match. A Treasure Hunt was deemed impracticable due to the petrol rationing.

Leaders of every Youth Movement in the town have always worked closely together, lending each other support and assistance where and when necessary.

Ronnie McDonald retired from Scouting in 1999 after over fifty years of service to scouting. There is no doubt at all that he will be much missed, but scouting in the town will still go from strength to strength with, no doubt, Ronnie keeping a watchful eye on its progress.

### SCOUT MASTERS

|  |  |
|---|---|
| 1909 - ? | Sergent Major Toyer |
| 1919 - 1922 | Rev J. Walker |
| 1922 - ? | Rev J. Walker & Rev Groundwater (joint Scout Masters) |
| 1934 - 1936 | No Scout Master |
| 1936 - 1937 | Wm C. Thomson, Troop Leader and Acting as Scout Master. |
| 1939 - 1940 | Patrol Leaders Harry Bruce & Ian Grewar "looking after the troop". |
| 1941 - 1943 | R. A. Murray, assisted by Murray Gray & R. S. Gray |
| 1943 - 1944 | F. W. Doig, assisted by Murray Gray, R. S. Gray, T. L. Brown & William Young |
| 1944 - 1945 | F. W. Doig, assisted by George Meldrum, T. L. Brown & R. S. Gray |
| 1946 - 1947 | F. W. Doig, assisted by George Meldrum & Chas Wilson |
| 1947 - 1948 | Charles Wilson |
| 1948 - 1951 | Alan Blyth |
| 1952 - 1953 | William Thomson assisted by Jack Scott |

### Lochnagar

In 1948 a character by the name of Davy Glen, who lived at Tealing, began, what was to become an annual event, a climb to view the sunrise from the summit of Lochnagar as a tribute to a friend who had been killed in the Second World War.

The climb took place on the nearest Saturday night to mid-summer and among the vast throng that took part on the first occasion were members of our

Group led by the Scout Leader Alan Blyth. The climb became an annual tradition in our Group and representatives from the Group have been at the summit on nearly every occasion since. The year 1997 due to very inclement weather conditions was the only year we missed out leading up to the 50th anniversary in 1998 when the climbing party from the Group accompanied by friends who had joined with them on the successful ascent *(no sun however)* were joined by Alan Blyth and had a celebratory breakfast at the Spittal of Glenshee Hotel before returning home.

*A debt of thanks is due to Linda McGregor, Jack Scott and Ron McDonald for their information.*

## THE BOYS' BRIGADE

The Boys' Brigade was formed by Sir William A. Smith in Glasgow in 1883 its purpose being "The advancement of Christ's Kingdom among Boys and the promotion *(encouragement)* of habits of Obedience, Reverence, Discipline, Self Respect and all that tends *(leads)* towards a true Christian Manliness". Their Motto is "Sure and Stedfast".

From Glasgow the movement quickly spread worldwide.

Every Company is free to work in its own way but most programmes include a Bible class and a weekly parade with emphasis on physical fitness.

We know from the booklet - "Coupar Angus - Historical and Ecclesiastical Associations - Strathmore Souvenir Sketch" by Rolland J. Miller and printed by John Leng & Co Ltd, Bank Street, Dundee in the early years of the 20th century, that the Boys' Brigade in Coupar Angus dates from the Rev Finlay Robert Macdonald's ministry (1881 - 1901) in the Parish Church, for he "instituted" a Company during his ministry. The Reverend Macdonald, who had been born in Canada of Scottish parents, was a man of great energy and enthusiasm, working tirelessly, not only for the members of his congregation, but for all the townspeople of Coupar Angus.

On his death the Boys' Brigade played a prominent part in his funeral and led the procession of pupils from the Burgh School, in what was recorded as being "in orderly line".

In the early days the Coupar Angus Boys' Brigade had its own pipe band which was founded with Mr Robert Dawson (the father of Jim Dawson) as Pipe Major. Mr John Robertson, a retired army Drum Major became drumming instructor. It was of such a high standard that the boys were frequently asked to supplement the town's pipe band. The Dawson family have had several generations of service in the Boys' Brigade in Coupar Angus.

Unfortunately details of the initial Boys' Brigade Company, which so far have come to hand, are rather sketchy. The present 1st Coupar Angus Company was founded in 1926 by the Rev J. E. Walker in what was then the North United Free Church.

It consists of three sections, each with its own leader and programme of activities - the Anchor Boys aged from 6 to 8 years; the Junior Section from 8 to 11 years; the Company Section for boys aged from 11 to 18 years of age.

The founding Officers in 1926 were - Mr C. M. Chalmers, Mr C. M. Taylor and Mr J. Cameron who had considerable experience in the Boys' Brigade in Glasgow.

In 1927 the Rev. Walker left the town and Mr C. M. Chalmers became Captain. At this time the Union of the North and the South United Free Churches took place, and the Coupar Angus Free Church was formed with Rev J. E. Adam as Minister.

*(Top) Jim Dawson looks on as Captain S Cowper presents Sergeant Clive Robb with the Queens Badge.*
*(Above) The last Provost of the Burgh, J. L. B. Apedaile, with Battalion President J Whittet, Secretary Janice Brown and Rev W Cochrane at the saluting platform.*

In 1929 further union saw the 1st Coupar Angus St.Andrews Company being formed. The Rev Adam was very Boys' Brigade orientated and under his and Mr Chalmer's Captaincy, flourished as an unattached company. In 1936 both the Rev Adams and Mr Chalmers left the district and the new Chaplain, the Rev F. Levison arrived. He was described as *"a bit of a whirlwind, breezing along at full speed ahead with robes flying out behind him"*.

World War II created many problems for Companies throughout the land, with halls being requisitioned by the Army and B.B. officers being called up. As a result of this the 1st Coupar Angus Company went into abeyance until 1946 when it was revived on the return from the forces of the Rev F. Levison.

Mr J. Tully took over as Captain with Mr J. Anton and Mr J. Dawson as his Lieutenants. Miss Murray became Leader in Charge of the Life Boys which had been formed during the Captaincy of Mr Chalmers.

In 1948 the Company became a Member Company of the Perth Battalion and is now one of the fourteen companies which makes up the Perth & Kinross Battalion.

*(Top) Mr Jim Dawson (right of centre) who as well as being a Captain in the Boys Brigade was a very active member of the Gardens and Allotments Association, for which this photograph was taken at a prize-giving session.*
*(Right) The Boys Brigade on a parade through the town.*

In 1948 St.Andrew's and the Abbey Church united and the Rev J. E. Logan became the Company's Chaplain.

In 1956 Mr Jim Dawson took over as Captain, a post he was to hold until 1972 when ill-health forced his retirement. Mr Dawson had served the Battalion as both Junior and Senior Vice-President and totalled over forty two years of service in the Boys' Brigade which is a quite outstanding achievement.

The Company has always been very active, and over the years has had many successes in Battalion competitions with particular emphasis on Bible Class; Physical Recreation and Football.

Battalion events which are held regularly include the following:

**Five-a-side Football - Chess-Badminton - Volleyball - Bible Quiz**

Badge Schemes include the following topics:

**First Aid, Fire and Crime Prevention, Wayfaring and Sports**

During the winter session the company compete monthly in many of these events at Bell's Sports Centre in Perth but the highlight of the year is the Battalion Sports which are held as the Grand Finale on Perth's North Inch. The Coupar Angus Officers have played an important part in the Battalion Council and Executive, with Janice Taylor *(nee Brown)* as a most efficient Battalion Secretary.

The Coupar Angus Company was presented with their Colours in 1971 by the Woman's Guild at a time when the Rev W. Cochrane was Chaplain.

In 1972 Mr J. Kidd took over as Captain and his experience as an Officer in the Dundee Battalion proved to be of great value.

The present Captain Mr R. Fraser was appointed in 1990 by the Session, when the Rev J. Drysdale was Chaplain. Captain Fraser's wife Moira, nee Dawson, is in charge of "the Anchor's Boy's" section.

As we enter the 21st century, the Company still actively pursues the Objectives of the Boys' Brigade, and are still taking part in all events at Battalion level, in all Sections and are as 'Sure and Stedfast' now as the Boys were when the Brigade was formed over a century ago.

## THE GIRL GUIDES AND BROWNIES

The Girl Guide movement is run along similar lines to that of the Boy Scouts. When Sir Robert Baden-Powell *(later Lord Baden-Powell)*, started the Scout movement in 1909, such was the interest shown by girls, that he asked his sister Agnes to work out a scheme for them along similar lines. So popular did the movement become that it spread from country to country and became a Worldwide Association.

In 1921 the first Guide Company was formed in Coupar Angus, which was followed by the introduction of 'Brownies' for younger girls. Their first meeting place was the Drill Hall *(now the Red Cross Hall)* in Causewayend.

From the very start Guides and Brownies proved to be very popular, and this over the years has never waned, despite so many modern day distractions.

The Coupar Angus Company's first Guider was Miss Bruce, a school-teacher in the town, and a member of a well known local family. She was joined by Miss Margaret Buist, whose record of over fifty years in Guiding is quite outstanding. Mrs Deuchar and Miss Bell ran the Brownie Pack.

In the early days, Miss Brodie Wood of Keithick was a staunch supporter. Many former Guides have fond memories of the games and other activities in which they took part in the grounds of Keithick House.

Sadly Miss Brodie Wood died in 1953 and was greatly missed. She had been District Commissioner from 1921-1946 and President of the Association from 1946-1952. As a memorial to her dedication and support to Guiding in Coupar Angus over many years, the Association presented "Colours" to the Coupar Angus guide company.

From the hall in Causewayend the Guides and Brownies moved to Calton Street, then in 1937 a Guide Hut was built in School Road and this is still their meeting place.

Uniforms for both Guides and Brownies have changed quite a bit over the years, but the aim of Guiding has not, and through work and play the girls are encouraged to be good and useful citizens, caring for their fellows. Guides still enjoy outdoor activities, and show great enthusiasm in cooking on an open fire, an essential requirement if their patrol is to gain their cooking pennant. Summer camps are still popular where the Guides enjoy a range of activities including abseiling, archery, wall-climbing and tie-dying.*

The two Brownie Packs in Coupar Angus are as popular now as in the days before television made so many traditional pastimes less attractive. Apart from the usual Brownie Badge Work, they find time for a variety of learning games and are very active fund raisers for the sick and less privileged in our society. In this sophisticated age they still wholeheartedly enjoy their parties at Hallowe'en and Christmas. They take part in Brownie Revels and are visited by experts in topics such as Animal Welfare and First Aid.

The Coupar Angus folk can be really proud of their Guides and Brownies but this has only been accomplished by the dedication of the leaders who selflessly give up their time week after week, month after month and year after year.

*A form of Batik.*

*(Top) A rather cold looking group of Guides with their colours outside the Abbey Church.*

---

62  The Stormont and Strathmore Annual for 1906.

### MISS C. R. SYMONS,
### GEORGE STREET,
### COUPAR ANGUS
### BABY LINEN AND ART NEEDLEWORK DEPOT.

Courteous and Prompt Attention always given to Business.

.. A SPECIAL FEATURE ..

Every endeavour made to procure, with the least delay, any desired Article not in Stock.

### J WILSON,
### BOOKSELLER AND STATIONER,
### COMMERCIAL STREET, COUPAR ANGUS

Fancy Goods, Pictorial Post Cards, and Artistic Stationery.

... CIRCULATING LIBRARY . .

In England public houses have for long been places where friends and families have met for a social drink and get-together. In many villages the "Pub" was the main meeting place - an attractive place where drinking to excess was hardly ever heard of.

# AN INTRODUCTION - to the evils of the demon drink.

Perhaps the reason for this was because by law, the beer could not be over a certain strength.

The family atmosphere in Scottish Pubs however, until after the second World War, was very different. They were regarded as the province of the male, and any female who dared to enter was looked on as a scarlet woman,

Nowadays, throughout Scotland, Pubs and Hotel bars generally have been given a face-lift in decor and atmosphere, and as a result have become friendly places frequented by men and women alike, serving both liquid refreshments and good quality food.

*The Stormont and Strathmore Annual for 1906.*

**STRATHMORE SUPPLY STORES**
**THE CROSS**
**COUPAR ANGUS.**
JAMES McNEILL, Proprietor.

GROCERIES AND PROVISIONS . . .
WINES, WHISKIES, and
MALT LIQUORS . . . . . . .
BISCUITS and CONFECTIONS . . .
PATENT MEDICINES . . . . . .
PROPRIETARY GOODS . . . . .
TOBACCOS, CIGARS, CIGARETTES.

**WHISKIES.**

We would direct special attention to the fine quality of our Standard Blends of Old Scotch Whisky. These Blends are justly celebrated for their age and uniformity of style and character; and they possess properties only to be found in thoroughly matured High-Class Medicinal Whiskies.

Prices 2/6, 2/8, and 3/- per bottle.
15/-, 16/-, and 17/- per gallon.

*"Tam lo'd him like a very brither - they had been fou for weeks thegither"* - from Tam O' Shanter

In the 18th Century, Coupar Angus stood on the north-south Military Road and because of this, licensing laws were relaxed. This led to an abundance of taverns and houses, some of which brewed their own ale. Whisky smuggling too was rife and a great deal of very unsocial drinking took place, especially among the poorer classes.

Many of the town's upright citizens were shocked at the plight of those families and throughout the country Temperance Societies were formed to bring home to the community the evils of the DEMON DRINK. To be poor in Victorian times was thought to be ones own fault. To be poor through an excess of drink was considered to be disgraceful and not a lot of sympathy, if any, was extended to the poor children who suffered pain and indignity through no fault of their own.

## THE GOOD TEMPLARS

The first Scottish Lodge of the Order of Good Templars was established in Glasgow in August 1869 in an attempt to combat the 'Demon Drink', for alcoholism then, and the misery and deprivation it caused, was a very great problem.

The following year in Coupar Angus, the Strathmore Lodge of the Independent Order of Good Templars was formed with forty members, most of whom were active Church people. It was reported at the time that:

*"their opening 'Soiree' was held in the Masons Hall with the Rev Robert Wallace in the Chair, and supported by members of the Lodge, dressed in the regalia of the order"*.

By April 1871 their membership had risen to over one hundred. By 1876 there were 1,171 Lodges throughout Scotland with a membership of nearly 84,000.

For many years the Good Templars were a force to be reckoned with as they spread their message of the evils of drink. Their campaigning paid off for they were successful in having the Licensing Laws changed and tightened up.

In 1922 Edwin Scrimgeour became Britain's first and only Prohibitionist Member of Parliament.

As the 1920's progressed, membership declined and had completely dwindled away by the end of World War 11.

In 1976 the Licensing (Scotland) Act swept away much of the legislation brought in as the result of pressure from the Templars and other Temperance Societies.

Now in the 21st century, further changes to existing legislation means that public houses may open on Sundays and, with certain provisions, licensed grocers also can sell alcohol.

---

A song my Grannie sang to me as a child, did not exaggerate the plight of many children of earlier times:-

A wee bit ragged bairnie,
 gaed wanderin' doon the street
Shiverin' in the cauld blast,
 wi' wee hackit feet

Blawin' on his handies,
 an' greetin' wi' the pain
There's nae a body lo'es him,
 'cause he's the drunkard's wain

---

*The Stormont and Strathmore Annual for 1906.*

### THE FAMED Old Scotch Whisky, ABBEY BLEND.

#### CERTIFICATE OF ANALYSIS.

ANALYTICAL LABORATORY,
11 & 12 GREAT TOWER ST., LONDON.

I hereby certify that I have submitted to very careful chemical analysis a sample of "The Famed Scotch Whisky" received from Mr James Dron, Coupar Angus, and find that it possesses great purity of composition, is thoroughly matured, and entirely free from all constituents of an injurious or undesirable character. It is soft and pleasing to the palate, possesses a fine aroma and bouquet, and I have every confidence in pronouncing it to be a perfectly sound and wholesome Whisky.

GRANVILLE H. SHARPE, F.C.S., Analyist,
Late Principal of the Liverpool College of Chemistry.

### JAMES DRON, George Street, Coupar Angus.

---

Published at 3s. 6d., for 1s. 6d.

### SCOTTISH REFORMATION and the COVENANTERS.

### INSCRIPTIONS

ON THE

### TOMBSTONES AND MONUMENTS

ERECTED IN MEMORY

OF THE

### COVENANTERS,

BY

### JAMES GIBSON,

*Editor of "Burns' Calendar," "Burns' Birthday Book," &c.*

Illustrated, foolscap 8vo, 292 pp., cloth, bevelled boards, gilt title.

"Every available source of information has been consulted which could throw light upon the names of the martyrs."—*Preface.*

### JOHN GRANT,
31 GEORGE IV. BRIDGE, EDINBURGH.

This is almost certainly the oldest hotel or hostelry in Coupar Angus for it dates from the early 18th century. It is a 'B' Listed Building and has an interesting cellar which may be an indication that it was built on the site or foundations of a much earlier structure, perhaps one dating from Abbey times.

# TAVERNS OF THE TIMES

## THE STRATHMORE HOTEL OR WHITE HOUSE

It is said that long ago it was called the White Horse Inn, but from an old map of the mid 19th century, it was called 'Howieson's Inn', whom we know were the owners at that time.

When Mr & Mrs Howieson retired in 1871 the name changed again, this time to the Strathmore Hotel. It was not the first Strathmore in Coupar Angus however for the 'Royal Hotel' until 1870 had been called the Strathmore Hotel.

The present Strathmore Hotel, or White House as it is more popularly called, is a handsome building with a quaint and unique porch of natural tree trunks bearing the weight of its roof, which could possibly be an early 19th century addition.

In the days before the railways the White House was a Coaching Inn, and some remnants of the stables can still be seen in the yard behind the hotel.

## THE ROYAL HOTEL

The hotel dates from the end of the 18th century when horse travel was the only mode of transport apart from Shanks pony. It was called the Defiance Inn after the stage-coach which passed through Coupar Angus on its way to Aberdeen.

When the railway arrived in town in the first half of the 19th century, the Defiance Coach was rendered redundant and the name of the hotel changed to the Strathmore Arms Hotel, but was known locally as the 'Strathmore'.

On 11th September 1844 Queen Victoria and Prince Albert stayed overnight in the then Defiance Inn, en-route from Balmoral Castle. In May 1861 it was reported in the local paper that the Strathmore Arms Hotel with Hall, Stabling and Shops, were sold by public auction to Mr William Simpson for £1100 which was little more that one seventh of its original cost. The paper went on to say:

*"Property in Coupar Angus has now arrived at its lowest level"*.

At this period Coupar Angus was undergoing a period of wealth for some, poverty for others. The factories had not yet been built and the hand-loom weaving industry was very depressed and the weavers suffering great hardship. The hotel was described as having been First Class at one time but had deteriorated. This was only a temporary phase however, for soon after it seems to have regained its previously excellent reputation.

In 1878 the name changed again, this time to the Royal Hotel. It has been believed locally that this took place after the Royal visit, but this is not the case. At this time the hotel was owned by representatives of George Gill - Miss Gill, Mrs Pringle and Mrs Rae, possibly his daughters, and the tenant was John Clark. The ground floor shops were rented to two Drapers, one Tailor and a Baker, the Loft to D. Brodie and the Stables to A. Stirton.

*(Top) The White House in Queen Street.*
*(Left) The Royal Hotel on the Cross.*

Angus, for the White House was called Howieson's Inn, and what is now the 'Vic', was the Hay Arms, after the owner there.

In the second half of the 19th century the Town Commissioners, the forerunners of the Town Council, and various other Clubs and Societies held their meetings in 'Smeiton's Inn'.

Although now-a-days the 'Athole' as it is called locally, is a modern and comfortable pub with a public bar, a lounge bar and a pool area, it still retains an old world charm and atmosphere befitting an ancient and historic building.

Until the Town Hall was built the hall of the Strathmore, then later the Royal Hotel, was in great demand for all manner of social gatherings, lectures and concerts.

As the 20th century progressed people no longer shopped exclusively in the town, so all but one of the shops on the ground level of the hotel were turned into a Public Bar.

Although this historic hotel has every modern amenity, it has retained many of its original features. Its seven bedrooms are well appointed and the function suite is in demand for weddings and other functions.

The former coaching yard is now the hotel car park.

## THE ATHOLE ARMS

It is unclear just how old the Athole Arms is, but in an antiquarian book "Ancient Things In Angus" there is record of a local historian seeing a stone engraved with the crest of the Earls of Errol with the motto "SERVA JVGVM", on the front of a local public house in Athol (now Athole) Street some years before 1840.

*(Top) The Athole Arms in Athole Street.*
*(Above) The Victoria Hotel in Gray Street.*

This would seem to indicate that the Athole Arms was built of Abbey stone and could possibly date from the late 18th century. The building was refaced a number of years ago, and if indeed the stone was built into the wall, it must have been rendered down and covered over for it can no longer be seen.
In the early days the Athole Arms was a Coaching Inn, and brewed its own ale until late into the 19th century.

Around 1860 it was known as 'Smeiton's Inn' after the owner then, and was described in the Valuation Roll as an "Inn and Brewery".

Calling hostelries after their owner seems to have been the fashion in Coupar

## THE VICTORIA INN

Known in Coupar Angus as the 'Vic', this public house is rumoured to have been the stable block for the Cumberland Barracks which stood opposite. As no recorded evidence has been found to confirm this however, it is impossible to prove or disprove this theory, but it certainly is a very old building standing on what was formerly the main route through the town.

From the Title Deeds we have learned that long ago a Police Station was housed in part of the building. The address of the first Police Station in the Valuation Role is Calton Street then a

## THE RED HOUSE

**T**he Red House Hotel was built in 1849 by Banker David Anderson, to meet the needs of an emerging. lucrative and rapidly expanding trade, catering for the needs of rail passengers.

Not unsurprisingly it was named the Railway Hotel, and was a solidly built but rather unpretentious building, then consisting of six bedrooms, a dining room and bar. For the duration of the railway in Coupar Angus, business was brisk, then on 4th September 1967 passenger services through the town were withdrawn by Dr Beeching, and the name was changed from the Railway to the Red House Hotel.

Despite the closure of the railway, the Red House still enjoyed a great deal of local trade, but by 1990 when the Bannerman family became the owners, it was in a very run down state. Immediately however, massive improvements commenced which saw the original hotel gutted, and the building extended to join up with the Nortel Leisure Centre which they had built in 1980 on the site of the former Lyburns Potato Store and previous to that, the Parish School.

In place of the rather cramped former hotel premises, there is now a spacious restaurant and bar with an attractive sun lounge, and a large and airy function room with first class facilities is situated to the rear of the premises.

For more than a decade the Leisure Centre had been a real boon to the sport orientated people of Coupar Angus, but as the nineties progressed, the Bannermans saw that needs were changing, and in 1997 part of this Complex was converted to first class hotel accommodation. The popular ground floor bar however was retained in its original form, and Pool, Squash, Sauna and Gym facilities are still available. A further hotel extension has been added for ten en-suite bedrooms, making a total of twenty in all.
The Red House has an attractive landscaped garden and a large car-parking area. On the completion of the Relief Road through the town, the Bannermans have had a very fine stone wall built by a local stone-mason, Jock Davidson, which not only adds a finishing touch to the improved and extended Red House Hotel, but compliments this area of the town.

little later, Hay Street, but most likely the two are one and the same and both wrong as the 'Vic' is in Gray Street. The explanation may be that those who did the survey were not natives of the town, and street names were neither clearly marked nor defined then.

The exterior, like that of the Athole Arms, has been resurfaced and painted over, but the Inn is very likely built of stone from the site of the former Cistercian Abbey.

The earliest available records show that around the middle of the 19th century, it belonged to a family called Hay, and was suitably named the 'Hay Arms'.

It may also have been a Coaching Inn for we also know from the Valuation Rolls of last century, that there were stables attached.

In 1875 James McLagan was the registered Innkeeper, and it was known as the 'Inn'. It was not until Queen Victoria's Jubilee in 1887 that it became the 'Victoria Inn'. At that time Mrs Brough was the Innkeeper and the owners were Ogilvy Brewers, Blairgowrie.

It is now a modern and comfortable public house with public bar, spacious lounge bar, and pool area occupying the ground floor. Upstairs is the Licensees' living accommodation

*(Top) The Red House, or Railway Hotel on the Forfar Road.*
*(Right) A more modern view of the Red House.*

# ENVERDALE COUNTRY HOUSE HOTEL

What is now Enverdale Country House Hotel was called Mount Pleasant* when built in 1875 by the father of David McFarlane, an Industrialist in the town, and first Provost of Coupar Angus. It remained in McFarlane ownership until 1894.

From 1895 until 1898 it belonged to James Logie an Insurance Agent, then in 1899 ownership changed to Charles Anderson, a Potato Merchant. In 1920 the house passed to Lindsay Anderson, described as a Merchant who before taking up residence, had lived at Greenside. When he became owner the name was changed to 'Enverdale House'. In 1928 the registered owner was Mrs E. B. Anderson which may be an indication that Lindsay Anderson had died.

The following year 1929 Mathew S. Walker, a retired gentleman, bought the house, then in 1940 the property was described as being owned by the 'Representatives of Mathew S. Walker' and the 'Tenant' was the War Department. For the duration of the war Enverdale was used by the War Department for the billeting of troops. In 1947 it was sold to Mr & Mrs James B. Mollison who ran it as a Guest House until 1968 when it was bought by the Bannerman family. At that time the house was surrounded by large gardens, lawns and an orchard. There was also a stable block which had survived from the days of horse drawn transport.

After several years of planning and alterations, Enverdale House Hotel opened in 1973 and was an instant and overwhelming success. It was quite outstanding in layout and decor, and far ahead of the others in the field of newly refurbished hotels at that time.

Gone were the stables, the lawns and the orchard and in their place was a function room with a sunken dance floor, and a purpose built kitchen planned to ensure that no matter how many were to be catered for, the service would be efficient and first class.

Much of the remaining garden ground was turned into a spacious carpark, but mature trees and shrubs were left in place to compliment what had been a very fine house, and which now was a first class hotel.

Six years on, the Bannermans moved to a new venture and Mr & Mrs Forbes, formerly of Tayside Hotel, Stanley, took over as mine hosts. In 1987 Mr & Mrs Martin Price became the owners.

In 1995 Mr & Mrs Robinson from Ireland bought the hotel and soon massive improvements and refurbishment was underway. The sunken dance floor so popular when installed, but which had proved to be a hazard for the accident prone, was replaced by a safer flush floor. The garden area was landscaped and there is now a delightful rose garden with comfortable seating, designed so that guests can relax over drinks or a light meal in pleasant and tranquil surroundings, when the weather is clement.

Enverdale Country House Hotel now has 'Three Crown' status and not only is it a popular venue for the people of Coupar Angus and district, it increasingly attracts visitors from many parts of the U K, Europe, and further afield.

* At present there is a house named Mount Pleasant close to Enverdale House which initially led to some confusion. Miss Johan Brodie however could remember when Enverdale House was known as Mount Pleasant.

(Top) Enverdale House in Precinct Street.
(Below) A more modern view of the Royal Hotel on the Cross.

# THEIR ROOTS WERE HERE

## THE MAYOR OF OTAGO

After the disastrous defeat at Culloden Moor which ended forever the hope of restoring a Catholic Monarch to the throne, many of the Highlanders who had supported Bonnie Prince Charlie left their homelands, and with their families made the slow and torturous journey to the lowlands and safety.

The route was fraught with difficulty and danger as they had to keep well away from the military roads, for if seen by the troops who patrolled them they would have suffered brutal death.

Many of these soldiers had been thieves and vagabonds before taking the Kings Shilling and had been ordered to show no mercy to the refugees be they old men, women or young children and babies. London government were determined to put to an end once and for all, Highland opposition to the Hanoverian King.

In many cases it took groups of Highlanders years of miserable toil to reach the comparative safety of lowland Scotland.

There was an ancient sanctuary at Dull in Perthshire, and many members of the Clan McLean reached its safety and settled there. For many years there was quite a large population of former Highlanders who had become weavers and small farmers. With the decline in the hand-loom weaving industry they would eventually disperse and make for the town and cities.

*Bill McIntosh*

Quite a number of the Clan McIntosh found their way to the Parish of Bendochy where they were given food and shelter on the farms in return for work, while others moved on to Eassie and Nevay on the border of Perthshire and Angus.

As time passed and the political situation became more stable, some of them moved on in the hope of finding better work and conditions. Quite a number of former Highlanders emigrated to Canada, Australia and New Zealand in the hope of a better future for themselves and their children.

The Newspapers of the mid 19th century carried advertisements inviting people to come to a brighter future in the Colonies. One young man who decided to take up this invitation and set sail for Otago in New Zealand, was the ancestor of Bill McIntosh. Bill, until he retired recently, was a successful and prosperous sheep farmer who has been involved in local government for over twenty years. It is interesting to note that local government in New Zealand is non-political and people vote for whom they think is the best man for the job. He has been the Mayor of Otago since 1989 and has met the Queen, Prince Philip and Prince Charles on several occasions on their visits to New Zealand.

Bill and his wife Verna have visited Scotland on several occasions tracing their roots and would be very pleased to be put in touch with relatives who it appears settled in and around Coupar Angus.

## JAMES CRAIGIE

JAMES CRAIGIE met and married local girl AGNES McFARLANE in the mid 19th century when he was stationed in Coupar Angus as a soldier in the 'Seventy Eight Regiment of Foot'.

In 1867 they and their family emigrated to South Island, New Zealand where they prospered, but never forgot their Scottish roots.

Their son James Junior, was an authority on Robert Burns. He became Mayor of Timaru and presented a statue of the bard to the city. He went on to become a Member of the New Zealand Parliament. He dedicated his life to the betterment of Timaru and its inhabitants and succeeded in obtaining a grant from the Andrew Carnegie Trust to build a Library there. He presented the town with chiming bells for the clock-tower, and also a fine collection of pictures for the planned City Art Gallery.

*These details were supplied by Mrs Ann Benson, New Zealand, the great, great, grand-daughter of James and Agnes while on a visit to Coupar Angus during the summer of 1995.*

## A COUPAR ANGUS BOY

**Jock Sutherland was born at 9 Calton Street, Coupar Angus on 21st March 1889.**

He went firstly to school in the town, then to the Roman Catholic School in Blairgowrie. In his spare time he worked as a Porter at the local railway stations, and also did a bit of caddying at the nearby Rosemount Golf Course.

His older brother Archie had emigrated to the United States of America some time previously, and when he wrote offering to pay Jock's fare should he wish to come out, he accepted with alacrity.

He arrived in Pittsburg in July 1907 and immediately started work in Dixmont State Hospital. During the next six years he had several jobs, then with the help of friends he had made, he enrolled at Oberlin Academy in Ohio where he obtained the preparatory education which would enable him to enter the University of Pittsburg.

**Always an outstanding sportsman, Jock was awarded an athletic scholarship for Soccer and Field sports, and four years on he graduated from the Pitt School of Dentistry as Dr John Sutherland.**

In 1917 Dr Sutherland became a naturalised American Citizen, enlisted in the United States Army, and was sent to Camp Greenleaf. There he drilled, played football and became the Coach of the camp team.

When he left the army in 1919 he was made head football coach at Lafayette, but was also a lecturer/instructor at the Pitt Dental School.

Jock Sutherland was to become a national figure in the world of American football and in the next fifteen years became something of a legend.

He had several nick-names - *"the dour Scot"*; the *"staid Scot"* and *"Stoneface"*.

He was tall and well-built, rather quiet and somewhat aloof, but this did not detract in any way from his success as a coach for his team won championship after championship in 1927, 1929, 1936 and 1937 and "Best in the East" honours in 1925, 1927, 1929, 1931, 1932, 1934, 1936 and 1937. He made "Rose Bowl" appearances in 1928, 1930 and 1933 with a victory which was something of a highlight at Pasadena in 1937. In nine seasons, Jock Sutherland's lads lost only one game.

Jock Sutherland never married and has been described as "a perfectionist". From the book 'College Football Legends' by Jim O'Brien, published by Touchdown Publications, 1988 we know that a photograph of this Coupar Angus lad, is hung in the National Football Foundation's College Football Hall of Fame, Kings Island, Ohio.

There is also a photograph of this famous son, hanging in the present day Coupar Angus Council Chamber.

## THE PEOPLES' PROVOST

From the moment he arrived in Coupar Angus in 1926 John or 'Jock' Davidson as he was better known, threw himself whole-heartedly into the life of the town.

True, he had come from a very public spirited family but Jock and his wife Helen McGeorge were quite outstanding in this respect.

A man of outstanding energy and enthusiasm, Jock was a first class Pharmacist of great compassion for his fellow man. No task was too large or too small for him to undertake, if it meant the well-being of someone in need. In these pre Welfare State days, not everyone could afford to go to, or to call out the doctor at the first sign of illness, and Jock Davidson the Chemist, was the one they went to for help and advice. He was looked on by many as a father figure, not only in health matters but when problems arose concerning the town and its people.

His interest in local politics spanned many years and he served as Provost on two separate occasions for a total of twenty three years.

*1939 - 1952*
*1961 - 1970*

Coupar Angus had for long been known in the past for the generosity of its prominent citizens, and Mr & Mrs Jock Davidson were no exception for not only did they give freely of their time to a multitude of deserving causes, they gifted several very fine pieces of furniture to the Town Council which still grace the present day Council Chamber.

*A mahogany side table*
*A very fine oval mahogany pedestal table*
*A grandfather clock in an oak case*
*(Menzies of Coupar Angus)*
*A silver plated inkstand*

During World War II, Jock served tirelessly on various committees. Not only were those pertaining to the running of the town, its various charities and comforts for the troops, but also on several Scottish and National War Committees.

Jock Davidson for a time was a County Councillor and a member of the Licensing Appeal Board. A Justice of the Peace, he was accorded the much deserved honour of being made a Freeman of Coupar Angus.

Deeply interested in local history, he compiled the 1954 Statistical Account of Coupar Angus, which contains a wealth of material of great value to the present day historian.

For the bi-centenary of the ancient curling club of Coupar Angus and Kettins, he took snippets from their minutes and records, and produced a very interesting booklet to mark the historic anniversary of 1949.

Jock's son Douglas, who lives in Blairgowrie, has inherited many of his late father's attributes. He also is a very public spirited figure and a highly respected local historian who shares his knowledge with all who are interested in this field. His collection of old photographs and postcards is quite unique.

### JOHN (Jack) DUNBAR

After Coupar School, Jack spent one year at Perth Academy then went on to Dundee Technical College to study Electrical Engineering.

The last of six musically minded sons, Jack was sent to Bertha McCulloch *(the organist at St Andrews Church)* for piano lessons as a matter of course, rather than an option.

*"At my first public performance at a Sunday School concert"* he recalls *"I played, and sang, "The Glory of Love". Everybody politely clapped, which made me big-headed enough to buy some more music. After all, you're not going to get far with the girls with only one number".*

With his pals Bill Young and Harry Bruce, his interest in music flourished with the formation of the DYBBC producing musical arrangements for the songs and choruses. This attracted the attention of Dod Michie who asked Jack to come and play at the Saturday Night Hop as one leg of his trio. It is one thing performing a single song you have practiced, but quite another to keep up with an experienced trumpet player and drummer with a steady beat.

He remembers being terrified the first time he played, when a complete piano arrangement was stuck in front of him to sight-read, in a trio where the melody relied on the piano. It was terrible. After the first night he wanted to crawl away and hide, but Dod would have none of it and gradually Jack developed a more professional and sophisticated style over the years.

Because of Dod Michie's encouragement, and Bertha MacCulloch's initial teaching, he went on to play as part-time pianist with some of the RAF Dance Bands in England, *(once briefly with Ray Ellington)*, all round the Arakan and Burma *(the RAF bought him a piano and crated it round the war zone)*. When lack of transport held up the return of troops from the far east, he produced and played in a weekly live show in the American Forces Radio Station in Calcutta *(CO Melvyn Douglas)*.

Back in England, he played in several of the north-east Clubs, and Manchester, had his first song published by Columbia Records, had an entry in one of the first Eurovision Song Contests, all as a part-time activity, because after the war, he graduated in Dundee, and started a professional life in Electrical Engineering in Manchester, London, Glasgow, Newcastle, Zambia then South Africa - all with a strong leaning towards marketing.

In Zambia, he wrote the music for one complete Pantomime, each year for five years, while building up a business as Managing Director of Allenwest. The success in Zambia led to promotion as MD for the same company in Johannesburg, then MD of an ailing electronic's company which he cured, then 'retired' at the age of 59 to form his own marketing company - which is still in operation at the present time after over twenty years.

With the aid of an electronic keyboard, and a couple of Apple Mac computers, Jack has published a book of music he has written for the children of St Columba's Presbyterian Church, and is working on the production of a CD.

**He never forgets his musical development all stemmed from that initial training, launch and encouragement in Coupar Angus.**

*(Top L to R) Canadian group the 'Three Deuces' with the late Norrie Paramor and Ray Martin, with Jack looking on after recording his first song 'Snuggle Up' with Columbia.*
*(At Right) Posing for the glamour shot in RAF 'uniform' in Burma, to send home.*

A cat with folded over ears is known to have existed in China in the 18th century where it was bred purely as meat. Since then however it has disappeared without trace.

# THE COUPAR ANGUS fold-eared cat

In 1961 William and Mary Ross who lived in the white cottage on the sharp bend of the Bendochy-Meikleour Road at Easter Banchory, saw that their neighbours Mr & Mrs George MacRae, had a strange fold-eared barn cat called Susie. They asked the Macraes that if the cat ever had kittens, could they have one. The Rosses owned a seal-point Siamese female from whom they bred and sold the occasional litter of Siamese kittens.

The strange cat intrigued them and about a year later, she produced two kittens, one male and one female, and both had folded ears. The male was given to a friend who had him neutered and kept him as a family pet, and the Rosses took the female who had a snow white coat like her mother, and called her 'Snooks'. Sadly, Snooks' mother was killed on the road and the Rosses made up their minds to try and perpetuate the breed through Snooks. When she started to produce kittens, they acquired a white Shorthair female called Lady May to breed from one of her sons and the breed was launched. They applied to register the breed with the Governing Council of the Cat Fancy (GCCF) but were turned down, which means that the breed cannot be shown at any of their shows. It has been accepted by the Cat Association of Britain however, who have enforced strict breeding policies.

How this cat with the folded forward ears, which gives it the look of a an owlish pixie or teddy-bear, arrived in the United States remains a mystery. It is much loved by American cat fanciers who took it to their hearts, and is a registered breed in the Cat Fanciers Association there.

page 148

## SOURCES

Blairgowrie & Coupar Angus Libraries, Local History, Reference & Archive Departments of the AK Bell Library, Perth.
Collins Encyclopaedia of Scotland . . . . . . . . . . . . . . . . . . . . . . . . . . . . . . . . . . . . . . . . . . . . . . . .by John Keay and Julia Keay
Published by Harper Collins 1994
Scottish Towns . . . . . . . . . . . . . . . . . . . . . . . . . . . . . . . . . . . . . . . . . . . . . . . . . . . . . . . . . . . . . . . . . . . . .by David Moody
BT Batsford, London 1992
The Advertiser - Blair, Rattray, Coupar Angus, Alyth, Kirriemuir, Strathmore & Stormont . . . . . . . . . . .Price 1d from 1861
Scotland in the 19th Century . . . . . . . . . . . . . . . . . . . . . . . . . . . . . . . . . . . . . . . . . . . . . . . . .by A. Hawthornthwaite
Scholar Press 1993
The British Fire Mark 1680 1879 . . . . . . . . . . . . . . . . . . . . . . . . . . . . . . . . . . . . . . . . . . . . . . . . . . .by Brian Wright
Woodhead, Faulkner, Cambridge 1982
The Child and the State in Scotland . . . . . . . . . . . . . . . . . . . . . . . . . . . . . . . . . . . . . . . . . . . . . . . . .Published 1909
Stormont and Strathmore Annual for 1906 . . . . . . . . . . . . . . .Printed and Published by Wm Culross & Son Coupar Angus
By Brian Wright Sponsored by Commercial Union Assurance . . . . . . . . . . . . . . .Published by Faulkner, Cambridge 1982
The Fortified House in Scotland Vol IV . . . . . . . . . . . . . . . . . . . . . . . . . . . . . . . . . . . . . . . . . . . . . . .by Nigel Tranter
Mercat Press, Edinburgh 1962 - 1986 . . . . . . . . . . . . . . . . . . . . . . . . . . . . . . . . . . . . . . . . . . . . . . . . . . . . . . . . . . . . .
Annual Report of Register General of Scotland
HMSO Scottish Banking ' A History 1695' . . . . .1973 by S. G. Checkland, Published Collins, Glasgow & Edinburgh 1975
The Anglo Boer Wars . . . . . . . . . . . . . . . . . . . . . . . . . . . . . . . . . . . . . . . . . . . . . . . . . . . . . . . .by Michael Barthorp
Published Blandford Press, Poole, New York, Sidney 1987
Perthshire Cess Book 1746 - 1747 No 12
The Vale of Strathmore - Its Scenes and Legends . . . . . . . . . . . . . . . . . . . . . . . . . . . . . .by James Cargill Guthrie
Published Wm Paterson, Edinburgh 1875
Strathmore Past and Present . . . . . . . . . . . . . . . . . . . . . . . . . . . . . . . . . .by Rev R. J. McPherson MA BD Phd FRSE
Published S. Cowan & Co, Printers and Publishers, Perth 1885
Historic Scenes in Perthshire . . . . . . . . . . . . . . . . . . . . . . . . . . . . . . . . . . . . . . .by Wm. Marshall, DD. Coupar Angus
Published Wm Oliphant & Co, Edinburgh 1875
Collins Encylopaedia of Scotland . . . . . . . . . . . . . . . . . . . . . . . . . . . . . . . . . . . .Ed by John Keay and Julia Keay
Published Harper Collins, London 1994
The Scottish Year . . . . . . . . . . . . . . . . . . . . . . . . . . . . . . . . . . . . . . . . . . . . . . . . . . . . . . . . . . .by David Murison
Published The Mercat Press, Edinburgh 1982
A Companion to Scottish History . . . . . . . . . . . . . . . . . . . . . . . . . . . . . . . . . . .by Ian Donnachie and George Hewitt
Published by Batsford Ltd, London 1989
Scotland 1689 to the Present . . . . . . . . . . . . . . . . . . . . . . . . . . . . . . . . . . . . . . . . . . . . . . . . . . . .by Wm. Ferguson
The Edinburgh History of Scotland Vol 4 . . . . . . . . . . . . . . . . . . . . . . . . . .Published Mercat Press, Edinburgh 1987
The Scottish Linen Industry in the 18th Century . . . . . . . . . . . . . . . . . . . . . . . . . . . . . . . . . . . . .by Alistair Durie
Published John Donald Publishers Ltd, 138 St Stephen Street, Edinburgh
Scotland 1689 to the Present . . . . . . . . . . . . . . . . . . . . . . . . . . . . . . . . . . . . . . . . . . . . . . . . . .by William Ferguson
The Edinburgh History of Scotland Vol 4 . . . . . . . . . . . . . . . . . . . . . . . . . . . . . . . .Mercat Press Edinburgh 1987
Mercat Cross and Tolbooth . . . . . . . . . . . . . . . . . . . . . . . . . . . . . . . . . . . . . . . . . . . . . . . . . . . . . .by Craig Mair
Published John Donald Publishers Ltd, Edinburgh 1988
Chronicle of the 20th Century . . . . . . . . . . . . . . . . . . . . . . . . . . . . . . . . . . . . . . . . . . . . . . .by Dorling Kindersley
London, New York, Stutgart, Moscow . . . . . . . . . . . . . . . . . . . . . . . . . . . . . . . . .Ed in Chief Derek Mercer 1995
Kessingís Record of World Events . . . . . . . . . . . . . . . . . . . . . . . . . . . . . . . . . . . .Consulting Ed Robert Fraser
Catermill Publishing
Inqvistionvm Ad Cappellam Domini Regis - Retornatarvm - Qvae - In pvblicis Archivis Scotiae . . . . . . . . .Adhvc Servantvr
Printed by command of his majesty King George III In pursuance of an address of the House of Commons
Great Britain MDCCCXVI
Rentall of the County of Perth . . . . . . . . . . . . . . . . . . . . . . . . . . . . . . .Ed by William Gloag Depute Collector of Cess
Perth 1835 Morisons Printers
Childrens Games ~Throughout the Year . . . . . . . . . . . . . . . . . . . . . . . . . . . . . . . . . . . . . . . . . . .by Leslie Daiken
Published BT Batsford Ltd, London 1949 R 394-3
Dundee Advertiser founded 1801
The Silver Bough, A Calendar of Scottish National Festivals . . . . . . . . . . . . . . . . . . . . . . . . . . . .by Marian McNeill
Published Wm MacLellan, 240 Hope Street, Glasgow 1959
Cambridge Historical Encyclopaedia of Great Britain and Ireland . . . . . . . . . . . . . . . . . . . . .Editor Christopher Haig
Published Cambridge University Press
A Dictionary of Scottish History . . . . . . . . . . . . . . . . . . . . . . . . . . . . . . . . . . . . . . . . . . . . . .Editor J. P. Kenyon
Published Seeker and Warburg, London
Our Meigle Book . . . . . . . . . . . . . . . . . . . . . . . . . . . . . . .Published Wm Kidd & Sons, Whitehall Street, Dundee 1932
The Parish of Coupar Angus . . . . . . . . . . . . . . . . . . . . . . . . . . . . . . . . . . . . . . . . . . . . . . . . . . . .by John Davidson
1st Stat Acc of Scotland 1790
2nd Stat Acc of Scotland 1843
The Presbytery of Perth . . . . . . . . . . . . . . . . . . . . . . . . . . . . . . . . . . . . . . . . . . . . .by Rev Robt Small, DD Edinburgh
Published D. Small, 3 Howard Street, Edinburgh 1904
The Scottish Congregational Ministry 1794 - 1993 by Rev Dr Wm D. McNaughton, Archivist Congregational Union of Scotland
Published The Congregational Union of Scotland

## SOURCES continued

Church House, 340 Cathedral Street, Glasgow 1993
Fasti of the U F C Of S 1900 -1929 . . . . . . . . . . . . . . . . . . . . . . . . . . . . . . . . . . . . . . . . . . Edited by Rev Alexander Lamb
Published Oliver & Boyd Edinburgh 1956
Rental Book of the Cistercian Abbey of Coupar Angus . . . . . . . . . . . . . . . . . . . . . . . . . . . by Rev Charles Rogers LLd Vol 1 and 2
Printed for the British Topographical Society 1880 London
The Scottish Provincial Banking Companies . . . . . . . . . . . . . . . . . . . . . . . . . . . . . . . . .by Charles W Munn BA Ph D Dip IB (Scot)
Pub John Donald Publishers Ed
Bank of Scotland A History 1695 -1995 . . . . . . . . . . . . . . . . . . . . . . . . . . . . . . . . . . . . . . . . . . . . . . . . .by Richard Saville
Edinburgh University Press
1847-1997 150 years of Banking in Coupar Angus . . . . . . . . . . . . . . . . . . . . . . by Archive Section, Corporate Affairs October 1997
The Royal Bank of Scotland
The Hiram key . . . . . . . . . . . . . . . . . . . . . . . . . . . . . . . . . . . . . . . . . . . . . . . . . . . . . . . . by Christopher Knight & Robert Lomas
Published by Arrow Books Ltd 1997
Printed in Great Britain by Cox & Wyman Ltd, Reading, Berks
Dundee & Its Textile Industry 1850-1914 . . . . . . . . . . . . . . . . . . . . . . . . . . . . . . . . . . .by Bruce Lenman, Charlotte Lythe, Enid Gauldie
Dundee Abertay Historical Soc Publication 1969 . . . . . . . . . . . . . . . . . . . . . . . . . . . . . . . . . . .Harley & Cox Printers Ltd, Dundee
The Celts . . . . . . . . . . . . . . . . . . . . . . . . . . . . . . . . . . . . . . . . . . . . . . . . . . . . . . . . . . . . . . . . . . . . . . .by Nora Chandwick
Penguin Books 1971
The Victoria & Albert Museum, London
Fasti of the United Free Church of Scotland

## LISTED BUILDINGS - COUPAR ANGUS BURGH

Cistercian Abbey, remains of - Queen Street
Abbey Church, Parish Church of Coupar Angus, Queen Street
Abbey Churchyard
The Steeple, Queen Street
Strathmore Hotel, Queen Street
Abbey hill, Precinct Street
Dunn, Tweedside
Pleasance Farmhouse
Klydon House Union Street
YWCA Union Street former original Secession Church
SE corner, The Cross, Commercial Street and Union Street
NE corner, The Cross, Commercial Street and Union Street
3 Commercial Street
Royal Hotel, High Street and 2 George Street
Millburn 38 George Street
Bannerman and Cuthill, George Square and 2 Causewayend
3 Causewayend
7 Gray Street
Masonic Buildings (St John Operative no 105) Gray Street
18, 20, 22 Commercial Street
2 Hay Street
Cumberland (or Yeomanry) Barracks, 2 Calton Street
1, 4, 6 Calton Street
Aviemore Calton Street
Union Bank Buildings and Bank House, Calton Street
Dalblair, Union Street
Princeland, Blairgowrie Road
Beech Hill Mansion House, Beech Hill Road
Gartloch Bank, Bogside Road

Keithick House
Keithick, North Lodge
Keithick House sundial
Kethick House, stables and steading
Keithick, South Lodge
Kemphill, Farmhouse and steading
Balgersho House
Bridge of Couttie
Larghan House
Isla Park
Viewbank, Farmhouse
Kinloch House steading
Kinloch House, walled garden and sundial
Kinloch House
Arthurstone House *(Butterstone School)*
Arthurstone House, sundial no 1 at SE front of house
Arthurstone House, Ice-house
Arthurstone House, walled garden
Arthurstone House, Summer-house in walled garden
Arthurstone House, Sundial no 2 in front of summer house
Arthurstone House, Sundial no 3 in front of greenhouse
Arthurstone House Castle Folly and greenhouse
Arthurstone House "Antiquarian Corner"
Arthurstone House, Dovecot
Ardler Church
Ardler Churchyard railings and gates
Ardler Churchyard, Carmichael enclosure
Ardler Manse (formerly)
Ardler (formerly Washington) School

# PERTH & KINROSS MUSEUM AND ART GALLERY DEPARMENT
## hold the following items which were originally in the Coupar Angus Museum

Wooden chair *(Baillie Ogilvy)*
Wash dolly, wooden handle and aluminium head
Singer sewing machine in case and stand
Memory Tickler tin shopping list
Iron and steel toaster with florette cut-out
Pair hinged wooden bats with string handles
Pendant
Iron shoe last
Small iron horse shoe
Bugle stamped 52 Henry Pottery & Co etc
Pair of small wooden clogs
Game of Flipperty Flop in wooden box
Large iron horseshoe, badly rusted
Pair large painted clogs
Travelling spirit stove
Iron corkscrew with wooden handle
12 Iron nails from Delvine
Chocolate box with postcards and photos
Greenfolder labelled "Coupar Angus ephemera" J M Richards
Cassell's Book of Knowledge Vols 1-8
Cyclist's touring club, British Road Book Vol IV
2 Flat irons stamped with stars
Miniature Union Jack on a steel pin
Brass pen knife
Horn pen knife
Rusted steel knife
78 Records
1 "I belong to Glasgow" by Will Fyffe
2 "O Scotland Bonnie Scotland" by Sandy MacFarlane
Pottery painted bowl commemorating the Crimeam French and English Alliance
Pair of iron scales with 7 weights and brass scale pan
Cotton flag, staff has wood worm
Varnished wooden ladle
Ransome's patent travelling inkstand
Travelling packman's weights brass
Embroidered silk watch pocket
3 brass tobacco stoppers
Glass medicine bottle found at Hallyburton in 1975

Papier-mache snuff box
Wooden snuff box
Flint and steel strikalight
Quill pen cutter
Pair of curling tongs
Gas mask in plastic case
Iron shoe last
Tin chest with initials DZHF
Brown's self-interpreting Family Bible bound in black leather
Copy of Eugenie Grandet by Balzac
AA Members Handbook for Scotland 1951-52
Coupar Angus Quoiting Club Accounts Book 1922
Coupar Angus Quoting Club Minutes Book 1923
Copy of Treasure Island by R L Stevenson
The Scripture Union Almanac 1913
Scripture Union Member's card for Margaret Forsan 1916
Octo-Centenary Order of Service for Coupar Angus Abbey Church and 2 copies of pamphlet, 30 August 1964
Charcoal drawing of Hammy the Bellman 1949 Pres. By Frank Benzies
2nd World War tin helmet
Pottery black cat
Coupar Angus Tennis Club Boys Junior Championship cup 1950-1958
Typed sheets, photos, etc connected with Mr Haig Forsan mounted on cardboard lids and sellotape
2 clay pipe bowls. One stamped "G Kean, Maker, Perth"
Silk ribbon and identify certificate of WAAC for Margaret Forsan 1917
Programme for the Playhouse, Coupar Angus, November 1947
Murray's Railway Map of Scotland
Iron Key *(for Black Tower)*
Shoe horn and button hook
Pair of glove stretchers
2 black glass bowls, tripod and 2 handles, one large, one small
Pocket watch made by Waltham Co Mass

The "Georgian Sealing Set" with wax and crucible
Cleaning pad for gramophone
Silver-plated desk set "Presented to Mr Steele by his bible class, Kinnoull, 13th March 1878"
Waffle irons
Tin candle moulds
Iron kettle
Framed photograph of Bowls Club, Blairgowrie 1st July 1921
Programme for Coupar Angus Public Buildings Bazaar 1895. 22nd, 23rd and 24th August "The Manse" written on the back
Coupar Angus British Legion and Pipe Band on Church parade. *(Photograph)*
Framed photograph of Coupar Angus Army Cadets, 1942
Pencil and wash framed drawing of back of Masonic Lodge, Coupar Angus. *
Pencil and wash drawing of buildings in Coupar Angus. *
Pencil and wash drawing of remains of Cisterion Monastery, Coupar Angus by Percy Home *
Drawing called "Old Coupar Angus" *
Drawing of street in Coupar Angus. *
Pencil and wash drawing of a Coupar Angus street by Percy Home. *
Coupar Angus bridge. Pencil and part drawing framed. *
Pencil and paint drawing of a Coupar Angus street by Percy Home. *
Pencil and wash drawing entitled "Coupar Angus, Perthshire, 1948" *
*(\* these items have a sticker on back with "Town Hall"written on it)*
Pair of child's black leather shoes
Wood and iron patten. With woodworm. Decorated leather strap
Nine newspaper cuttings of the bothy workers in large white frame
26 coloured Edwardian postcards, framed
Large framed photgraph. Broughty Ferry Rink Tournament, 1907
Framed sampler by Andrina Robbie age 12 years. Rosebank School, Dundee 1888
Framed photo of the laying of foundations of Coupar Angus new Public Buildings 1886.
Framed photo of the International Bowling Tournament, Cardiff, July 1913
Framed illuminated Script presented to the Rev Patrick James Stevenson, Minister of Coupar Angus in 50th the year of his Ministry. Sept 1878 - has woodworm.
Two wooden cases of Edwardian colour postcards.

*(Left) The Lake at Hallyburton House.*

# General Index

This index lists the names of subjects, places, businesses, streets and so on. Personal names, except where used in the names of businesses, are listed in the separate Index of Names.
On occasion, where it seemed justified, a subject is indexed in more than one place to increase access to topics.
Readers should also note that except where it is unavoidable, as in the case of certain proper names, "Coupar Angus" is not used as a prefix since far too many headings would appear in such a listing.

(ill./s) = illustration/s only
(+ill./s) = text and illustration/s

Abbey *see* Cistercian Abbey, monks etc.
Abbey Kirk  22, 23, 24 (+ill.), 25 (+ill.), 26
    choir  24 (ill.)
    churchyard  27 (ill.), 28
        Arthurstone Mausoleum  28
        watch house  27 (ill.), 28
    communion silver  26 (+ill.)
    construction  24-25
    decoration  25
    furnishings  25
    hall  31
    manses  26-27
    ministers, list of  26
    organ  25 (+ill.)
    Panel of Weepers  25
    pew rent receipt  27 (ill.)
    wedding party  26 (ill.)
Abbot's Burgh  10
Aberdeen-Angus cattle  36
Advertisements *see* Shops and businesses
Agricultural Association  36
Agriculture  9, 36-40
    Aberdeen-Angus cattle  36
    Agricultural Association  36
    berry pickers  37
    blackcurrants  37
    crops  36-39
    enclosure of land  36
    engineering works  51
    farm workers' houses
        Coupar Grange  38 (ill.)
    feeing markets  36, 53
    "ferm touns"  9, 36
    fruit preserving works  38, 51
    Horse Society  40, 123
    Industrial Revolution, effect of  41
    leases and tacks  38-39
    potatoes  37
    raspberries  37
    soft fruit  37-39
    strawberries  37
    tacks *see* leases and tacks
    trysts *see* feeing markets
Alcohol  139-140
    Independent Order
        of Good Templars  140
    prohibitionists  140
American football  146
Anti-Burgher Church *see* Secession Church
Armed forces
    Cameronian Regiment  35
    Home Guard  70 (ills)
    Perthshire Rifle Volunteers  110
    Polish Army  103 (ill.)
Athole Arms  142 (+ill.)
Athole Street Bakery  60 (ill.)
Auld Steeple *see* Tolbooth
Baillie Ogilvie's chair  13 (+ill.)
Balbrogie  9, 85
Balgersho
    bleachfield  49

    den  44 (ill.)
    House  45 (ill.)
Banks and banking  79-81
    Bank of Scotland  81 (+ill.)
    Citizen of the Year Award  81
    Lloyds TSB  81 (+ill.)
    National Bank of Scotland  80
    Perth Banking Company  80
    Royal Bank of Scotland  80 (+ill.)
    Savings Bank  81
    Union Bank Buildings  80 (ill.)
    Union Bank of Scotland  80 (+ill.), 81
Barlatch Street *see* George Street
Beechhill  9, 10
Belmont Castle Eventide Home  32 (ill.)
Bendochy Church  23 (ill.), 35 (ill.)
Bendochy Parish  35
    population  38
Bendochy School  38 (ill.)
Berry pickers  37
Blackcurrants  37
Blairgowrie Road  67 (ill.), 75 (ill.), 96
Boatlands Farm  45
Boer War  128-129, 134 (ill.)
Bowling  115 (ill.), 116-117 (+ills)
    Club House  116 (ill.)
Boys' Brigade  108, 136-137 (+ills)
    activities  137
    pipe band  136
Brewing  36
Brass Band  110 (+ill.)
Bridges
    Damhead bridge  95 (ill.)
    Couttie Brig  37 (ill.), 92 (ill.), 11 (ill.)
    Isla bridge (rail)  47 (ill.)
    Keithick bridge (little)  9 (ill.)
    Kitty Swanson's bridge  91, 97
British Legion  109 (+ill.)
Brodie's Yard  60
Brownies *see* Girl Guides
Bubonic plague  85
Buildings
    Arthurstone Mausoleum  28
    Athole Arms  142 (+ill.)
    Athole Street Bakery  60 (ill.)
    Auld Steeple *see* Tolbooth
    Balgersho House  45 (ill.)
    Bank of Scotland  81 (+ill.)
    Belmont Castle Eventide Home  32 (ill.)
    Bendochy Church  23 (ill.), 35 (ill.)
    Bendochy School  38 (ill.)
    Bowling Club House  116 (ill.)
    Clocktower *see* Tolbooth
    Coupar Angus School  61 (ill.)
    Cumberland's Barracks  92,93 (ill.)
    Defiance Inn *see* Royal Hotel
    Enverdale Country House Hotel  144
    Enverdale House  144 (ill.)
    Farina mill  37 (+ill.), 60, 111 (ill.)
    farm workers' houses
        Coupar Grange  38 (ill.)

    fire station  82 (ill.)
    Grayburn Bakery  60 (ill.)
    Hallyburton House  41 (ill.)
    Irvine and Co. (drapers)  59 (ill.)
    Keithick House  43 (ill.), 44 (ill.)
    Kinclaven Castle  19
    Lintrose House  38 (ill.)
    listed buildings  150
    Lloyds TSB (bank)  81 (+ill.)
    mills  51, 52 (ill.)
    Playhouse  103
    police station (former, Hill Street)  82 (ill.)
    power loom factories  50, 51, 52 (+ills)
    Red House Hotel  46 (ill). 47, 143 (+ill.)
    Royal Bank of Scotland  80 (+ill.)
    Royal Hotel  141-142 (+ill.), 144 (+ill.)
    St. Andrew's Church  31 (+ill.), 32, 35
    St. Anne's Scottish
        Episcopal Church  33 (+ill.)
        ministers, list of  33
        rectory  34
        subscribers  33
    St. Mary's Roman Catholic Church  34-35
    Secession Church (now Y.W.C.A.)  28-29
    souterrain (Pitcur)  42 (+ill.)
    Steeple *see* Tolbooth
    Strathmore Hotel  141 (+ill.)
    Strathmore Works  51 (+ill.), 52
    Tolbooth  10, 14 (+ill.), 15 (+ill.),
        16 (ill.), 58 (ill.), 83
        bell  14 (ill.)
        poem  16
    toll house (Forfar Road)  93 (ill.)
    Town Hall  20 (+ill.), 21 (+ill.), 67-68,
        102 (ill.)
        contents  20-21
        opening  99
        Polish Army connection  103 (ill.)
    Townhouse *see* Tolbooth
    Union Bank Buildings  80 (ill.)
    Union Bank of Scotland  80 (+ill.), 81
    Vic, The *see* Victoria Inn
    Victoria Buildings  47
    Victoria Hall *see* Town Hall
    Victoria Inn  14 (Ill.), 83, 142-143 (+ill.)
    White House *see* Strathmore Hotel
        *see also* Hotels and
        public houses
Burgh
    boundaries  11
    seal  19 (+ill.)
Burgh of Barony  10, 23
Burgh Police Act 1892  11
Burgh School  31, 61, 62, 63, 67
Burgher Church  30, 49
Burnside Road (Relief Road)  8
Businesses *see* Shops and businesses and
    business names and
    under names of
    industries

**Buildings con't**

Buttery Bank  86 (ill.), 93 (ill.)
Buttery Bank Road  93
C.A.R.A.  *see* Coupar Angus Recreation Association
Caddam  9
Caddam Road  92
Caledonian Barbecue Co.  52
Caledonian Railway Company  47, 50
Calton Street  96
Cameronian Regiment  35
Campbell Street  50
Caravan Club rallies  122
Casseyend *see* Causewayend
Causewayend  9, 45, 48, 49 (+ill.), 95 (ill.), 96 (ill.)
Chicken processing plant  52 (+ill.)
Cholera  85
Church of Scotland  22
Church Place  29
Churches  9, 10, 22-35
    Abbey Kirk  22, 23, 24 (+ill.), 25 (+ill.), 26
        choir  24 (ill.)
        churchyard  27 (ill.), 28
        Arthurstone Mausoleum  28
        watch house  27 (ill.), 28
        communion silver  26 (+ill.)
        construction  24-25
        decoration  25
        furnishings  25
        hall  31
        ministers, list of  26
        manses  26-27
        organ  25 (+ill.)
        Panel of Weepers  25
        Pew rent receipt  27 (ill.)
        wedding party  26 (ill.)
    Anti-Burgher Church *see* Secession Church
    Bendochy Church  23 (ill.), 35 (ill.)
    Burgher Church  30, 49
    Church of Scotland  22
    Congregational Church  29
        attendance certificate  29 (ill.)
        ministers, list of  29
        Covenanters  10, 23, 28, 35, 140
        developmental chart  23
    Ecumenical Union *see* Congregational Church
    Free Church of Scotland  22
    Gospel Hall  34 (ill.)
    Parish Church *see* Abbey Kirk
    Roman Catholicism  34-35
    St. Andrew's Church  31 (+ill.), 32, 35
        ministers, list of  31
        union with Abbey Kirk  25, 31
        use as Abbey Kirk hall  31
        Women's Guild  30 (ill.)
    St. Anne's Scottish Episcopal Church  33-34 (+ill.)
        ministers, list of  33
        rectory  34
        subscribers  33
    St. Mary's Roman Catholic Church  30, 34-35
    Secession Church  10, 22, 28-29
        manses  29
        ministers, list of  29
    United Free Church  22
    United Presbyterian Church  22, 30
    *see also* Cistercian Abbey, monks etc.
Cinemas  30, 35
Cistercian Abbey, monks etc.  9 (+Ill.), 22 (ill.), 28 (ill.), 86 (ill.)
    Abbey seal  19 (+ill.)

    agriculture  38
    chapels  23
Civic regalia  17 (+ill), 19 (+ill.)
    Burgh seal  19 (+ill.)
    Committee for Provost's chain  17
Clocktower *see* Tolbooth
Coaching  (horse drawn transport)  94
Coal  37, 47 (ill.), 90
Commerce  53-60
    *see also* Shops and businesses
Commercial Street  11 (ill.)
Commissioners *see* Local government
Common  70 (ill.)
Communications  84
    postal services  84
    telegrams  84
    telephones  84
Community Council *see* Coupar Angus, Ardler and Bendochy Community Council
Company names *see* Shops and businesses and Company names
Concerts  102, 104 (ill.)
    Mulberry Bush  104 (+ill.)
Congregational Church  29
    attendance certificate  29 (ill.)
    ministers, lits of  29
Coronation (1953)  105-106 (+ill.)
Coronation Works Store *see* Eassie and Balkeerie Supply Co. (EBSCO)
Coupar Angus and Newtyle Railway Co. *see* Newtyle and Coupar Angus Railway Co.
Coupar Angus, Ardler and Bendochy Community Council  12, 81
    Citizen of the Year award  81
    *Coupar Angus Newsletter*  35
Coupar Angus Junior Football Club  119 (ill.)
*Coupar Angus Newsletter*  35
Coupar Angus Recreation Association  118
Coupar Angus School  61 (ill.)
Coupar Fair  100
Coupar Grange
    Mansion House  41 (ill.)
    farm workers' houses  38 (ill.)
"Coupar Parliament"  49
Couttie Brig (bridge)  37 (ill.), 92 (ill.), 111 (ill.)
Covenanters  10, 23, 28, 35, 140
Cricket  113-114 (+ill.), 120
Crops  36-39 *see also* Agriculture
Cross, The  (all ills)  53, 57, 59, 79, 84, 108, 141
Cuddies' Wynd  95
Culross, William and Son (Printers)  57-58 (+ill.)
    printing press  58 (ill.)
Cumberland's Barracks  92, 93 (ill.)
Cupar - name change  11
Curling  100 (+ill.), 111-113 (+ill.)
Damhead bridge  95 (ill.)
Dance bands  102
    Rennie Quartet  107-108
    Windsor Dance Band  102
Dances  102-103
Davidson, Walter and Sons (Chemists)  59
Defiance Inn *see* Royal Hotel
Diet  86
Diphtheria inoculation  70
Diseases  85, 87
Domestic service  41, 43
Drainage of land etc. 37, 85
Dramatic Society  105, 106 (ill.)
Dunbar, William T. (Baker)  60 (ill.)

Dunbar-Young-Barclay Broadcasting Co. *see* D.Y.B.B.C.
Dundee and Newtyle Railway Co.  32, 47
Dundee Road  95 (ill.)
Durie and Miller (Jute Works)
    coronation celebration 1953  106 (ill.)
    fire  50, 51
D.Y.B.B.C. (Dunbar-Young-Barclay Broadcasting Co.)  104, 105
Eassie and Balkeerie Supply Co.  52
Easter Myreriggs  39
EBSCO *see* Eassie and Balkeerie Supply Co.
Eccesliastical affairs/history *see* Churches and Cistercian Abbey
Ecumenical Union *see* Congregational Church
Education  31, 32, 61-78
    Bendochy School  38 (ill.)
    Burgh School  31, 61, 62, 63, 67
    church schools  61
    classes  62 (ill.), 63 (ill.), 66 (ill.)
    community education  74
    condition of school buildings  63
    Coupar Angus School  61 (ill.)
    Episcopal School  33
    evening classes  65, 67
        syllabus  65 (ill.)
    fees  74
    football team  76 (ill.)
    Free Church School  31, 32, 62, 63
    Gaelic language  76
    gifts (James Coates of Paisley)  100
    half-timers  61, 62
    head teachers, list of  69
    Industrial School  62-63
    inspectors' reports  64 (ill.), 65
    McRitchie Memorial Prize  68
    Parish School  32, 61
    Parochial School *see* Burgh School
    pupil teachers  31
    Savings Bank  68, 76
    School Board  62, 64, 100
    school fees  64
    School Hero Fund  69
    school log book  62 (ill.)
    school milk  71
    school visits  66, 75-76, 77
    schools (all ills)  61, 62, 63, 66
    Scotch Education Department  61
    speech therapy  73
    teachers' salaries  64
    Tweedie Prize  75
Emigration  36, 145
Enclosure of land  36
Entertainments  102-110
    cinemas  30, 35
    concerts  102, 104 (ill.)
    coronation (1953)  106-106 (+ill.)
    dance bands  102
    dances  102-103
    Dramatic Society  105, 106 (ill.)
    D.Y.B.B.C. (Dunbar-Young-Barclay Broadcasting Co.)  104, 105
    Farmers' Dance  102
    festivals  98-101
    films  103
    Five Dimes (singers)  104
    Mulberry Bush concerts  104 (+ill.)
    pipe bands  108-109 (+ill.), 136
    Playhouse  103
    Rennie Quartet  107-108
    Spitfire Fund  104 (+ill), 105 (ill.)

**Education con't**

    Three Deuces (musical group) 147 (ill.)
    Windsor Dance Band 102
    World War II 103-104
Enverdale Country House Hotel 144
Enverdale House 144 (ill.)
Episcopal Church *see* Scottish Episcopal Church
Episcopal School 33
Estates 41-45
    Coupar Grange
        Mansion House 41 (ill.)
        farm workers' houses 38 (ill.)
    Hallyburton 41-43
        arboretum 42
        community woodland 43
        fête 43
        forestry 42
        House 41 (ill.)
            gardens 42 (ill.)
        staffing 43
    Keithick 43-45
        House 43 (ill.), 44 (ill.)
        Keithick den 44 (ill.)
        meteorite 45
        owners, list of 45
Farina mill 37 (+ill.), 60, 111 (ill.)
Farm workers' houses Coupar Grange 38 (ill.)
Farmers' Dance 102
Farming *see* Agriculture
Feeing markets 36, 53
"Ferm touns" 9, 36
Ferries 91
Festivals 98-101
    Coupar Fair 100
    horse market 53, 99
Films 103
Fire Service 82
    fire station 82 (ill.)
Five Dimes (singers) 104
Flax industry 48, 49, 51
Flooding 42 (ill.)
Fold eared cat 148 (+ill.)
Folk medicine 86
Football 118-121 (+ills)
    school team 76 (ill.)
    team lists 119, 120
    teams 118 (ill.), 120
Fords (across rivers) 91
Forfar Road 93 (ill.), 96
    toll house 93 (ill.)
Foxhall Park 119, 123
Free Church of Scotland 22
Free Church School 31, 32, 62, 63
Freemasonry 131 +ills.), 132
Fruit preserving works 38, 51
Gardens and Allotments Society 77, 101 (ill.), 137 (ill.)
Gas lighting 50
Gasometer 50
Geekie and Black (flax and linen works) 50, 51 (ill.)
George Square 50, 81 (ill.), 109 (ill.)
George Street 13 (ill.), 49 (ill.), 50, 84 (ill.), 93 (+ill.), 95
Girl Guides 45, 138 (+ill.)
Gospel Hall 34 (ill.)
Grampian Country Food Group 52
Gray Street 96, 131 (ill.)
Grayburn Bakery 60 (ill.)
Guides *see* Girl Guides
Hallyburton Estate 41-43
    arboretum 42
    community woodland 43
    fête 43

    forestry 42
    House 41 (ill.)
        gardens 42 (ill.)
    staffing 43
Hay Arms *see* Victoria Inn
Health centre (Trades Lane) 85 (ill.), 88
Health services 85-90
    bubonic plague 85
    cholera 85
    diphtheria inoculation 70
    diseases 85, 87
    drainage 85
    folk medicine *see* Herbal and folk medicine
    health centre (Trades Lane) 85 (ill.), 88
    herbal and folk medicine 86
    immunisation 87
    poliomyelitis inoculation 73
    sewage works 85, 86, 88
    vaccination (BCG) 73
    water supply 72, 85, 87
    whooping cough 87
Herbal and folk medicine 86
High Street 47 (ill.), 82 (ill.)
Highland games 123
History of town and parish, general 8
Hockey 119, 121 (+ill)
    East Perthshire Hockey Club 121
    team 121 (ill.)
Holidays 98-101
    coronations 99
    Handsel Monday 98
    "tattie" holidays 100, 101
Home Guard (World War II) 70 (ills)
Horse biscuit 53
Horse drawn transport 94-95
Horse market 53, 99
    candy 53
Horse Society 40, 123
Hotels and public houses 139-144
    Athole Arms 142 (+ill.)
    Defiance Inn *see* Royal Hotel
    Enverdale Country House Hotel 144
    Hay Arms *see* Victoria Inn
    Railway Hotel *see* Red House Hotel
    Red House Hotel 46 (ill.), 47, 143 (+ills)
    Royal Hotel 141-142 (+ill.), 144 (+ill.)
    Strathmore Hotel 141 (+ill.)
    Vic, The *see* Victoria Inn
    Victoria Inn 14 (ill.), 83, 142-143 (+ill.)
    White House *see* Strathmore Hotel
Immunisation 87
Independent Order of Good Templars 140
Industrial Revolution effects on agriculture 41
Industrial School 62-63
Industries *see under names of industries*
Inoculation 70
Irvine and Co. (drapers) 59 (ill.)
"Jeelyworks" *see* Fruit preserving works
Justice, administration of 10, 11, 13, 14
    pillory 11
Jute industry 48, 50-51
Keithick 9
Keithick bridge (little) 9 (ill.)
Keithick Estate 43-45
    House 43 (ill.), 44 (ill.)
    Keithick den 44 (ill.)
    meteorite 45
    owners, list of 45
Kinclaven Castle 19
Kirks *see* Churches
Kitty Swanson's bridge 91, 97
L. O. Tractors 52 *see also* Olding, Jack and Co.

Ladies' Society 106
Laing Crescent 49
Larghan Victory Park 40, 113, 122 (+ills)
League of Horsemen 121
Leather industry 36, 47, 60
    saddlers 36, 60 (ill.)
    shoemakers 36
    tannery 36, 47, 60
Linen industry 48, 50-51
Lintrose Estate 37
    House 39 (ill.)
Listed buildings 150
Local government
    Abbot's Burgh 10
    Burgh
        boundaries 11
        seal 19 (+ill.)
    Burgh of Barony 10, 23
    Burgh Police Act 1892 11
    Civic regalia 17 (+ill.), 19 (+ill.),
        Burgh seal 19 (+ill.)
    Committee for
        Provost's chain 17
    Commissioners 11, 14
    fire service 82
        fire station 82 (ill.)
    Parish Council 11
    Parochial Board 11
    Police Burgh 11
    police service 82-83
    police station (former, Hill Street) 82 (ill.)
    Provosts 17-18
        chain of office 17-18 (+ills)
        list of subscribers for 18
        list of Provosts 18
        regalia 17 (+ills)
        robes 17 (+ill.)
    Sewage works, 85, 86, 88
    Town Commissioners 11, 14
    Town Committee 10, 11, 14
    Town Council 11, 12 (+ill.)
        minutes 12
Lodging House *see* Poor House
Manufacturing industries *see under names of industries*
Markets 53
    horse market 53
Marshall Food Group 52
Meigle Road *see* Forfar Road
Middlehills (mill) 50
Monkmyre Loch 39, 91 (ill.)
Monks *see* Cistercian Abbey, monks, etc.
Motor transport 95, 96 (ill.)
Mugs, commemorative 71 (ill.)
Music *see* Entertainments
Myeridge *see* Myreriggs
Myreriggs 39
New Road *see* Union Street
Newtyle and Coupar Angus Railway Co. 47, 80
Nortel Leisure Centre 143
North United Free Church *see* St. Andrew's Church
Occupations, list of (1794) 53
Olding, Jack and Co. (textile works) 48 (ill.), 50 (ill.), 52
Parish Church *see* Abbey Kirk
Parish Council 11
Parish school 32, 61
Parochial Board 11
Parochial School *see* Burgh School
Paterson, Charles B. (saddler) 60 (ill.)
Paths *see* Road transport
Patronage Act, 1712 22

page 155

**Local Government con't**

Perth Road 48 (ill.)
Perthshire Rifle Volunteers 110
Pillory 11
Pipe bands 108-109 (+ill.), 135, 136
Pitcur (fortified tower house) 41-42
    souterrain 42 (+ill.)
Playhouse 103
Pleasance Road 36
Police Burgh 11
Police service 82-83
    police station (former, Hill Street) 82 (ill.)
Poliomyelitis inoculation 73
Polish Army (World War II) 103
Poor House 11
Population 12 (bar graph), 36, 38, 60
Postal services 84
Potatoes 37
Poverty 11, 45, 50, 90, 141
    soup kitchens 45, 50, 69
Power loom weaving see Textile industry
Precinct Street 49
Preserve works see Fruit preserving works
Prices 60, 86
Printing 57-58
    press 58 (ill.)
Provosts 17-18
    chain of office 17-18 (+ills)
        list of subscribers for 18
    list of Provosts 18
    regalia 17 (+ills)
    robes 17 (+ill.)
Public houses see Hotels and public houses
Quarries 32
Queen Street 14 (ill.), 22 (ill.), 94 (ill.)
Quoiting 114-115 (+ill.)
Railway Hotel see Red House Hotel
Railways 32, 37, 46-47
    Coupar Angus and Newtyle Railway Co.
        see Newtyle and
        Coupar Angus Railway
        Co.
    Coupar Angus station 46 (ill.)
    Dundee and Newtyle Railway Co. 32, 47
    Isla bridge 47 (ill.)
    level crossing 46 (ill.), 47 (ill.)
    Newtyle and Coupar Angus
        Railway Co. 47, 80
    Scottish Midland Junction Railway Co. 47
    Station Hotel 46 (ill.) see also Red
        House Hotel
Raspberries 37
Red Cross 88-90 (+ills)
Red House Hotel 46 (ill.), 47, 143 (+ills)
Relief Church see Congregational Church
Relief Road see Burnside Road
Rennie Quartet 107-108
Right of way dispute (Boatlands) 91
Road transport 91-97
    coaching 94
    fords 91
    ferries 91
    horse drawn 94-95
    Kitty Swanson's bridge 91
    motorised 95, 96 (ill.)
    right of way (Boatlands) 91
    toll houses 93 (ill.), 94 (+ills)
    tolls 94 see also Roads and streets
Roads and streets
    Barlatch Street see George Street
    Blairgowrie Road 67 (ill.), 75 (ill.), 96
    Brodie's Yard 60
    Burnside Road (Relief Road) 8
    Buttery Bank Road 93
    Caddam Road 92
    Calton Street 96
    Campbell Street 50
    Casseyend see Causewayend
    Causewayend 9, 45, 48, 49 (ill.),
        95 (ill.), 96 (ill.)
    Church Place 29
    Commercial Street 11 (ill.)
    Cross, The (all ills) 53, 57, 59, 79, 84,
        108, 141
    Cuddies' Wynd 95
    Dundee Road 95 (ill.)
    Forfar Road 93 (ill.), 96
        toll house 93 (ill.)
    George Square 50, 81 (ill.), 109 (ill.)
    George Street 13 (ill.), 49 (ill.), 50,
        84 (ill.), 93 (+ill.), 95
    Gray Street 96, 131 (ill.)
    High Street 47 (ill.), 82 (ill.)
    Laing Crescent 49
    list of 97
    Meigle Road see Forfar Road
    New Road see Union Street
    Perth Road 48 (ill.)
    Pleasance Road 36
    Precinct Street 49
    St. Catherine's Lane 32
    street plan 8
    Timber market see George Square
    tolls and toll houses 93 (ill), 94 (+ills)
    Trades Lane 50, 95
    Union Street 31 (ill.), 50, 81 (ill.),
        92 (ill.), 94 (ill.), 96 (+ill.),
        108 (ill.)
Roll of Honour (World War I) 21 (ill.), 124 (ill.)
Roman Catholicism 34-35
Royal Hotel 141-142 (+ill.), 144 (+ill.)
Saddlers 36, 60 (ill.)
St. Andrew's Church 31 (+ill.), 32, 35
    ministers, list of 31
    union with Abbey Kirk 25, 31
    use as Abbey Kirk hall 31
    Women's Guild 30 (ill.)
St. Anne's Scottish Episcopal Church 33-34 (+ill.)
    ministers, list of 33
    rectory 34
    subscribers to building 33
St. Catherine's Lane 32
St. Mary's Roman Catholic Church 30, 34-35
Savings Bank see Education
Saw mill 60
Schools see Education and names of schools
Scotch Education Department 61
Scottish Episcopal Church 32-34 see also St.
    Anne's Scottish
    Episcopal Church
Scottish Legal Burial Society 132
Scottish Midland Junction Railway Co. 47
Scout Movement 133-136 (+ills)
    pipe band 135
    Scoutmasters, list of 135
Secession Church 10, 22, 28-29
    manses 29
    ministers, list of 29
Sewage works 85, 86, 88
Shoemakers 36
Shops and businesses
    advertisements (all ills) 30, 51, 52, 59,
        60, 65, 74, 83, 90, 101,
        103, 104-105, 109, 138,
        139, 140
    Athole Street Bakery 60 (ill.)
    Caledonian Barbecue Co. 52
    Caledonian Railway Co. 47
    Coronation Works Store see Eassie and
        Balkeerie Supply Co.
    Coupar Angus and Newtyle Railway Co.
        see Newtyle and
        Coupar Angus Railway
        Co.
    Culross, William and Son (Printers)
        57-58 (+ill.)
        printing press 58 (ill.)
    Davidson, Walter and Sons (Chemists) 59
    directories and listings 54-56
    Dunbar, William T. (Baker) 60 (ill.)
    Dundee and Newtyle Railway Co. 42, 47
    Durie and Miller (Jute works)
        fire 50, 51
        coronation celebration 1953
        106 (ill.)
    Eassie and Balkeerie Supply Co.
        (EBSCO) 52
    Geekie and Black (flax and linen mills)
        50, 51 (ill.)
    Grampian Country Food Group 52
    Grayburn Bakery 60 (ill.)
    Irvine and Co. (drapers) 59 (ill.)
    L. O. Tractors 52 see also Olding, Jack
        and Co.
    Marshall Food Group 52
    Newtyle and Coupar Angus Railway Co.
        47, 80
    Nortel Leisure Centre 143
    Olding, Jack and Co. (textile works)
        48 (ill.), 50 (ill.), 52
    Paterson, Charles B. (saddler) 60 (ill.)
        see also Commerce
Skating 100
Soft fruit industry 37-39
Soup kitchens 45, 50, 69
Souterrain (Pitcur) 42 (+ill.)
South United Free Church see United
    Presbyterian Church
Spitfire Fund 104 (+ill), 105 (ill.)
Sports 111-121, 123
    American football 146
    bowling 115 (ill.), 116-117 (+ills)
    Bowling Club House 116 (ill.)
    Coupar Angus Recreation Association 118
    cricket 113-114 (+ill.), 120
    curling 100 (+ill.), 111-113 (+ill.)
    football 118-121 (+ills)
        Foxhall Park 119, 123
        Juniors 119 (ill.)
        school team 76 (ill.)
        team lists 119, 120
        teams 118 (ill.), 120
    Highland Games 123
    hockey 119, 121 (+ill.)
        East Perthshire Hockey Club 121
        team 121 (ill.)
    quoiting 114-115 (+ill.)
    skating 100
    tennis 117-118 (+ill.)
    team list 118
Steeple see Tolbooth
Stone of Destiny 19
Strathmore Hotel 141 (+ill.)
Strathmore Works 51 (+ill.), 52
Strawberries 37
Street list 97
Street plan 8
Streets see Roads and streets see also Transport
Supernatural beliefs 28
    witch knowe 87

**Shops and businesses con't**

Tannery 36, 47, 60
Telegrams *see* Communications
Telephones *see* Communications
Tennis 117-118 (+ill)
    team list 118
Textile industry 48-52
    Balgersho bleachfield 49
    "Bucky" 49
    "Coupar Parliament" 49
    flax 48-49, 51
    jute 48, 50-51
    linen 48, 51
    Middlehills (mill) 50
    Olding, Jack and Co. (textile works) 48 (ill.), 50 (ill.), 52
    power loom weaving 50 (ill.), 51-52 (+ill.)
    spinning school 48
    Strathmore Works, 51, 52
    waulkmill 49
Three Deuces (musical group) 147 (ill.)
Timber market *see* George Square
Tinkers 37
Toc H 132 (+ills)
Tolbooth 10, 14 (+ill.), 15 (+ill.), 16 (ill.), 58 (ill.), 83
    bell 14 (ill.)
    poem 16
Tolls and toll houses 93 (ill.), 94, (+ills)
Town Commissioners 11, 14
Town Committee 10, 11, 14
Town Council 11, 12 (+ill.)
    minutes 12
Town Hall 20 (+ill.), 21 (+ill.), 67-68, 102 (ill.)
    contents 20-21

    opening 99
    Polish Army connection 103 (ill.)
Townhouse *see* Tolbooth
Trades Lane 50, 95
Transport *see* Railways, Road transport, and Roads and streets (list) and by name
Trysts *see* Feeing markets
Union Bank Buildings 80 (ill.)
Union Street 31 (ill.), 50, 81 (ill.), 92 (ill.), 94 (ill.), 96 (+ill.), 108 (ill.)
United Free Church 22
United Presbyterian Church 22, 30
Vaccination (BCG) 73
Vic, The *see* Victoria Inn
Victoria Buildings 47
Victoria Hall *see* Town Hall
Victoria Inn 14 (ill.), 83, 142-143 (+ill.)
Voluntary organisations
    Coupar Angus Recreation Association 118
    Freemasonry 131 (+ills), 132
    Gardens and Allotments Society 77, 101 (ill.), 137 (ill.)
    Ladies' Society 106
    League of Horsemen 121
    Red Cross 88-90
    Toc H 132 (+ills)
    Women's Guild 30 (ill.) *see also* Youth organisations
Wage levels (c1800) 60
War memorials 21 (ill.), 23 (ill.), 25, 68 (ill.), 124 (ills), 125, 126, 127
Water supply 72, 85, 87
Weaving *see* Textile industry

Welton 9
Whisky distilling 60
White House *see* Strathmore Hotel
Whooping cough (pertussis) 87
Windsor Dance Band 102
Witch knowe 87
Women's Guild 30 (ill.)
World War I 43, 69, 89, 124
    memorials *see* War memorials
    Red Cross in 89-90
World War II 70-72, 78, 90, 124
    entertainments 103-104
    evacuees 70, 72
    Red Cross in 90
    War Weapons Week 70, 71
    Warship Week 71
    Wings for Victory Week 71
Wynd *see* Trades Lane
Young Women's Christian Association 28, 29
Youth organisations
    Boys' Brigade 108, 136-137 (+ill)
        activities 137
        pipe band 136
    British Legion 109 (ill.)
    Brownies *see* Girl Guides
    Girl Guides 45, 138 (+ill.)
    Scout Movement 133-136 (+ills)
        pipe band 135
        Scoutmasters, list of 135 *see also* Voluntary organisations
Y.W.C.A. *see* Young Women's Christian Association
Young Women's Christian Association 28, 29

# Index of Personal Names

In this index only the names of persons who were significant in the history of Coupar Angus and round about, directly or indirectly, are listed. This means that some well known names mentioned in the text to give historical context are not listed here. Also, where group photographs appear, for example a football team, in most instances no attempt has been made to list all the names associated with such photographs.

Where necessary and possible, to assist the reader to identify people, a brief description of the person has been appended to their name.

**(ill.) = illustration only**

**(+ill.) = textual mention and illustration**

Abernethy, Bill (Footballer) 120
Adams, Captain D. (Fire Officer) 82
Agger, Frank (Town Councillor and Baillie) 21, 122
Albert, Prince (Consort of Queen Victoria) 15
Allan, Rev. Alexander 28
Allan, Andrew (School Attendance Officer) 62, 63
Anderson, Andrew (Slater) 24
Anderson, J.R. 111 (ill.)
Anderson, James (Wright: a trade) 24
Anderson, Captain James (of Balbrogie – Home Guard) 70 (ill.)
Angus, John 88
Apedaile, J.L.B. (Len) (Provost) 12 (ill.) 20, 52, 81, 135, 136 (ill.)
Arneil, Mrs. Georgie (Compositor) 58
Balmerino, 3rd and 6th Lords 10
Bain, Rev. Thomas 62
Baxter, Ali (Drummer) 103
Baxter, Charlie 114 (ill.)
Baxter, Jean 104
Benzies, Bob 58
Benzies, Douglas 58
Benzies, Frank, M.B.E. 57 (+ill.), 58, 123
Benzies, Frank, S. 58
Benzies, Pat 104
Bishop, Rev. James 28
Black, Andrew (Headmaster) 74, 77
Blyth, Alan (Scout Master) 134, 135, 136
Blyth, Archie 100 (ill.)
Boyd, Charles (Solicitor) 62
Boyd, Sgt. Neil, (Military Cross) 69
Brodie, Miss Johan 87 (+ill.)
Brown, Mrs. G. (of Blairfield) 25
Brown, Jimmy (Footballer) 118 (ill.), 119
Bruce, David ("Brasso") 134
Bruce, Gertrude 104
Bruce, Harry 105 (ill.)
Buchan, Andrew (Abbot) 12
Buist, Miss Margaret (Guide Leader) 138
Burrie, Will 114 (ill.)
Cameron, Miss Margaret (Head Teacher) 77
Cameron, Peter 100 (ill.)
Campbell family (of Argyll) 10
Campbell, Donald (Abbot) 10, 44
Campbell, Ian 120
Campbell, Nicol (of Keithick) 44
Carmichael, Rev. Robert 28
Carver, John (Architect) 24
Chalmers, James (Provost) 17 (+ill.)
Cheape, Willie (Footballer) 119 (+ill.)
Clark-Barnacle, Canon A. 33, 34
Cochrane, Rev. William 25, 27, 75
Collingswood, Edward (of Kinloch) 33
Collisto, General 23
Coogan, Jean 68 (ill.)
Copeland, Douglas (Footballer) 120
Coupar, Lord 10, 14, 23
Craig, James 73 (ill.)

Craigie, James 145
Crichton, James 133, 134
Crockett, John (Curler) 111-112
Croll, Albert (Postman) 84 (ill.), 114, 120
Culross, David (Printer) 57
Culross, William (Founder Printer) 47, 57
Davidson, Douglas (Chemist) 59
Davidson, John D. (Chemist and Provost) 20, 59 (ill.), 100 (ill.), 103 (ill.), 115 (ill.), 120, 122, 146-147 (+ill.)
Davidson, Walter (Chemist) 59
Dawson, Jim (Boys' Brigade Captain) 136 (+ill), 137 (+ill.)
Dawson, Robert (Bob) (School Janitor) 76 (ill.)
Dewar, Bob 100 (ill.)
Doig, Miss Annie (Teacher) 72
Doig, Bob (Printer) 57, 58
Doig, R.G. (Dramatic Society) 105
Doig, William 134
Donaldson, Bert 114 (ill.)
Donaldson, John 120
Dow, Sandy 73 (ill.), 120
Dudman, Len (Footballer and Cricketer) 120
Dun, Rev. William 29
Dunbar, John (Jack) (Pianist) 103, 147 (+ills.)
Dunbar, William T. (Fiddle Player and Provost) 102, 103 (ill.), 116 (ill.)
Elphinstone, Lord 10
Ferguson, Mrs. Charlotte A. 20, 122
Ferguson, John (Manufacturer) 62
Fiddes, Ian (Footballer) 120
Fraser, Hugh (School Janitor) 75
Gatt, Alex 111 (ill. curling), 112
Geekie, Robert 11
George xxxxxx, Bishop of Aberdeen 24
Gibb, Peter 100 (ill.
Gilzean, Alan (Footballer) 73 (ill.), 74, 120
Goldie, Rev. Thomas 30
Gow, William (Contractor) 24
Granger, Rev. Thomas 29, 30
Grant, Alan 73 (ill.)
Gray, David, (Footballer) 120
Gray, Davie (Quoits player) 114 (ill.)
Gray, Stuart (Footballer) 120
Gray, T.B. (Baker) 60 (ill.)
Gray, Tommy (Footballer) 119 (ill.), 120
Grimond, Rev. James 29
Haliburton, George (Bishop of Aberdeen) 24
Hally, R.G. (Bob) 40, 100 (ill.), 123
Hallyburton, Lord Douglas 37
Harness, Roy 106
Harrison, Jock 120
Hay, Rev. George 24, 26
Hay, Sir Thomas (7th Lord Errol) 25
Henderson, Pat 111 (ill. curling)
Hill family
    Legal dispute with Abbey Kirk 24-25
Hill, General Sir Basil 33
Hope, Dr. Gilbert (G.P.) 88

Hume, David (Provost) 20
Hynd, R. (Quoits player) 114 (ill.)
Jackson, Mrs. Dorie (Infant mistress) 75
Johnston, Bruce G. (Head Teacher) 74
Keay, Sandy (Footballer) 120
Kusza, Richard (Watchmaker) 15
Kusza, Victor (Watchmaker) 20
Laing, Gordon (Footballer/Cricketer) 120
Lamb, John (Band conductor) 110
Lawson, James C. (Builder) 62
Lindsay, Colonel M.J. (of Hallyburton) 113 (+ill.)
Llewellen Palmer, Julian (of Hallyburton) 43
Logan, Rev. J.B. 31
Louise, Princess
    marriage celebrations in 1871 15
Loutet, John (Teacher) 64, 65, 67
Low, William (Contractor) 24
Lowe, Dr. R. (G.P.) 14
Lowe, Thomson (of Winnipeg) 14
McCoull, Donald (Alleged Criminal) 13
McCulloch, Bertha (Organist) 147
Macdonald, Alexander 134
MacDonald, Alexander Colkitto see Collisto, General
MacDonald, Rev. Finlay Robert 15, 108, 136
McDonald, Ronnie (Scout Master) 133 (ill.), 134, 135
McFarlane, David (Commissioner and Provost) 11, 20, 52
McFarlane, George 52
McGeorge, David (Chemist) 59
McGeorge, W.S. (Artist) 20
Macgregor, William (Baillie) 17
McIntosh, Bill (Mayor of Otago, New Zealand) 145 (+ill.)
McKenzie, Alistair (Scout) 135
Mackenzie, James Stewart or Stuart (of Keithick) 44
McKenzie, Will (Groundsman) 120
McLean, Rev. Daniel 30
McPherson, Dr. Alex. (G.P.) 88
Macpherson, Private Alex. (Military Medal) 69
McRitchie, Miss Annie (School Teacher and Town Councillor) 66, 67
Marshall, Daniel B. (Marshall Food Group) 52
Marshall, Isobel 104
Marshall, Rev. Dr. William 28
Marshall, Wilson (Marshall Food Group) 51 (ill.)
Martin, Nan 104
Mason, William (Pipe Major) 109
Mason, Rev. James 31
Menzies, William Dudgeon Graham (of Hallyburton) 21
Michie, Dod (Trumpet player) 103 (ill), 147
Milne, Dr. Frank (G.P.) 87 (+ill.), 88
Moray (Earls of) 10
Morris, Pat (Curler) 100 (ill.)

Muirhead, Rev. Charles  28
Murray, Jean  68 (ill.)
Murray, Mungo (of Lintrose)  33, 34
Murray, Patrick (of Simprim, Meigle)  39
Niven, George (Footballer)  120 (+ill.)
Ogilvie, Rev. Thomas  26
Ogilvy family  10
Ogilvy, John (Baillie)  13
Orr, Mrs. Margaret (Head Teacher)  77
Parsons, Mrs. Betsy (of Ohio, U.S.A.)  78
Paterson, Lt. Ralph, (Military Cross)  69
Paton, James (Banker)  62
Petrie, George (Dramatic Society)  105
Pithie, Dave (Curler)  100 (ill.)
Pitkeathly, Robert (Pipe Major)  109
Pratt, Mrs. Barbara (Head Teacher)  75, 77
Ramsay, John (Schoolmaster)  61
Reid, David (Builder)  32
Rennie, Adam (Fiddle player)  107 (+ill.), 108
Reston, Rev. David  29
Robb, Mike (Quoits player)  114 (ill.)

Roberts, Rev. David  34
Robertson, Annie (Provost)  20, 71
Robertson, Mrs. Betty (Teacher)  76
Robertson, Jimmy (Curler)  100 (ill.)
Robertson, Sandy  120
Robertson, W.B. (Headmaster)  71 (+ill.), 73
Rodger, Harry  120
Scott, Jack (Scoutmaster)  134, 135
Simpson, Len  120
Slidders, James  110
Small, Rev. Thomas  28
Smeaton, John (Quoits player)  114 (ill.)
Smith, Rev. A. Wylie  107
Steen, David C. (Provost)  116 (ill.)
Stevenson, Rev. Patrick James  62
Stewart, Rev. James  29
Strain, G.W.F. (Headmaster)  67, 68
Sturrock, Eddie (Edwin) (Teacher)  76 (ill.), 77
Sutherland, D. (Quoits player)  114 (ill.)
Sutherland, John (Quoits player)  114 (ill.)
Sutherland, Dr. John (Jock) Bain  21, 146

Swanson, Hugh (Mason)  37
Thomson, Pat (Mr.)
Torry, Very Rev. John  33, 62, 63
Tuckwell, John (Headmaster)  73
Wallace, Rev. Robert  140
Wann, Tom (Footballer)  119 (+ill.)
Watson, George (Teacher)  63
Watson, Hugh (Tenant of Keillor)  36
Wedderspoon, Sir Thomas  52
West, William (Tenant farmer)  39
Whitson, James (of Isla Park)  62
Whytock, Colin (Quoits player)  114 (ill.)
Wimberley, Major General Douglas (of Foxhall)  130 (+ill.)
Wineberry, Mike (Footballer)  120
Wood, Admiral Sir Andrew (1455-1515)  44
Wood, Miss Brodie (of Keithick)  45, 138
Young, Bill ("Professor Halfloafskie")  104 (+ill.), 105 (ill.)
Young, George (Businessman)  49